Third Grade Language Arts

Reading Book 2
Lessons 81 to 160

Visit **McRuffy.com** for helpful resources to teach this curriculum!

Reading Book 2
ISBN 978159269-2590

McRuffy Press Third Grade Language Arts Curriculum
ISBN 978159269-2118

Written and illustrated by
Brian Davis M. A. Ed.

Graphic Design by
Sherylynn Davis

McRuffy Press, LLC
P.O. Box 212
Raymore, MO 64083

816-331-7831

sales@mcruffy.com

www.McRuffy.com

Book 2　　　　　　　　　　　　　　　**Table of Contents**

Story		Page	Lessons
1	Elijah's Coming		
	Part 1	4	81-85
	Part 2	17	86-90
	Part 3	30	91-95
2	Matthew and Goliath		
	Part 1	43	96-100
	Part 2	57	101-105
3	The Bobcat Cowboys Steal the Show		
	Part 1	70	106-110
	Part 2	81	111-115
	Part 3	94	116-120
4	The King is Coming	103	121-125
5	Big Tom's Cafe	117	126-130
6	Pigs in the Pancakes	129	131-135
7	The Case of the Missing Trumpeter		
	Part 1	141	136-140
	Part 2	154	141-145
8	The Bobcat Cowboys Take the Cake		
	Part 1	167	146-150
	Part 2	181	151-155

Elijah's Coming
Part 1

Table of Contents

Chapter		Page
1	Elijah Alone	5
2	The Storm	8
3	The Stranger in the House	11
4	The Stranger Awakes	14

Vocabulary Words

blacksmith

conductor

continue

distance

encourage

mistreat

underground

by Brian Davis

In the year 1851, a ten-year-old boy is left in charge of his family's farm for an afternoon. Suddenly, a storm changes everything. What will Elijah do when two unexpected strangers need his help?

Chapter 1
Elijah Alone

Elijah watched his family travel down the road. The big wagon wheels kicked up a little dust behind them. His three brothers and one sister waved. Elijah's mother held her other little baby girl in her arms. His father held the reins and stared straight ahead.

Although Elijah was only ten, he was not afraid. That's what he told himself. The truth was he was a little afraid. This was his first time to stay home alone. Normally, his older brother Joseph stayed.

Someone always stayed behind when the family went to town. He had begged to stay behind. Going to town was exciting. But Elijah wanted to prove he was almost a man. He wanted his father to see how responsible he was.

Joseph jumped at the chance to go to town. He planned on seeing if his grandfather needed any chores done. He owned the blacksmith shop. Joseph liked to work, as long as he got paid. His grandfather always made him work hard for his money. That way, Joseph wouldn't be wasteful.

Still Elijah's big brother did promise to bring some candy back. Joseph wanted to encourage his brother to stay home more often. A piece of candy was a rare treat. Elijah thought he was getting the best part of the deal.

The jangling wagon climbed to the top of the hill. The wagon paused. Elijah's father turned his head. He pulled off his wide brimmed hat. He waved to Elijah, turned, and shook the reins. The wagon was soon out of sight.

Elijah felt all alone as he waved back. He glanced down the empty road. Then he turned to the field behind his home. In the distance was another small log cabin. It was just like his home.

A tiny puff of smoke arose from the chimney. It reminded him that he was not so alone after all. It was the home of his uncle Jermain. Elijah's mother told him to go there if he got too afraid.

Elijah wanted to go. Yet he wanted his father to see that he was a man. He didn't want anyone to know he was afraid. If he went to his uncle's house, all his cousins would tell on him. Still, it was good to know they were so close.

Feeling so alone made him think about his great-grandfather, Levi. When he was only nine years old, Levi was captured in Africa. Slave traders took him aboard a ship. He never saw his family again.

The slave traders took him to America. There, he became a slave on a farm in Pennsylvania in 1773. It was his owners that named him Levi. He was owned by a family that became Quakers. The Quakers were a group of Christian people. They had started the colony that became the state of Pennsylvania.

Many Quakers felt it was wrong to own slaves. They told the other Quakers to set their slaves free. The people that owned Levi finally agreed. Levi was made a free man.

Still, he wasn't taken back to Africa. He was all alone in a new country. Levi was only fourteen when he was freed. He continued working for the Quaker family.

This time, they paid him. Levi saved most of his money. When he was twenty years old, he moved to Ohio. He bought some land. Levi started his own farm.

It was the same farm that Elijah lived on. He was glad he had never been a slave. Elijah had heard stories from escaping slaves. His father and his Uncle Jermain helped runaway slaves.

Escaping slaves crossed the Ohio River from Kentucky. Elijah's father would hang a lantern out by the barn. The lantern had a blue shade. This let the runaways know that all was safe.

Sometimes late at night, Elijah would hear three light knocks on the door. His father would softly ask, "Who's there?"

Someone would answer, "A friend with a friend."

That's how the Underground Railroad worked. It was risky. Elijah's father told the children to never let anyone know they had guests. Elijah's father could go to jail. It was illegal to help runaway slaves.

Elijah's father said it was more wrong to own slaves. The slaves were fed. They were allowed to rest. But, Elijah's father always had them tell their stories. All the children listened in. Elijah's father said this was part of their education.

Many of the slaves had been mistreated. Some had scars from beatings. They didn't have good homes to live in. They had to work long hours. Others told how family members had been sold.

Most didn't know how to read or write. Elijah was grateful that his parents taught him. Elijah loved to read books. His parents didn't have a lot of money. Yet they spent money for books.

Elijah liked to read to their guests. Many would ask him to read scriptures from the Bible. They always seemed amazed that a young black boy could read. Elijah also liked to write. He would write down the runaways' stories.

The runaway slaves never stayed long. Most would be gone the next day. Sometimes slave hunters would comb the woods. They wanted to catch the slaves to get a reward. The slaves would stay in the root cellar until it was safe to move on.

Elijah's father made a hole in the floor of the cellar. If anyone looked in they would think it was empty. The hole led to a tunnel. The tunnel led to the woods. The end of the tunnel was covered by what looked like a stack rocks.

The stack was hollow. A few rocks covered the door. Still it was light enough for Elijah's younger sister to open. Elijah's father made the tunnel. He didn't want the runaways to feel trapped in the cellar.

He was also sneaky when he gave the runaway slaves rides. Elijah's father would place some boards eighteen inches above the floor of the wagon. This created a space for the slaves to hide. He would then toss some bags of grain on top. He would scatter some straw to hide the boards.

He would then take the slaves to the next stop on the Underground Railroad. Most of the slaves now went to Canada. The Fugitive Slave Law of 1850 made it dangerous for the slaves to stay. They could be captured even in free states.

Elijah was glad his father was a conductor. A conductor was someone who helped people on the Underground Railroad get to the next stop. Elijah wished he could do more. He wanted to go into the south and free all the slaves.

"Someday I will," thought Elijah. "Someday, they'll say Elijah's coming. He'll take us to freedom."

Chapter 2

The Storm

Thick clouds rolled overhead. Lightning flashed in the distance. The wind was picking up dust. It blew across the field.

Elijah hoped his parents would be home soon. Maybe they stayed in town. They were always welcome at his grandfather's little cabin. Elijah's mother wouldn't want the baby out in the storm.

Elijah finished his chores. He made sure the barn door was latched. A strong wind might blow it off its hinges. His father would say he was careless if that happened.

Uncle Jermain's cabin looked very tempting. Elijah almost bolted across the field. Then he heard the squealing sound. At first he thought it was the wagon returning.

Then Elijah saw the lantern. It was the one with the blue shade. The wind was catching it. There was no use lighting it. Elijah picked it off the hook.

He carried it into his house. His father would be glad Elijah remembered to bring it in. Then Elijah began to worry. What if a runaway needed a place to hide? That was especially true on a stormy night. Could he be responsible for a slave's safety?

The thick clouds made it darker. Elijah didn't like this. He didn't like it at all. Maybe he wasn't ready for this. He was all alone. Then there was a storm.

The cabin was pitch black inside. Elijah lit the lantern with the blue shade. He placed it in the window. He hoped it would guide his family home.

Elijah grabbed some of the bread his mother had left for him. He pulled the quilt off his bed. Elijah curled up in his mother's old rocking chair. He rocked and waited.

He soon drifted off to sleep. The rain pelted the roof of the cabin. Elijah would have slept through the storm. A loud clap of thunder made him jump.

Suddenly he was awake. He looked around the cabin. His parents still weren't home. Elijah realized he had been asleep several hours. It was the middle of the night.

Over the rain, he thought he heard a sound. Elijah walked to a window. He peered into the darkness. A flash of lightning lit the barnyard.

He saw something near the barn. It was under a tree. But now it was dark again. He could see nothing. Elijah waited for another flash.

It came at the same time as the thunder. It was so loud, the cabin shook. It was followed by a loud cracking sound. Lightning had struck a tree. A limb hung down.

More lightning revealed a standing horse. Its reins were caught in a branch. The frightened horse pranced. Elijah knew it needed help.

He slipped on a hat and jacket. Elijah ran toward the barn. Part of the branch was now leaning against it. Elijah untwisted the horse's reins. The animal was free.

Elijah was leading it toward the barn. Suddenly, another flash of lightning lit up the night. The flash revealed a man's face. Elijah jumped. Someone was trapped under the branch.

The limb was thick and heavy. It wasn't something a boy could move. Then he heard the man moan. Elijah had an idea.

A rope was hooked to the horse's saddle. Elijah grabbed the rope. He tied it to the limb. He wrapped the other end around the horn of the saddle.

Elijah carefully led the horse. It strained to pull the limb. It wasn't broken completely free of the tree. Finally, the branch snapped. It was off the man.

The injured man lay in the mud. He didn't move. Elijah was afraid that he was dead. He didn't know what to do.

Finally, the man started moving. He struggled to his feet. Elijah could see he was about to fall. Elijah rushed to the man.

He propped him up. Elijah thought he was going to fall under the man's weight. The man must have thought that too. He tried harder to stand. The two of them staggered to the cabin.

Elijah helped the man to a mat on the floor. The man fell on it. Elijah built a fire in the fireplace. He pulled an old green blanket over the man. Then he remembered the horse. It was still tied to the limb.

Elijah rushed back outside. He untied the horse and led it into the barn. He unhooked the saddle and slid it off. That's when Elijah noticed the saddle bags.

The man might need them, Elijah thought. He put the horse in a stall. He made sure it had some fresh hay. The horse seemed grateful. It neighed happily. Then it took a big bite.

Elijah tossed the saddle bag over his shoulder. He flopped it onto a barrel. Elijah ran as fast as he could back to the cabin. Once he reached the door he was safe from the rain.

He started to enter the cabin. Suddenly, he thought about the man inside. He was a stranger. He was a white man. He might even be dead.

Elijah wasn't sure he wanted to go inside. He peeked in the window. The man was right where Elijah had left him. The man looked like he was asleep.

Elijah carefully opened the door. He kept his eye on the stranger the whole time. He watched the man closely.

"Mister," said Elijah. The man didn't move. "Mister!" Elijah said more loudly.

The man's fingers moved.

"Are you all right?" asked Elijah as he took a step forward. "I brought your saddle bags to you."

The man's chest moved slowly up and down. He was breathing. Elijah stepped closer. The man's clothing look charred. He had been struck by lightning along with the tree.

"Would you like some water? Some food?" Elijah asked.

The man didn't answer. He seemed to be asleep. Elijah got a blanket for him. Then he put another log on the fire.

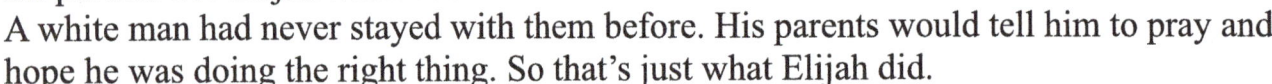

What else could he do? Elijah thought. What would his parents do? Elijah wasn't sure. A white man had never stayed with them before. His parents would tell him to pray and hope he was doing the right thing. So that's just what Elijah did.

Chapter 3
The Stranger in the House

The old rocking chair creaked. Elijah was rocking to stay awake. He kept his eyes on the man. Elijah wished his parents would come back.

He thought about going to his Uncle's house. The storm was still raging. Elijah remembered the flash of lightning that hit the man. It wasn't safe to cross the field.

Elijah looked at the door. How he wished it would open. How he wished his father would step through the doorway. Elijah knew the truth. His parents wouldn't be back until morning.

He lowered his eyes. That's when he noticed the saddlebags. Elijah was curious. Who was this man? What was he doing on their farm? He would ask the man if he were awake.

Elijah eyed the bags. Should he? It wasn't his. Still, what if the man was dangerous? Elijah needed to know. He had a right to know.

If he waited for the man to wake up it could be too late. Elijah decided to look in the saddlebags. He studied the man for a minute. The man was sound asleep.

Elijah lit another lamp. He placed it on the dinner table. Elijah picked up the saddlebags. He pulled out a bench.

The buckle on the strap was a bit tight. It had been soaking in the rain. Elijah worked the leather loose. He pulled up the flap on the first bag.

It had all the things a traveler would use. There was a shaving cup, brush, and knife. Some cheese and bread were wrapped in a cloth. There was a box of bullets. Elijah remembered the rifle holster on the saddle.

There was one surprise. It was a badge. It was thick and heavy. Elijah ran his fingers over the words. The man was a U.S. Marshal. At least, he had the badge of a U.S. Marshal. But if he were a marshal, he would be wearing the badge, Elijah thought.

Elijah opened the other bag. It was filled with papers. Elijah recognized them. He had seen them in town. The papers were wanted posters.

They described runaway slaves. Rewards were given for found slaves. The posters told how much. There were dozens stuffed in the bag.

"So you're a slave hunter," said Elijah as he looked at the sleeping man.

Part of him was sorry he had rescued the man. Elijah could have left him trapped. Maybe the man would have died. Perhaps, God was trying to kill the man. That's why lightning struck him.

Then Elijah thought of the Bible stories his father and mother had told him. He remembered how people's lives were changed when they realized how wrong they were.

"There's still hope for you, Mister," said Elijah.

Of course, the man didn't hear Elijah. Still, Elijah wanted to speak it. He stuffed the papers back into the bag. He didn't notice a poster that fell to the floor.

Next, he started to fill the other bag. Then he saw the bullets again. That reminded him of the rifle. Elijah decided to make one more trip to the barn.

It was still pouring rain. Elijah crossed the barnyard. He slid back the latch to the barn. The horse pranced around the stall.

The rifle was still with the saddle. Elijah thought about taking it with him. Instead, he decided to hide it. He pulled it out.

It was a fine rifle. In looked very expensive. That's when Elijah noticed the saddle. It too looked very expensive. The man must be rich, thought Elijah. He tucked it under the hay.

Elijah noticed something else. Tied to the saddle was an old cloth bag. It was heavy. Elijah untied it and looked inside.

It was full of pieces of iron. There were chains. There were locks. It also had handcuffs and ankle irons. The man must have used them on slaves he captured.

Elijah sighed. How could he help such a man? He thought about the rifle again. Then he thought of how his father taught him to love his enemies.

Elijah didn't understand this at first. His father explained the problem with hatred. He said it just takes everything over, love, joy, peace. Soon, all you can do is hate. His father told him it was a choice to not hate. Sometimes it was a tough choice. Yet, it was always the right choice.

It was a talk he often gave to runaway slaves. He explained that they needed to forgive. If not, they would still be slaves. "Slaves to the devil himself," his father often said.

"I'm not a slave," said Elijah as he walked past the gun's hiding place.

He stomped through the pouring rain. The boy stopped on the porch again. Elijah peeked through the window. The man had not moved. He slid the latch on the door.

Elijah walked to the man. The man was still breathing. He was still asleep. Elijah put another log on the fire.

"That's the strangest runaway slave I've ever seen," said another voice in the room.

Elijah jumped.

"That's what the blue lantern is for? Isn't it? Runaways are welcome here aren't they?" Somewhere in the shadows the voice came again.

Elijah looked at the window. The blue lamp was still glowing. His heart sank. He had given the safe signal. He didn't mean to have any slaves come this night. Especially with a slave hunter laying on the floor.

He still couldn't see the person speaking. Elijah picked up the blue lantern. He walked toward the corner of the cabin. Someone was sitting in his mother's rocking chair.

"You're the youngest farmer I've ever seen, too," said the woman.

She seemed to be in her early twenties. Her clothing looked familiar. It was also dry. That would be difficult with all the rain.

"I borrowed your wife's clothes," said the woman.

Elijah had to giggle. "I don't have a wife. I'm only ten years old."

"You must have a wife. A ten year old boy couldn't run this farm all by himself," she teased.

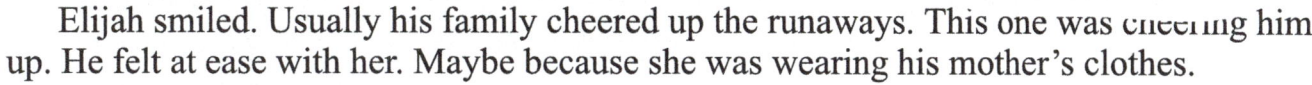

Elijah smiled. Usually his family cheered up the runaways. This one was cheering him up. He felt at ease with her. Maybe because she was wearing his mother's clothes.

"My parents left me in charge. They'll be back soon."

Elijah looked back at the sleeping man. Suddenly he grew concerned. He had to get the woman to the cellar. If the man woke up she would be in danger.

Elijah noticed something under his feet. It was another wanted poster. He stooped to pick it up. The word Runaway Slave was real big at the top.

"What do you have there boy?" asked the woman.

"Elijah. you can call me Elijah. It's a poster. I found it in the man's saddle bag."

"You shouldn't be nosing around other people's things," said the woman.

Elijah thought that was strange. She had nosed around his cabin. She had helped herself to his mother's clothes. Now, she was telling him he was wrong to do the same thing.

"What does it say? Read it to me," commanded the woman.

Elijah stared at the poster. "Fugitive Slave. Five feet, two inches tall called Lizzy. Dark skin wearing a red and blue dress."

"Like the one drying by the fire?" asked the woman.

"Like the one drying by the slave hunter," said Elijah.

"I know," said Lizzy. "He chased me here. I saw what happened at the tree. I wanted to see if he survived. When I looked in the window, I saw you were alone with him. I didn't want him to hurt you on account of me."

"I don't think he could hurt anyone tonight," said Elijah.

"That lightning bolt made sure of that," said Lizzy. "Anyway, you did all you could for him. It's up to the Lord now."

Chapter 4
The Stranger Awakes

"Where am I?" said the voice in the dark.

Elijah woke up. He could see the man laying by the fireplace. He was rubbing his face. The man was very confused.

"Is anyone here?" asked the man.

Elijah didn't say anything. The room was dark again. Elijah lit a lantern. He walked toward the man.

The man turned toward him. "Who are you?"

The man winced as he looked at Elijah. The boy stepped closer. He held the lantern close to his face. He tried to sit up, but groaned loudly.

"You're hurt," said Elijah. "It might be best if you lie still for awhile longer."

"How did I get here? Why does my head feel like it's about to split open?" asked the man.

"Don't you remember the storm?" asked Elijah.

"Storm?" the man repeated with a confused look on his face. "I don't remember anything, anything at all."

"This boy saved your life," said Lizzy. "You were struck by lightning. Most of the tree took the hit. But it got you too. I was in the woods. I saw the whole thing. You were pinned beneath a tree limb."

"You got a pretty severe blow to the head from the tree. It was the boy's smart thinking that saved you. He used your horse to lift the branch. You would still be out there in the storm if it weren't for him."

"And what were we doing out in the woods?" asked the man.

"You should know," said the woman. "You were looking me, Mr. Shepard."

"So you know me. Is that my name, Shepard?" asked the man. "Are we friends? Did you get lost?"

Now, Lizzy looked confused, "You don't remember, do you?"

"Like I told the boy, I don't remember anything at all."

Elijah handed the marshal's badge to Mr. Shepard. "I think this is yours."

The man frowned. At first Elijah thought it was the pain from the injury. But it seemed to be something deeper. He sighed deeply and handed the badge back to Elijah.

"Did you remember something?" asked Elijah.

He suddenly seemed very tired. He rubbed his eyes. He hoped to make the pain go away. It didn't help. The man laid flat. He rested his arm on his forehead. Elijah thought he could see tears in the man's eyes.

"I guess I owe you thanks," the man spoke to Elijah. "Thank you for saving my life."

Everyone was quiet for a few minutes. The man spoke again. "My memory is coming back. I once was a U. S. Marshal. I did capture a few slaves in my day."

"I thought I was doing the slaves a favor," said the man. "I told myself their masters would take better care of them. In the free states, they starve. They have no place to live. The have no jobs."

"But they do have freedom," added Lizzy. "Isn't that worth the risk?"

"I didn't see it that way at the time, I was just doing my job. It's a U.S. Marshal's duty to uphold the law. Without laws, there is no freedom. That law says that slaves are to be returned to their masters. Maybe that is a bad law. Still, the law was on my side."

Elijah didn't understand why the man talked the way he did. It sounded like he was no longer a U. S. Marshal. Then Elijah remembered the badge. The man wasn't wearing it.

"The law says I can be sold," said Lizzy. "That's what was going to happen to me. I was going to be sold like a cow or a pig. I'm not an animal. I'm a person."

"Mister Shepard," Elijah interrupted. "It's not good to be a slave. It's terrible. You and I, we've always been free. Some folks only dream of that. They'll do anything to live that dream. Why do you want to stop them?"

"I'm thirsty, Son. Could I get some water?" asked the man.

Elijah dipped a cup in a bucket. He started to walk to the man. Lizzy took the cup from his hands. She placed it on the table.

"Let the man get his own water," said the woman.

"Bring me the water, Boy," said Mr. Shepard.

Elijah didn't know what to do. Lizzy looked like she wasn't going to let him get the water. He stood there looking at Lizzy and the man. He could understand why she was so mean to the man. Mr. Shepard had chased her. She thought he wanted to put her back in slavery.

"The boy's not bringing you the water," said Lizzy. "I'm bigger than he is. If you want water, get it yourself. He's not your slave."

"Then I'll just get it myself," said the man calmly.

He pulled himself to his feet. His arms and legs were stiff. His head ached so terribly that he could barely see. It took a great effort just to stand up.

"It's over here. It's right next to me," said Lizzy. "The nice cool water is waiting on the table. Just help yourself. With all this rain, there's plenty of water."

Elijah thought Lizzy was being very mean. He wanted to grab the cup. He wanted to hand it to Mr. Shepard. He knew Lizzy would stop him.

Mr. Shepard found the table. He felt the bench. His legs were still shaky. The man was glad to have a place to sit.

Lizzy scooted the cup toward him. Mr. Shepard reached out a shaky hand. It brushed the cup. The tin cup clanked on the floor.

Mr. Shepard pounded his fist on the table, "Please get me some water!" he moaned.

Lizzy didn't get the water. She pulled out the other bench. She sat down. The woman stared at the man.

"You're a slave to your pain," she spoke calmly. "Now, you have a master. You can't get away. It keeps you from doing what you want to do. Now do you know why I ran away?"

Mr. Shepard didn't answer. Lizzy picked up the cup. She walked to the bucket. Lizzy dipped the tin cub into the water.

She took it to the table. Lizzy took Mr. Shepard's hand. The man looked very surprised. She placed the hand on the cup.

"I got you the water," said Lizzy. "What you're feeling is a terrible feeling. I know you're in pain. You'd do anything to get away from it. That's how I've felt all my life."

Mr. Shepard sipped from the cup. The water was cool and good. He drank the rest of it. He placed the cup on the table.

"Thank you, Lizzy," he said softly.

"Would you like some more?" asked Lizzy.

"No, I would like something else," said the man. "Bring me my saddle bag."

Elijah brought it to him. The man dug through the bag. He smiled as he pulled out an object. Lizzy's jaw dropped.

Elijah's Coming
Part 2

Table of Contents

Chapter		Page
5	Slave Hunters	18
6	The Flooded Creek	21
7	A Bit of Hope	24
8	Elijah on the Trail	27

by Brian Davis

Vocabulary Words

accident

miracle

disguise

protection

curious

Elijah's parents still haven't returned home. The slave hunter and the runaway slave both need his help. Who will Elijah decide to help?

Chapter 5

Slave Hunters

Lizzy didn't know what to think. In her hand was a hand carved doll. It was only about four inches long. It was painted with a pink dress. It was worn like it had been played with.

Elijah spoke up, "Did you carve that, Mr. Shepard?"

"No," interrupted Lizzy, as if she were just coming out of a fog.

"I retired after the Fugitive Slave Law was passed," said Mr. Shepard. "It was right after I was told to arrest a free black man accused of being a runaway slave. I wasn't an abolitionist at the time, but I never liked injustice. A man was almost enslaved simply on the word of two liars."

"Fortunately, the man escaped," Mr. Shepard smiled for the first time. "With a little help. That man gave me this doll and asked me to help him find his daughter. It so happened that she had been taken, too."

Tears welled up in Lizzy's eyes, "You know my daddy?"

"He would have continued searching for you himself, but it just wasn't safe," said Mr. Shepard.

Lizzy turned to the window. She didn't want anyone to see her cry. She watched the rain fall outside. The sky was getting lighter. The rain was slowing.

"Someone's coming," said Lizzy as she moved away from the window.

Mr. Shepard walked to the window. His feet were still a little shaky. He pulled back the curtain. Mr. Shepard then turned around.

He walked to the fireplace. He picked up the dress Lizzy had been wearing. The dress hung near the fireplace. It was now dry.

Mr. Shepard rolled it up. He hid it under a blanket. He looked around the room. Everything else looked fine, except Lizzy and Elijah. They looked terrified.

"Who is it?" asked Elijah.

Mr. Shepard didn't answer. "Where is the next stop on the Underground Railroad?"

Elijah didn't want to say. He also didn't know. Elijah did know the direction his father went. Still, he promised not to tell. He especially didn't want to tell a U.S. Marshal.

Mr. Shepard looked panicked. "What direction. Just tell me the direction."

"Northeast," said Elijah.

Lizzy looked worried. "Don't let those men take me away."

Mr. Shepard handed her a broom. "Keep sweeping. Act like you belong here."

Suddenly there was a knock on the door. Mr. Shepard unlatched the wooden door. He opened it wide. Two men were standing on the porch.

"Hello, Gentlemen," the two men were surprised by who answered the door.

"What are you doing here, Shepard?" asked one of the men.

"I was after the same runaway you were," answered Mr. Shepard. "Before I ran into a tree. This lady and her brother helped me out."

The men looked at Lizzy and Elijah. Elijah wasn't sure they believed the marshal. One poked his head in the door. He looked all around.

"Which direction was she heading?" asked the other man.

"Northeast," said Mr. Shepard with a smile.

"Northeast," said the man as he smiled back.

The men got back on their horses. Mr. Shepard stepped out on the porch. He watched them ride off. Mr. Shepard had a big smile on his face.

Elijah couldn't believe Mr. Shepard had told them the right direction. He stepped out on the porch with the marshal. He looked at the man. Elijah was very disappointed.

"You promised not to tell," said Elijah.

Lizzy stood behind them. She was in the doorway. She didn't want the men to see her. She had a very angry look on her face.

"Elijah," said Mr. Shepard as he pointed to the men. "What direction are they riding in?"

Elijah thought a minute. The sun was shining on the backs of the riding men. He seemed confused. Elijah looked at Mr. Shepard.

"West," said Elijah.

"Those two slave hunters never believe anything I say," explained Mr. Shepard. "I say northeast, and they go any other direction. Usually, I do tell them a lie. So this time they believed the truth was a lie. If I find a slave first, they don't get money. So we don't help each other out."

"Well, I'll be," said Lizzy. "You outfoxed those old wolves."

"It's not the first time. Now, when I find an escaped slave, they always manage to escape to freedom, before they're returned to their owners. I try to get them onto the underground railroad as quickly as possible.

Those two are trouble. One time they captured a runaway I had found while I was asleep. Now, if I am helping a runaway, I shackle us together at night.

"They may be back," said Mr. Shepard. "It would be best if we could keep moving. I think I can travel if we take it slow."

He looked at Lizzy. Mr. Shepard thought as he rubbed his chin. He looked at Elijah. Then he looked at Lizzy.

"It's too bad the two of you aren't the same size," said Mr. Shepard. "We could have disguised Lizzy as a boy. That would have helped. Lizzy's master has a big reward out for her."

Elijah smiled, "I have an older brother. His clothes should fit her. He's outgrown some overalls and a shirt. My mother was saving them for me. They should be just right for her. Besides, I think my mother would want her dress back."

"Good," said Mr. Shepard. "Now, I'll need some scissors."

"Scissors?" asked Lizzy.

"You're going to need a haircut," explained Mr. Shepard.

"Oh, no," said Lizzy. She started backing to the door. "I'm not letting you take scissors to my head with your shaky hands."

"Would you like your hair or your freedom?" asked Mr. Shepard.

"I can do it," offered Elijah. "I've watched my mom cut my brother and dad's hair."

Lizzy sighed. She sat on a bench. She lifted her hair off her neck. Lizzy looked like she was about to cry.

"Cut away," she said to Elijah.

Chapter 6

The Flooded Creek

Within an hour, Lizzy looked like a young boy. Mr. Shepard asked Elijah to get a hoe. He asked if Lizzy could borrow it until they were ready to travel. Lizzy asked why she needed to carry a hoe.

"Why would a runaway slave stop to weed a garden?" asked Mr. Shepard. "If a slave hunter saw you, he would think you're just a local farm boy. It's part of your disguise. If someone sees you, just start working."

"I'm going to follow the slave hunters for a bit to make sure they don't double back on us."

"What if someone from around here sees her? They'll know she doesn't belong here," said Elijah.

"She can tell them she's your cousin Sam. She's, I mean, he's here for a visit," explained Mr. Shepard. "Now all you have to do is show her the garden. If something happens to me, tell her where the next stop on the underground railroad is."

"Oh," said Elijah. He lowered his head. "I don't really know where the next stop is." Then his face brightened, "Uncle Jermain knows. I'll take Lizzy to him if I need to."

"Good," said Mr. Shepard. "I feel like I can ride. If you would kindly show me to my horse, I'll be leaving."

Elijah led Mr. Shepard and Lizzy to the barn. Mr. Shepard saddled up his horse. Elijah found a hoe for Lizzy to carry. He was sorry to see the man leave. He felt safer with the marshal around.

Lizzy and Elijah watched Mr. Shepard ride toward the town. Then they turned and began walking across the field. Uncle Jermain's cabin wasn't far. Elijah could see some of his cousins doing their morning chores.

Elijah's Aunt Mary met him at the porch. She didn't seem to notice Lizzy. Mary seemed very upset. Elijah thought she looked like she had been crying.

"Go out to the barn, Elijah. You're Uncle was just coming to get you," said Aunt Mary.

Elijah was now afraid. Maybe Uncle Jermain had found out he had helped a white man. He began trembling as he reached the barn. All his cousins stopped working. They all stared at Elijah. None of them said a word.

Inside the barn, Uncle Jermain was putting a bridle on his old mule. He didn't have a saddle. He said he didn't need one. That was a good thing. Uncle Jermain couldn't afford a saddle.

Uncle Jermain pulled himself onto the back of the mule. He reached down his hand. "Climb up, Son," he said. Elijah took his uncle's hand. A strong arm pulled him up. Uncle Jermain shook the reins. They rode out of the barn.

They rode for several minutes. Uncle Jermain said nothing. Elijah became more worried. He also became more confused. If he were in trouble, he would have known about it before now. What else could it be?

They neared a creek. Water was almost over the bridge. The heavy rains had made the little creek look like a roaring river. From the mud and sticks on the bridge, Elijah could tell the river had covered it in the last few hours.

"The creek level is dropping," said Uncle Jermain. He seemed very sad. "Mr. Jones was through here this morning. He saw something strange. He checked it out. Then he came to my place."

"This isn't easy son. I just didn't know how to tell you," said Uncle Jermain.

He guided the mule closer to the river bank. It normally dropped off ten feet. This morning, the creek was just a few feet below the bank. Elijah noticed the big tangle of branches.

They had been washed down the creek during the storm. The high winds blew them loose. The rushing water carried them away. They seemed to be caught on something.

Elijah studied the mess. There was something else in the pile. Just above the water was a wagon wheel. Elijah didn't understand why they were here looking at a wagon wheel stuck in the mud.

Uncle Jermain climbed down from the mule. He pulled Elijah down. They walked along the bank. Uncle Jermain got as close to the wagon wheel as he safely could. Elijah was still very confused.

He spoke softly to Elijah, "That's your folk's wagon. See the place on the wheel I fixed." He pointed through the brush. "Something bad has happened."

Elijah felt numb. This couldn't be true. This couldn't be happening. How could everyone leave him all alone?

"I've been down the creek. There's no sign that any of them made it to shore. Rushing water is a dangerous thing. I don't think there's any hope."

Elijah stood up. He took off his jacket. "They could still be in the wagon. They could be stuck. They need help!"

Uncle Jermain grabbed Elijah tightly. "You can't go in there. If they're still in the wagon, it's already too late." Tears streamed down Uncle Jermain's face.

He hugged Elijah tightly. The two of them cried. Suddenly, they heard a rustling sound. Someone was coming out of the woods next to the road.

The two watched hopefully. Maybe it was Elijah's family. Maybe they had made it to land. The two searched the woods with their eyes.

Elijah saw a familiar face appear. It was not his family. It was Mr. Shepard. He was leading a team of mules. Elijah recognized the mules, too. They were his father's.

"Mr. Shepard!" shouted Elijah. Uncle Jermain seemed surprised that Elijah knew the man.

Mr. Shepard looked at Uncle Jermain. "Do you know anything about these mules?"

"They belong to my brother," said Jermain. "I thank you for returning them. I'm afraid there's been an accident. You didn't happen to see any people along the creek?"

"Not a sign of anyone," said Mr. Shepard.

Jermain sighed, "I'm afraid they all drowned: my brother, his wife, and five children. My nephew, Elijah, is their other son. You seem to know each other."

"I owe my life to the boy," said Mr. Shepard.

Uncle Jermain didn't seem to understand. He started to ask a question. Mr. Shepard interrupted.

"We can save that story for another time. First of all, your brother is not dead."

Uncle Jermain stared at Mr. Shepard. He didn't know what to think of the white man. He seemed to know a lot. Elijah's uncle crossed his arms.

"What would you know about that?" asked Uncle Jermain.

"Hop on your mule. I'll show you."

Chapter 7
A Bit of Hope

Mr. Shepard led them up the road. They were heading back toward town. Mr. Shepard stopped and turned off the road. He pointed to some tracks.

"Your brother's wagon stopped here. It looks like they came from the bridge. My guess is the water covered the bridge. They pulled off into the woods to get some protection from the storm."

Mr. Shepard then pointed out some more prints. "Another wagon stopped by. There are more hoof prints, see? There are the wagon wheel prints."

Uncle Jermain didn't understand what Mr. Shepard was saying. Neither did Elijah. Mr. Shepard rode to another set of prints.

"See all the footprints? There was some kind of struggle here. Now, let's follow the wagon tracks back to the bridge."

Mr. Shepard led them down the road. He pointed to where the wagon tracks went into the creek. Behind the wagon were three sets of footprints. The footprints were filled with water.

"Those footprints are behind the wagon. They're also very deep. It shows that the wagon was pushed in the creek. That's why the mules got free. Someone set them free."

"So, did someone make my family drown?" asked Elijah.

"Like I said, your family's not dead. They've been kidnapped. I've seen this kind of thing before. Free black people are taken south. They're sold into slavery."

"How do you know all this?" asked Uncle Jermain.

"Until recently, I was a U.S. Marshal."

"How recent?" asked Uncle Jermain.

"Two months ago," said Mr. Shepard. "I spent many years catching lawbreakers, then the new Fugitive Slave Act was passed. It would have made me hunt down women, and children just because they wanted to be free. I couldn't justify that."

"I took off my badge. It's still in my saddle bags. However, I never want to wear it again. Not when it means I have to arrest innocent people."

"He was looking for Lizzy," added Elijah.

"Who's Lizzy?" asked Uncle Jermain.

"The young boy Elijah brought to your farm," explained Mr. Shepard.

"A boy named Lizzy?" asked Jermain.

"You can call her Sam," said Mr. Shepard.

Elijah was very relieved to find out his family hadn't drowned. But he was worried. They had been kidnapped. He still hadn't gotten his family back.

"We'll need to go after them," said Mr. Shepard.

"We'll?" said Uncle Jermain. "I'll need to go after them. This isn't any of your business."

"You'll end up a slave yourself," warned Mr. Shepard. "You don't want to travel in the slave states alone. Besides, how will you get them back when you find them? I need you to help me identify them. You need me to keep you from ending up a slave yourself."

"I'll come to," said Elijah.

Mr. Shepard and Uncle Jermain both said no to that. "It's just too dangerous. You can stay at our house. Aunt Mary will take care of you and Lizzy or Sam. We'll take care of the rest."

"We'll?" said Mr. Shepard.

"I don't want to end up a slave. I guess we're stuck with each other."

Mr. Shepard put out his hand. Uncle Jermain shook it. They started back for Uncle Jermain's farm. They would need some supplies to get started.

Mr. Shepard and Jermain packed quickly. They needed to get some food and water. Uncle Jermain didn't have a fancy saddlebag like Mr. Shepard. He had two cloth bags. They hung over each side of the mule.

Seeing the bags gave Mr. Shepard an idea. Mr. Shepard opened his own cloth bag. Elijah knew what was in it. It had the chains and the irons that were used on slaves. He pulled out a set of handcuffs.

Uncle Jermain was afraid he was going to be handcuffed. Mr. Shepard held out the handcuffs. Uncle Jermain reached out and grabbed them. Next, Mr. Shepard pulled a string around his neck. The string had a key tied to it.

He handed that to Uncle Jermain also. Elijah watched his uncle take them. His uncle had a very curious look on his face.

"Put the handcuffs in your bags. Put the key around your neck," explained Mr. Shepard. "If I tell you to put the cuffs on, do so. You might have to wear them in some towns. I gave you the key. Try it out. I'm not trying to trick you."

Uncle Jermain put the key in the lock. The cuffs opened. Jermain put the key around his neck. He stuffed the handcuffs in one of the cloth bags.

"No one will try to catch you if you've already been caught," said Mr. Shepard. "This has been some day. First, I disguise a runaway as a free person. Now, I'm disguising a free man as a slave. Anyway, those chains may keep you from becoming a slave."

"Are you sure I can't come along?" asked Elijah.

"Who would run the farm?" asked Uncle Jermain.

Elijah knew that was just an excuse. He knew his cousins could do his chores. The really hard work, like plowing, he couldn't do anyway. That would have to wait until his father came home. Elijah didn't argue. He knew it would do no good.

Uncle Jermain had his mind made up. Elijah never knew him to change it. That didn't matter to Elijah. Nobody was going to kidnap his family and get away with it. Uncle Jermain said he couldn't come along.

His uncle didn't tell him he had to stay. Elijah wasn't planning on staying. Not from the second he heard Mr. Shepard tell what happened. Elijah noticed something about Mr. Shepard's saddle. It made him feel even braver.

"I'd better do my chores," said Elijah. "When will you be back?"

"It may take a few days," said Uncle Jermain. "Just do as your aunt says. We'll take care of the rest."

"Thank you," said Elijah.

"No," said Mr. Shepard. "Thank you. I owe you my life."

"Mr. Shepard, if you get my family back, you don't owe me a thing!" Elijah said as he ran toward his barn.

Chapter 8
Elijah on the Trail

Elijah knew he would have to hurry. He fed the chickens. He didn't bother to collect the eggs. He made sure their water trough was full.

The little donkey was waiting for his breakfast. "Eat fast. I have plans for you," Elijah said to the donkey.

The hogs and cows had their own little ponds. He threw the pigs some rotting vegetables and a few ears of corn. Elijah put the mules in the pasture.

Next, he ran to the house. He tried to think fast. Uncle Jermain and Mr. Shepard would be passing through any minute. Elijah didn't want them to get too far ahead.

Elijah packed some food and matches. He took a blanket. Then he remembered to grab his papers. They would prove he was free.

There was also a small tin can above the stove. It had a few coins in it. His mother saved it for emergencies. Elijah thought this was the biggest emergency his family had ever had. He took the can.

He threw everything into a white flour sack. In the barn, he grabbed some rope. He thought he might need it to tie up the kidnappers.

Elijah dug into the hay. He found what he was looking for. There was Mr. Shepard's rifle. The man hadn't noticed it was missing. He wrapped it in a brown burlap sack.

A small saddle was in the barn. It had been a gift from his grandfather. He had traded it for some work in his blacksmith shop. The saddle came with the little donkey. It was just right for a boy Elijah's size.

He strapped the saddle on the donkey. Elijah tied on his supplies and the rifle. He knew that if his uncle caught him, he would be in big trouble. He thought he could just say he was bringing Mr. Shepard the rifle.

Elijah came out of the barn when his uncle and Mr. Shepard rode by. He waved. His uncle told him to be good. He also said to be brave. Everything would be all right.

"I'll be brave," yelled Elijah.

Soon, they were over the hill. Elijah ran into the barn. He led the little donkey out. Elijah swung his leg over the saddle.

Elijah stayed out of sight. He wouldn't ride on the road.

He rode in the woods alongside the road. Uncle Jermain and Mr. Shepard were heading toward the town. They would cross a bridge into Kentucky.

Elijah watched the two men cross the bridge. He waited. A smile came across his face. A large cargo wagon was crossing the bridge. It had a tall load of boxes.

"Just what I was waiting for," said Elijah.

He could hide behind the large wagon as it crossed. If his uncle turned around, he couldn't see Elijah. All he would see was the full wagon.

Elijah did sneak a quick peek around the wagon a few times. His uncle and Mr. Shepard were almost to the other side. He was peeking when he reached the other side. Suddenly a loud noise made the donkey stop.

A small wooden box had fallen off the wagon. Elijah started to call out to the driver. He stopped. He didn't want his uncle to hear him. Elijah got off his donkey.

No one else was crossing the bridge. The box had broken open. Elijah was curious. He looked inside the box.

It made him smile. "Firecrackers!"

He picked them up and threw them in his sack. The wagon was now farther away from him. It had passed Uncle Jermain and Mr. Shepard. They were deciding which road to take.

If they turned around, they would see him. Elijah led the donkey across the bridge. He hid in a ditch at the side of the road. He walked toward his uncle. The tall grass helped hide him.

He got close enough to hear them talking. A man had a covered wagon full pots and pans. He was trying to sell them to people who passed over the bridge. Mr. Shepard was asking the man if he had seen wagons full of slaves pass through.

"I saw a wagon late last night. I couldn't believe they would be out in this storm. There was a whole family. I saw a man and a woman with a baby."

"And three boys and another girl?" asked Uncle Jermain.

"That sounds about right," said the man. "It was dark and raining. I couldn't see very well. Still, that sounds right. They went toward Newport. I suppose they were runaways. Most likely they were being taken to the judge."

"That makes sense," said Mr. Shepard. "They'll be put on trial there."

"Trial?" asked Uncle Jermain. "For what?"

"For being runaway slaves," said Mr. Shepard.

"But they're free," said Uncle Jermain. "They've been free all their lives!"

"I hope they have their papers," said Mr. Shepard. "The judge doesn't like to let any black people go free if he can help it."

Uncle Jermain and Mr. Shepard rode off. Elijah was about to climb out of the ditch. Then he heard hoof beats. He thought maybe they had come back to the old man. Elijah listened carefully.

The horses were coming from the other direction. They stopped at the wagon. A man was yelling for the old man to come out. The man poked his head out.

"Would you like to buy some pans?" he asked.

One of the men flipped him a coin. "Just tell me what those last two men wanted," said the man.

"They were just looking for some slave hunters," said the old man. "It seems like there was some kind of mix-up. Something about a free black family that someone thought was a slave. I'm sure the judge will get it worked out."

Elijah listened as they rode off. He hurried out of the ditch. Elijah saw the men ride away. They were following Mr. Shepard and Uncle Jermain. The little donkey couldn't keep up with the horses.

Elijah watched from a distance as three men on horses caught up with them. They had guns pointed at Mr. Shepard and Uncle Jermain. Elijah hid in the woods. The men found the handcuffs in Mr. Shepard and Uncle Jermain's bags.

They made them put them on. One of the men searched Mr. Shepard for the key. Mr. Shepard said that he had lost it. Uncle Jermain and Mr. Shepard were led into the woods.

Elijah's Coming
Part 3

Table of Contents

Chapter		Page
9	Captured	31
10	Saving the Family Papers	34
11	A Chicken to the Rescue	36
12	The Proof	39

by Brian Davis

Vocabulary Words

biscuits

decision

identify

instructions

plantation

Mr. Shepard and Uncle Jermain are in trouble. Will Elijah be able to help them and save his family? Find out in the conclusion of *Elijah's Coming!*

Chapter 9
Captured!

Elijah tied up his donkey behind some bushes. He knew how to be quiet in the woods. Elijah liked to hunt with his father. Any noise would scare the animals away. So he learned to be very quiet.

He got close enough to see what was happening. Mr. Shepard and Uncle Jermain were led down a hollow. Their waists were tied around a tree. Gags were put in their mouths. They wouldn't be able to yell for help. They were then blindfolded.

One man rode on toward town. Another one led Mr. Shepard's horse and Uncle Jermain's mule into the woods. The other man guarded their prisoners. Elijah was hoping they would just go away. He would then be able to free his uncle and Mr. Shepard.

Elijah found a small cliff he could lean over. He watched them all afternoon. The two men sat by a fire. They looked at Mr. Shepard and Uncle Jermain once in awhile. Elijah could hear the men talking.

"I sure hope the sheriff doesn't come looking for us," said one of the men.

"Why would he come out here?" said the other.

"Well, someone will be missing these two. They'll come looking."

Elijah could tell they were worried about getting caught. Still, by nighttime, they hadn't left. The other man never came back. Elijah wanted to ride on to town. He wanted to save his family. Mr. Shepard and Uncle Jermain would need to be rescued first.

The woods were soon dark. The only light was from a small campfire. Elijah went back to his donkey. He opened his sack. He took out what he needed.

Elijah unwrapped the rifle. He had never thought of shooting at a man. The thought made him shake. He hoped his plan would work.

Elijah crept to the cliff. The men were still at the campfire. Elijah took out some firecrackers. He lit a match. Elijah tossed the firecrackers.

The popping sound echoed through the woods. Elijah took out the rifle. He fired it toward the camp. But he was careful not to aim at the men. By this time the men were jumping and running for cover.

Elijah tossed some firecrackers into their campfire. The explosions made sparks fly out. Elijah was glad it had rained that morning. He didn't want to set the woods on fire.

Tiny sparks landed everywhere. The men were brushing them out of their hair. They were confused and afraid. One of them started yelling.

"It's the sheriff and his deputies. Get out of here!"

The two men hopped on their horses and rode off. Elijah watched his uncle and Mr. Shepard. Uncle Jermain reached the key to the handcuffs. Elijah watched as Uncle Jermain and Mr. Shepard freed themselves.

They looked around for the sheriff. The woods were now silent. Mr. Shepard untied his horse. Uncle Jermain hopped on his mule. Elijah sneaked back to the donkey and began to follow them again.

Before long they were riding into Newport. Mr. Shepard went right to the sheriff's office. Elijah hid in an alley between the jail and the newspaper office.

Elijah heard Mr. Shepard and Uncle Jermain talking to the sheriff. Elijah found out some good news. His parents were inside the jail. Mr. Shepard explained how they had been kidnapped.

Then Elijah heard some bad news. The sheriff wouldn't let Elijah's parents go. He explained that they were accused of being runaways. They would have to go to trial. That would happen in the morning.

Uncle Jermain was getting very upset. He told the sheriff that the kidnappers should be going to trial. The law was working for the wrong people. His voice got louder and louder.

The door to the sheriff's office opened. Mr. Shepard pushed Uncle Jermain out.

"You're going to land us in jail," explained Mr. Shepard. "You can't yell at the sheriff like that."

"But he," Uncle Jermain tried to argue.

"He's doing all he can," said Mr. Shepard. "It's up to the judge now. I'm sure everything will work out."

Uncle Jermain calmed down. "He didn't even let us see them. I wish we could tell them everything was going to be all right."

That gave Elijah an idea. He looked down the alley. There was a small window. It was high off the ground. It had bars on it. Elijah decided to send his parents a message.

"I just need some paper and something to write with," he said to himself.

Then he remembered the newspaper office. A light was still on. Elijah figured they were working on the next morning's paper. They had lots of ink and paper there. He noticed a back door to the office.

He decided to sneak in. Elijah tied up his donkey. He reached into the bag. Elijah pulled out the can of coins. He put them in his pocket. He didn't want to leave his money in the alley.

Elijah was in luck. The back door was unlocked. Inside was a desk. Nobody was around.

He found a sheet of paper on the desk. A feather quill sat in a jar of ink. He was going to write a message. He wanted to write: Elijah's coming to get you out of jail.

He had just finished the word "coming." Then he heard footsteps coming his way. Elijah grabbed the paper. He started to go to the door.

Then he saw the doorknob turning. Elijah dove under a table. He pulled his knees up to his chest. He didn't want to be seen.

The outside door opened and closed. Elijah saw a pair of cowboy boots. Another man came from inside the newspaper office. Elijah heard a match being struck. He began to smell cigar smoke. The man from the newspaper office whispered.

"Did you bring the money?" he asked.

"Fifty dollars for one piece of paper," said the man from outside. "Do you have the fake wanted poster?"

"I finished running tomorrow's paper first. I have the press almost set up. Why don't you go to the saloon for about a half hour? Meet me back here."

"Alright. Make sure it describes that black family, a man, woman, baby and four other children. It should say they escaped from a plantation in Louisiana. Here, take these. Get their names from the papers we took from them."

Elijah heard the rustle of paper.

"Make sure you burn those when you're done. That's the only thing that proves they're really free."

"I'll add the names to the poster," said the newspaper man.

Chapter 10
Saving the Family Papers

Elijah was left alone in the office. When it was safe, he sneaked out the back door. He knew what he had to do. Elijah needed to get his family's freedom papers back.

There was a window in the alley. Elijah rolled a wooden barrel up to it. He stood on the barrel and looked inside. The man was looking at Elijah's parents' papers.

The newspaper man was setting up the printing press. Elijah knew his timing had to be perfect. He counted on the printing press making just enough noise. He waited until the man was just starting to print the poster. The man tossed the papers on the table behind him. They landed next to a pile of freshly printed newspapers.

Elijah sneaked into the back door of the newspaper office. He moved as quickly as he could. His hand reached out to grab his parent's papers. Just then the newspaper man turned around. Elijah froze.

He was a big man. He puffed on a cigar. The man didn't notice Elijah at first. He placed the wanted poster on the table. Then he reached for the freedom papers. His hand touched Elijah's.

That startled both of them. They both jumped back. Elijah wanted to grab the papers and run. He knew he'd never get away.

Instead, he grabbed a newspaper and plopped it on the table. "My master would like a paper," said Elijah. He reached into his pocket and pulled out some coins. "How much?"

"Three cents," said the newspaper man.

The newspaper man took the coins. Elijah slid the newspaper off the table. He didn't know what to do next. He looked at his parent's papers.

The newspaper man saw Elijah staring. "What are you looking at boy?" said the newspaper man. He scooped up the papers. The man walked to a little potbellied stove.

A small fire was inside. The man tossed in the papers.

Elijah's heart sank. He turned and left the newspaper office. This time he went out the front door. Elijah remembered the kidnapper would be back soon.

He ran to the alley. Elijah stuffed the newspaper in his bag. Then he remembered the note. Elijah grabbed a small rock. He wrapped his note around it.

Elijah was good at throwing rocks. He could skip one four times across the pond. That skill came in handy. He wanted to get out of the alley before the man came back.

It only took one toss to get the rock and his note into the small jailhouse window. The rock landed on Elijah's father's lap. He jumped. Then he unwrapped the note.

"Elijah's coming," he whispered to his wife.

"What does that mean?" she asked.

"I hope it means he knows we were kidnapped," answered Elijah's father.

"I don't know if that makes me feel better," said Elijah's mother. "I was hoping he was safe at Jermain's house."

"Well, I guess the man we heard yelling was Jermain," said Elijah's father. "I'm sure they're together."

Elijah and his Uncle weren't together. Elijah was all alone. He wandered the streets. Now he wished he could find his Uncle. He knew something that could help his parents. He had to tell them about the fake wanted poster.

He came to a house at the edge of town. Something looked familiar about it. He didn't catch it at first. Then a feeling of relief came to him. Near a shed hung a blue lantern.

Elijah approached the door. He knocked softly three times. He heard someone walking slowly to the door.

"Who's there?"

"A friend with a friend," answered Elijah.

The door opened. A white woman was dressed in her sleeping gown. She looked at Elijah. Then she eyed the donkey. She pointed to the animal.

"That must be your friend," she said with a chuckle.

The house was a stop on the Underground Railroad. Elijah was fed. He was given a warm place to sleep. The woman started giving him instructions for the next stop.

"Once you cross the river, look for two cabins. They're not too far apart, just across a field from each other. I heard they're a nice black family."

"I know the place," smiled Elijah. The woman had described his home. He had heard about this woman from runaways.

"I sent a young gal that way just the other day. I sure hope she made it," said the woman.

Elijah smiled when he thought of Lizzy. He wanted to tell the woman about everything that had happened. Then he remembered how the kidnappers tied up Mr. Shepard and his Uncle. He didn't want anything bad to happen to this woman.

He thought it was better that she not get involved. Besides, Uncle Jermain and Mr. Shepard would get things fixed. Elijah was beginning to feel things would be fine. He was also feeling very sleepy.

Chapter 11

A Chicken to the Rescue

The smell of fresh baked biscuits filled the air. Bacon sizzled on the stove. Pots and pans clanked in the kitchen. It was all the things Elijah liked waking up to.

At first, he thought he was home. Then he opened his eyes. He was in a small bedroom. Sunlight poured through a window.

Elijah popped out of bed. He slid to the floor. Elijah pulled on his shoes. On the floor was his cloth bag. He snatched it and ran to the kitchen.

He started to run out the back door. The woman blocked it. "I cooked this breakfast just for you. Now sit down and enjoy it. Besides, a runaway needs his strength. You shouldn't go out in the daytime anyway."

The food did look good. "What time is it?" asked Elijah.

"Seven o'clock," said the woman. "Why?"

"I have to get to the courthouse," said Elijah.

"It won't be open for another hour. Sit down and eat. Why would a runaway slave go to the courthouse?"

"I'm not a slave. I got lost from my uncle. I need to meet him at the courthouse this morning," Elijah explained as he ate.

The woman didn't ask any more questions. Elijah didn't explain anything else. He just ate. He was glad he had some time. The food was wonderful.

Soon he was on his way again. Elijah rode the little donkey. This time he wanted Mr. Shepard and Uncle Jermain to find him.

The road was busy. Farmers were coming to town to sell things. Some had vegetables. Others had animals in crates. There were piglets, chickens, and even a few ducks.

The courthouse was easy to find. It was in the middle of town. People were gathered at the steps to go in. Elijah just caught a glimpse of his family.

They were chained together. Some deputies followed them with guns. Their backs were turned to Elijah. He jumped, yelled, and waved, but they couldn't hear him. Farmers were setting up a little market. People were gathered to shop.

Elijah tied up his donkey. He grabbed his white bag. Mr. Shepard and Uncle Jermain were on the courthouse steps. Elijah tried to get to them. He was getting bumped and shoved.

By the time he got to the courthouse the steps were empty. He opened the door. Just as he stepped in, a deputy stopped him.

"Stay outside, Boy. You have no business here," said the deputy. He gave Elijah a shove.

"I need to…" started Elijah.

It was too late. The deputy closed the door. That wasn't going to stop Elijah. He ran around the courthouse. There was a backdoor.

It was standing open. A deputy leaned against the doorframe. Elijah sighed. There just had to be a way.

He sat in the grass. Elijah watched the shoppers. There were families. Mothers shopped with their small children. Elijah missed his family. He stared up at an open courthouse window. Then he saw a crate full of chickens. He felt the coins in his pocket. Elijah hopped up from the courthouse lawn.

Inside the trial was beginning. The bailiff read the charges. Elijah's family was accused of being runaway slaves. The man in the cowboy boots handed the judge a poster.

It described Elijah's family. The poster said they were the property of Mr. Jonas. He said he came from a plantation in Louisiana. He claimed that Elijah's family lived there. The poster was proof of that.

Elijah's father spoke up, "That's a lie! My family has been free for four generations."

The judge pounded his gavel. He pointed at Elijah's father. "The law states that you cannot speak for yourself. If you yell in my courtroom again, I'll have you and your family whipped."

"Now," said the judge, "does anyone here have proof that this family doesn't belong to Mr. Jonas?"

Mr. Shepard stood up. "Yes, judge. This is a free family from Ohio. They were kidnapped yesterday."

"And you have proof of this?" asked the judge.

Uncle Jermain stood up, "I have proof. This man is my brother. What he said was true."

The judge looked at Jermain, "I asked do you have proof? If I just have your word, then how do I know who is telling the truth? This man claims they are his slaves. You say they're free. Whom am I to believe?"

Jermain knew the answer. The judge would believe the white man. The judge just shook his head.

"This is a simple matter of law. The Fugitive Slave Act states that all a person must do is identify his property. Nobody here can prove that these runaways are not his. I have to rule for…"

Just then, Elijah tossed a chicken through the window. The whole courtroom full of people started laughing. All the deputies rushed forward. They chased the chicken.

One deputy grabbed a foot. The chicken pecked him on the head. The man let go. Finally, a farmer in the crowd came forward.

He cornered the chicken. The farmer picked it up. He tucked it between his arms. The bird calmed down.

Nobody noticed that Elijah had sneaked into the back of the courtroom.

Chapter 12
The Proof

Everyone took their seats. The judge straightened out the table in front of him. He looked around the room. The judge cleared his throat.

"As I was saying there is no proof that…"

"I have proof," said Elijah from the back of the courtroom.

He walked forward. All eyes were on him. A deputy tried to stop him.

"Let the boy come," said the judge. "I want to see any proof he has."

Elijah pointed to his parents, "I am their son. I am free. I have papers to prove it."

Elijah dug into his bag. He pulled out the newspaper. He placed it on a table. Finally, he found his freedom papers. He handed them to the judge.

The judge looked them over. He handed them back. The judge looked at Mr. Jonas. Then he picked up the wanted poster.

"The poster says there are only five children in the family. The names of the parents on the boy's papers are the same as the wanted poster. How would you explain that?" the judge asked Mr. Jonas.

"The boy's papers could be faked. Or his parents might just have the same names. All I know is that those slaves are mine."

"And this boy isn't?" asked the judge about Elijah.

"I've never seen him before," answered Mr. Jonas.

The judge sighed. "I guess that could be the case."

Elijah spoke to the judge. "I have more proof."

The judge nodded. Elijah looked at his mother. "I brought a blanket. It's in this bag. You keep it on your rocker. What color is it?"

Mr. Jonas spoke up, "The law states that the runaways can't answer questions. You said so yourself, Judge."

The judge nodded. "True. It couldn't hurt to hear the answer."

"I didn't make the law," said Mr. Jonas, "but you promised to keep the law."

The judge sighed. He looked at Elijah. "Do you have any other proof?"

"I saw Mr. Jonas last night," said Elijah. "He didn't bring that poster from Louisiana. He had it printed at the newspaper office. He paid fifty dollars for it. Then the newspaper man burned my family's freedom papers."

"That's quite a story," said the judge. "I'd like to believe you."

Something startled the chicken. It fluttered away from a farmer who was holding it. The chicken landed on a table. As it did, Elijah's newspaper fell to the floor.

He reached down to grab it. As he picked it up he noticed something. A paper was stuck to the back. Elijah pulled it off. It was another copy of the wanted poster.

"I have proof," said Elijah as he waved the paper in the air.

He handed the newspaper and the poster to the judge. The judge studied the papers. Mr. Jonas tugged on his collar as he watched. He seemed to be getting very warm.

The judge looked up. "Mr. Jonas," the judge waved the newspaper. "Your name might be in the paper tomorrow." Then he looked at the people in the courtroom.

"The ink from the wanted poster stuck to the newspaper. That means the ink was wet at the time. This is today's paper. It was probably printed last night. It's the Newport News. The boy's story must be true."

He pointed to Elijah's family, "These people were kidnapped." Then he pointed to Mr. Jonas. "And there is the kidnapper."

The judged ordered the deputies to take the chains off Elijah's family. He then ordered them to put the chains on Mr. Jonas. Elijah's father told how they were kidnapped. He told how Mr. Jonas and two other men pushed the wagon into the creek.

"The boy is lying," Mr. Jonas yelled. "I brought that wanted poster from Louisiana. I didn't have it printed here." Mr. Jonas was very angry. He stood and shouted, "He has no proof of his story!"

The judge asked how much the wagon was worth. Elijah's father said twenty-five dollars. The judge ordered Mr. Jonas to pay Elijah's father one hundred dollars for the wagon. The judge didn't like being lied to.

Mr. Jonas told the judge where to find the other two men. The sheriff went to look for them. Soon they would be in jail. Elijah hugged his family. The judge started to leave.

"Sir," said Elijah.

The judge stopped.

"Could I have my chicken back?" asked Elijah.

The judge seemed surprised, "That's your chicken?" He grinned. "I'd take good care of that hen if I were you. She saved me from making a very bad decision."

"I will, sir," said Elijah.

Mr. Shepard and Uncle Jermain walked up behind Elijah. He looked up at them. They patted him on the back.

"I thought I told you to stay home," said Uncle Jermain.

"No, you said I couldn't come with you," explained Elijah. "You never said I couldn't come by myself."

"Well, we couldn't have done it without you," said Mr. Shepard.

Elijah agreed, "You would probably still be tied to that tree."

"You made all that noise?" asked Uncle Jermain.

Mr. Shepard shook his head, "You are one amazing young man."

Elijah got lots of hugs that day. His father said he was proud of him. Elijah's mother just laughed and cried. His older brother said that he would buy Elijah a whole store full of candy someday.

Elijah's father bought a new wagon. They hitched Mr. Shepard's horse and Uncle Jermain's mule to the wagon. Elijah tied the little donkey to the back. They headed toward home.

Outside the town, Mr. Shepard told them to stop. He hopped from the wagon. Mr. Shepard grabbed his rifle. The family watched him approach a large farmhouse just off the road.

Everyone was very curious. Mr. Shepard talked to a man on the front porch of the house. Elijah watched but they were too far away to hear. Mr. Shepard handed the man the rifle. The man wrote something on a piece of paper. Mr. Shepard seemed very happy when he returned.

"What happened?" asked Uncle Jermain.

Mr. Shepard grinned. "Nothing."

By evening, the new wagon rolled onto the farm. Everyone was very tired, except Mr. Shepard. He hopped from the wagon. Everyone else crawled out.

He unhitched his horse. Uncle Jermain unhitched the mule. Mr. Shepard walked to the back of the wagon. He untied the donkey.

"Elijah!" called Mr. Shepard. "Come with me. The day isn't over yet." He motioned for Elijah to get on the donkey.

Elijah knew something good was up. He didn't want to miss it. Elijah ran to the donkey. Mr. Shepard and Elijah followed Uncle Jermain across the field. Uncle Jermain looked very confused.

A young boy was hoeing in the garden. "Who is that?" asked Uncle Jermain.

"Lizzy!" called Mr. Shepard.

The boy turned. It wasn't really a boy. It was Lizzy.

"You're supposed to call me Sam!" she said.

Mr. Shepard reached into his pocket. He pulled out a paper. He handed it to Lizzy. She didn't know what it was.

"Read it for her, Elijah," said Mr. Shepard.

Elijah slid off the donkey. "It says Bill of Sale. It says Mr. Shepard owns you."

Elijah didn't quite understand. "You bought Lizzy?"

Mr. Shepard laughed, "No, I bought her freedom. That farmhouse we stopped at was her old master's home. I traded my rifle for her. I explained that getting a nice rifle for Lizzy was a good deal. She had already escaped. So, if he couldn't catch her, he would have nothing. He agreed."

Lizzy dropped the hoe. "You mean I'm free? I'm really free! No more running and hiding!"

"That's just the way it should be," said Mr. Shepard. "Everyone should be free."

Matthew & Goliath
Part 1

Table of Contents

Chapter		Page
1	Nathan Goliath	44
2	The Price of Peace	46
3	Matthew's New Diet	49
4	Three Smooth Baseballs	52
5	Batter Up	55

Vocabulary Words

compassion

distracting

inexpensive

murmur

nervous

opportunity

persecute

story by Brian Davis
illustrations by Ron Wheeler

A new boy causes big problems for Matthew Day and his friends. Will Matthew have the courage to face the bully and teach him a well deserved lesson?

Chapter 1
Nathan Goliath

Matthew Day could hear crying as he approached his third-grade classroom. The teacher had closed the door. He looked at his friends, Rail and Buzz. Rail had a puzzled look on his face.

"What's going on?" asked Buzz as he turned the doorknob.

The knob didn't turn.

"We're locked out. I guess we should all go home. Let's start our three-day weekend."

Buzz was the class clown. He never missed an opportunity to joke around. It was typical of him to miss the fact that someone behind the door was upset.

"You have no business in there," said the school nurse. She had just walked up behind them. She was carrying an ice pack.

"I was just going to get my spelling book," said Buzz. He was always quick with an excuse.

"You could certainly use the extra study time," said the nurse.

Buzz looked puzzled. How could she know? The nurse saw the surprised look on the boy's face.

"I am the school nurse," she explained, "and your spelling grade is not too healthy."

Matthew and Rail laughed. The nurse unlocked the door. She slipped inside without opening the door all the way. Buzz tried to follow her.

"O-u-t, out!" spelled the nurse with her finger pointed at Buzz.

• "Isn't out spelled o-w-t?" asked Buzz. He saw the stern look on her face. "Just kidding," said Buzz as he backed out of the doorway.

More classmates gathered around the door. School was about to start. The hallway was getting noisier. Buzz put his ear to the door.

"Get quiet," yelled Buzz. "I can't tell what they're saying."

Mrs. Anderson, their teacher, opened the door. "I can certainly hear what you're saying, Bradley." Bradley was Buzz's real name. "Now, clear a path and let us through."

The crowd around the door moved back. They parted like Moses parted the Red Sea. Everyone watched as the teacher, the nurse, and Stacy Lane walked out of the classroom. Stacy was one of Matthew's classmates. She was holding a bag of ice over her right eye.

• A murmur rose from the crowd. This had to be serious. "At least Stacy is walking," thought Matthew. But everyone had more questions than answers.

"I'll be back in a moment," said Mrs. Anderson. "Everyone go find your seats and begin your morning board work."

Mrs. Anderson always had something written for them to do on the chalkboard. Buzz started to go in. All of the sudden he stopped.

"I'd rather wait out here," said Buzz.

•Matthew looked over his shoulder. Only one person was in the room. It was Nathan Goliath. He was the biggest third grader Matthew had ever seen. This was Nathan's second day at Matthew's school.

Matthew thought Nathan was trouble the first time he saw him. He shuddered as he thought about it. What had the giant third grader done to Stacy's eye?

"I don't blame you," said Matthew.

"It's just too scary in there for me," said Buzz. "I…I can't believe our morning board work is spelling!"

Rail stepped right between the two boys. He put his lunchbox on the shelf. Rail calmly hung his backpack on a hook. He unzipped it and pulled out his folders. Matthew wasn't surprised. Rail was smaller than the other students, but he was fearless.

By now all the students had crowded just inside the door. They wanted to see what Nathan would do to Rail. They both sat in the same row by the windows. Nathan was in back, of course. He had to be. No other third grader could see around him.

Rail was in the front. He had to be. He couldn't see around any of the other students. Matthew sat in the next row, second desk back. They were still close enough to talk when the teacher let them. It was a near perfect seating arrangement, until yesterday.

Just as Rail walked by Nathan's desk, he tripped. Rail landed flat on his face. His folders slid across the classroom. The boys and girls in the classroom jumped back.

Nathan didn't seem to notice. He was staring out the window. The big third grader had a giant smile on his face. He even started waving to someone outside.

Matthew was getting angry. The new boy had just tripped his best friend. Nathan seemed to be very pleased with the mess he created. Then Matthew noticed who Nathan was waving at.

It was Stacy. She was walking out of the school with her mother. Matthew grew angrier. How could this huge kid be so cruel? Nathan's waving seemed to mock her. There was even a proud look on his face.

None of the other third graders rushed to help Rail. They were afraid of Nathan. Matthew was so stunned he didn't think of helping his friend at first. Then he realized that Rail needed him.

Matthew rushed over to him. He was careful to stay away from Nathan as much as possible. Rail seemed to be okay. He was more embarrassed than hurt. Matthew helped gather and sort the folders and papers.

Suddenly, Nathan turned around. "You should be more careful," Nathan warned. "You don't want to end up like Stacy."

"Uh…no sir," stammered Rail.

"I'll be careful too," said Matthew.

"That's a good idea," said Nathan. "There seems to be a lot of accidents happening around here." Then Nathan smiled.

Matthew and Rail scurried to their desks. The two boys peeked over their shoulders. Nathan was staring at Rail. Now, the huge third grader had a big frown on his face.

Matthew thought it was one of the meanest looks he had ever seen on a third grader. A cold chill ran down his spine. He glanced at Rail. He looked a little pale and swallowed hard.

Chapter 2
The Price of Peace

Mrs. Anderson seemed to be in a good mood when she came back to the classroom. The students didn't even notice her return. They were all busy doing the morning board work. Everyone was so afraid of Nathan. The normal distracting chatter between students was missing. There was nothing else to do but school work.

Still, Matthew was surprised that Mrs. Anderson didn't say something about Stacy. Why wasn't Nathan being punished? Matthew wondered if even Mrs. Anderson was afraid of Nathan. He was almost bigger than the teacher.

Trudy Upton, Stacy's best friend raised her hand.

"Yes, Trudy," said Mrs. Anderson.

"Is Stacy going to be all right?" asked Trudy.

"She'll be fine. I'm sure she'll be here Monday," said Mrs. Anderson.

"I hope the rest of us make it through the day," said Buzz. "There seem to be a lot of 'accidents' happening in this classroom."

Everyone turned and looked at Nathan. The big third grader smiled.

"I'll be careful," said Nathan. "I hope everyone else will be careful too."

Everyone quickly turned around. All the students worked quietly that morning. Soon it was time for morning recess. The class was afraid of what Nathan might do to them on the playground.

"Okay class, put away your work. It's time for recess," said Mrs. Anderson.

Buzz raised his hand, "May I stay in to study my spelling?"

Mrs. Anderson laughed, "Quit joking around, Buzz."

Ten other hands shot up. "Can I stay in, too?" everyone was asking.

"I must have the funniest class," said Mrs. Anderson. "I want everyone to line up, except Nathan."

"Except Nathan?" said Matthew. "I'm ready for recess!"

A line formed very quickly at the door. They waited for Mr. Morgan's class to pass. Then Mrs. Anderson's class followed behind. Mr. Morgan had recess duty that day. Four third grade classes had recess at the same time.

Mrs. Anderson's class was relieved to get outside. They all talked about what had happened to Stacy and Rail. Soon, all the third graders knew about the giant in Mrs. Anderson's class. They were all glad Nathan had to sit out this recess.

Then it happened. The door to the school building opened. Out stepped the biggest third grader in all the classes. He was even bigger than a lot of the fifth graders. Nathan Goliath seemed to fill the whole doorway.

"What do you suppose happened to Mrs. Anderson?" asked Trudy Upton.

"I don't know, but I'm really going to miss her," said Buzz.

"Stop it," said Matthew. "I'm sure there's a good reason he's out here."

"Nobody ever misses just part of a recess," said Rail. "Especially when you give someone a black eye."

"Something doesn't make sense here," said Matthew. He started walking toward Nathan.

"Come back," yelled Buzz. "It's not worth the risk!"

Matthew stopped. He was close enough to hear what Nathan was saying. The boy towered over another group of third graders. Matthew could see the fear in their eyes.

"I'm collecting money..." said Nathan.

All the students pulled out coins. They handed them to Nathan.

"Is this enough?" asked one of the boys. "I can bring more money Monday."

"Okay," said Nathan. "I'll look for you Monday at recess."

The students ran off. Matthew watched Nathan count the money. Nathan put it in his pocket. Rail, Buzz, and Trudy ran up to Matthew.

"What happened?" asked Rail.

"He took some money from those kids," said Matthew.

Nathan looked at Matthew, Rail, Buzz, and Trudy. He seemed to be watching them. Matthew had a sinking feeling in his stomach.

"Good-bye allowance," Matthew said as he reached for the change in his pocket.

"Oh, no," said Rail. "I don't have any money."

"Why don't you run to Mr. Morgan?" said Matthew.

"And tell on Nathan?" asked Rail.

"Are you crazy?" asked Buzz. "You'll really make Nathan mad if you tell on him. Besides, I don't want to see Mr. Morgan get hurt."

"No," said Matthew. "Don't tell on Nathan. Just hide from him. He won't pick on you if you're standing by a teacher."

"Why don't we all run?" asked Buzz.

"Because we must face Nathan sometime," explained Matthew. "We can't run all the time. Besides, I have some money. I'll give him some money for Rail, too. But, Rail, you better run just in case."

"In case of what?" asked Rail.

"In case I don't have enough money to satisfy Nathan," answered Matthew.

Rail ran over to the four-square game Mr. Morgan was refereeing. Rail got in line to take a turn. That way it didn't look like he was hiding out. But Rail watched his three brave friends. Nathan was talking to them now. Rail was too far away to hear what was being said.

"Do you have any money for Rail?" asked Nathan. "I'm…"

Matthew interrupted him,
"We know what you're doing. I hope I have enough." Matthew reached in his pocket. He pulled out two quarters, a dime, and four pennies.

"That's very kind of you," said Nathan. "What about you two?" He asked Buzz and Trudy.

Trudy was about to say, "You wouldn't hit a girl." Then she remembered Stacy's black eye. She reached into her pocket and pulled out a crisp one dollar bill.

Buzz only had eighteen cents. He had just bought a new joke book. Buzz handed Nathan the dime, nickel, and three pennies. Buzz knew it wasn't much. He closed his eyes and waited for the punch.

"Thanks," said Nathan as he walked off to another group of children.

Buzz opened one eye. "Is he gone?"

"Yes," answered Matthew.

"At least he's an inexpensive bully," said Buzz. "It only cost me eighteen cents to not get punched."

"Cheap! I paid him a whole dollar," said Trudy.

"Maybe it just cost more to not be mean to girls," said Buzz.

"I'm just glad it's Friday," said Matthew. "I don't have enough money for another recess."

By the time Mr. Morgan blew the whistle, Nathan had two pockets stuffed with money. He was the only third grader with a smile on his face. Every student now knew who the huge boy was. They all wondered how they would make it through the next week.

"He can't beat us all up," Matthew said to Rail as they walked to the line.

"I wonder if he'll just take turns," said Rail. "It would be pretty tiring fighting all the kids that don't have money."

"I wonder what I could sell to raise some money?" said Trudy.

"Maybe I could sell my spelling book," Buzz smiled. "Having a bully around may not be so bad after all."

Chapter 3
Matthew's New Diet

Clouds moved in over the next hour. Matthew watched the big raindrops pelt the windows. He had never been so glad to see rain before. This would cancel the after-lunch recess.

Now, he could eat in peace. That nervous feeling turned into a hungry feeling. The teacher always called rows to line up for lunch. Rail's row was the first one called.

Students buying hot lunch formed one line at the door. The rest walked to the coat rack and shelf. Lunch boxes lined the shelves.

It was normally like that every other Friday. Most of the students brought their lunch. It was tuna fish day. Only Rail ate the hot lunch every day. He seemed to be grateful no matter what they had for lunch.

Matthew watched and waited as the first row grabbed their lunches. He especially kept his eye on Nathan. That wasn't too tough. Nathan was so big it was hard to see anyone else. Still, he wasn't prepared for what happened next.

Nathan reached out for the red lunchbox. It was a red Super Squid Master Detective lunchbox. Matthew almost jumped out of his seat. He was about to yell, "That's my lunchbox!" Then he remembered how big Nathan was.

Still, he wasn't taking this lying down. The teacher called Matthew's row to line up next. He got in line behind Nathan. Nathan turned around. He noticed Matthew looking at the box.

"Do you like my new lunchbox?" asked Nathan. He had a big smile on his face. "Where's your lunch?"

Matthew felt that Nathan was just being mean. How could he be so cruel? Matthew's face was turning red. If only Nathan wasn't so big.

"Where's your lunch, Matt?" asked Mrs. Anderson.

"It's uh…" Matthew glanced at Nathan.

Nathan just smiled back. He patted the Super Squid Master Detective lunchbox. "It is the greatest lunchbox ever made," thought Matthew. It also contained something other than tuna fish.

"Why don't you get in the hot lunch line," said Mrs. Anderson. "I'll send a charge slip home. You can bring the money to pay for it Monday."

Matthew sighed. He hated tuna fish. He also hated starving. Then he thought of something else he hated: bringing money to school.

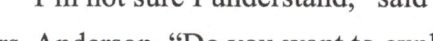

"Can my parents mail the money?" asked Matthew.

"I guess they can," answered Mrs. Anderson. "But they don't need to do that."

"Oh, they need to," interrupted Buzz. "If the school wants the money, it must be mailed."

"I'm not sure I understand," said Mrs. Anderson. "Do you want to explain?" she asked Matthew.

Matthew glanced at Nathan. He didn't believe the lunch money would make it to the classroom. Not in Matthew's pocket anyway. Matt could just picture Nathan waiting in some dark corner of the hallway Monday morning. The giant would be waiting to take the lunch money.

"Uh…my parents need to pay by check…in the mail," stammered Matthew. "It's for their taxes."

"Hmmm," Mrs. Anderson rubbed her chin. "I guess that would be fine. Just line up behind Rail."

The class marched down to the lunchroom. Rail and Matthew ate as far away from Nathan as possible. Matthew didn't eat. He was too angry to eat. He also didn't like the food.

Matthew watched Nathan at the next table enjoying the contents of the Super Squid Master Detective lunchbox. His mom must have packed a special lunch. The food looked better than ever. Every bite Nathan took made Matthew angrier.

"Are you going to eat your tuna?" asked Rail.

"You can have it," said Matthew. "If you help me out."

"What are you going to do?" asked Rail.

"I'm getting my lunch back!" Matthew gritted his teeth. "I don't care how big Nathan Goliath is!"

"You're going to just walk up and take it? I can't let you do that. I'd miss you too much. You can keep the tuna fish sandwich."

"All you need to do is distract him," explained Matthew. "I'll do the rest. Nathan won't even know who took the food."

"But it's almost all gone. He's about ready for that cupcake," pleaded Rail.

"It's the principle of the thing," explained Matt. "Besides, I love cupcakes."

Rail sighed. "What do you want me to do?"

"Just distract him," answered Matthew.

"How will I do that?"

"Just talk to him," said Matthew.

"Talk to him? What about?" asked Rail.

"I don't know. Ask him how he got so big. Just do something. We're running out of time."

"And food," said Rail. Nathan was gnawing on the core of a sweet, red apple.

Rail stood up. He took a deep breath. Rail walked to the other table. Just as he got there he tripped and fell.

Rail was face-to-toe with the biggest shoe he had ever seen on a third grader. Nathan leaned down under the table. The boy had a huge grin on his face.

"Did you lose something?" asked Nathan.

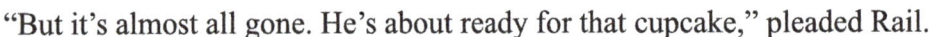

Matthew saw his chance. He hopped from his seat and made a dash for the Super Squid Master Detective lunchbox. Matthew snatched the cupcake and ran out the cafeteria door. He stopped in the hallway.

Matthew stuffed his face with the cupcake. It was the best tasting cupcake he had ever eaten. It was just what he needed to make it through the rest of the day. Matthew glanced back into the cafeteria.

Nathan was looking all around his table for the cupcake. That made the chocolate desert seem even better to Matthew. It was the sweet taste of revenge. Matthew was rather proud of himself.

He smiled as he walked back into the cafeteria. Matt had stood up to the bully. He had reclaimed his food. Matthew was feeling braver than he had all day.

"Looking for something?" asked Matthew as he walked by Nathan.

"Yes," answered Nathan as he continued looking down at the table. "I'm looking for a chocolate cup…" Nathan stopped when he looked up.

"Cake," Matthew finished the sentence. "A cupcake? Hmm, I saw it here just a minute ago. Maybe someone took it. There's been a lot of lunches coming up missing today."

Matthew strutted back to his seat. Nathan was still watching him. Rail was busy eating Matthew's tuna fish sandwich. He finally glanced at Matthew. Rail's mouth dropped open.

"Rail," said Matthew. "Close your mouth. I don't like looking at half-chewed tuna sandwiches. Want to hear something funny?" asked Matthew. "Nathan has no idea what happened to the cupcake. He's looking all over for it."

"I…I think he knows where it went," stuttered Rail.

"How could he?" asked Matthew.

"Your face is covered with chocolate icing," answered Rail.

Chapter 4
Three Smooth Baseballs

Matthew didn't feel so good after lunch. He felt like he was going to have a headache. Well, at least he thought his head would ache. He could just imagine Nathan's fist meeting his face.

There was only one thing to do: go home early. It was a matter of survival. Matthew didn't like to pretend he was sick. He didn't like to lie. Matt didn't have to do either one. He was so nervous, he really felt sick.

A half-hour later, he was home. Mrs. Day brought him a cup of warm soup. She took the thermometer out of Matthew's mouth. Mrs. Day held it up.

"You don't have a fever," she said.

"I think it was something I ate," answered Matthew remembering the cupcake.

"Well, you'll be up and around in no time," said Mrs. Day. "It's supposed to be a nice day tomorrow. I'm sure you'll want to play baseball."

Baseball, without Nathan. No school, no Nathan, no problem. That was the cure that Matthew was looking for. He felt great the next morning.

After breakfast, Matthew jogged to the baseball field. It was right behind the church his family attended. Several kids were already there. Team captains had been chosen.

"You made it!" said Rail when he saw Matt. "I thought you might be too sick to play. You can be on my team." Rail was one of the captains.

He liked to volunteer to be captain. That way he wouldn't be picked last. Although Rail wasn't that good of a player, he was a good captain. Some of the players would argue over playing different positions.

Rail was gifted in solving those kinds of problems. He would point out the good things he saw in the players. He would tell them why they were better playing in different positions.

Plus, he always let the other players bat before him. He played whatever position no one else wanted to play. But he always picked Matthew first. Of course, Matthew was picked last this time. He had almost missed the start of the game. But now Rail's team had one more player than the other team.

"You can have the next player that shows up," offered Rail.

There were always kids who came late. That's because there really wasn't an official starting time. The game started when there were enough players to play. The game always began with a coin toss.

Rail called tails. The shiny quarter landed heads side up. Rail's team would bat last. The boys on the other team cheered. Every team always wanted to bat first.

Rail told Matthew to pitch. He always let Matthew pitch. The other kids didn't mind. Matthew was a good pitcher. The most important thing about being the pitcher is being able to throw the ball over the plate. Games get kind of boring after twenty or thirty walks.

The game was just about to start. Matthew had just thrown a warm-up pitch. That's when it happened. He noticed the looks on the faces of the other team. They were all watching something.

Matthew had a sinking feeling he knew what it was. He slowly turned around. Matthew groaned. Walking toward the baseball field was the biggest third grader any of them had ever seen. Nathan Goliath had a baseball glove on his hand, a bat on his shoulder, and a big smile on his face.

The other team captain yelled out, "You're on our team."

"I'm glad he's on our side," said one of the boys.

"What's your name?" asked the captain.

"Nathan Goliath," said Nathan.

"You can bat first," said the captain.

"Thanks," said Nathan.

He tossed down his glove. Nathan strolled to the plate. The catcher backed up against the fence. He wanted to give Nathan as much room as possible.

Nathan had a huge bat. He took a few practice swings. Matthew thought it stirred up a breeze. The leaves on the trees rustled. Matthew began to have that sick feeling from the day before.

"I'm not afraid," Matthew told himself. But he didn't believe himself. He was afraid. He felt so small and weak compared to Nathan.

Then Matthew thought of David and Goliath in the Bible. David stood up to a giant that was trying to kill him. Nathan just wanted to hit a baseball. At least that's what Matthew hoped. Matthew tossed the other two practice baseballs to the dugout.

Matthew slapped the remaining baseball in his glove. "I'll show him. He's not getting a hit off me!" he mumbled to himself. He didn't say it loudly. He didn't want Nathan to hear.

He decided to throw the ball harder than he had ever thrown it before. He wanted to let Nathan Goliath know the he couldn't be pushed around. Matthew remembered the bravery of David.

Matthew went into his wind-up. He released the ball. Matthew threw it so hard, he almost fell over. The ball zoomed toward the plate. It was the hardest, fastest pitch Matthew had ever thrown.

It was also the wildest. Nathan couldn't swing. He couldn't even move, until it was too late. The baseball smacked him right in the forehead. Nathan looked like a Giant Redwood tree that had just been chopped down.

He fell flat on his back. Dust rose from the batter's box. Matthew thought he felt the ground shake. Everyone was stunned, everyone, except Nathan. He was completely still. The baseball had knocked him out.

The new pastor at the church had seen the whole thing. He ran over. Nathan was starting to wake up. His giant hand was rubbing his forehead. The pastor helped him to his feet and led him to the church.

The other boys didn't follow. They just watched. Matthew watched the closest. He noticed something the other boys didn't. There was a dusty streak down Nathan's face. Matthew thought he saw tears.

Matthew didn't know how he felt. Suddenly, Nathan looked weak and…well…human. He had never thought of Nathan as someone who had feelings. Some of the kids who lost money the day before came up to him.

"You showed him!" smiled Buzz. "He won't mess with us again!"

"He had it coming," said another. "You're a hero, Matt."

Matthew wasn't so sure. He didn't feel like a hero. He just felt tired. The slaying of the giant ended the baseball game before it really began. At least for Matthew it did. He told the others he didn't feel well. They thought he just felt sick from the day before. Matthew knew differently.

Chapter 5
Batter Up

"That was a quick ball game," said Matt's father as Matthew came in the kitchen door. Then he saw the look on Matt's face. "Are you feeling all right?" He put his hand on Matthew's forehead. "You don't feel too warm."

"I don't feel well, but it's not that kind of sick," answered Matthew. "I...I may have hurt someone. Not too badly. I mean, they didn't need an ambulance or anything."

Mr. Day could tell it wasn't an emergency. Matthew would have come running into the house. He didn't. So, Mr. Day pulled out a chair at the kitchen table. He motioned with his hand, "Step into my office."

Matthew sat down. Mr. Day pulled out another chair. He could tell that Matthew was feeling guilty. "Tell me what happened."

"I was pitching. I hit a player in the head," explained Matthew.

"Does an adult know about this?" asked his father.

"Yes. The new pastor led the boy to the church," answered Matthew. "The boy seemed okay. He was walking and everything. But I think he was crying."

"That would be natural if he were hurt. That's a good sign. I mean, he could have been knocked out," said Mr. Day.

"I think it did knock him out. But he woke up," said Matthew.

Matthew's father could see how terrible Matthew felt. "It was an accident. That happens sometimes when you play."

Matthew sighed, "I'm not sure it was an accident."

"Not sure?"

"Well," explained Matthew. "I don't like this boy very much."

"I thought you like all the kids in the neighborhood. Who don't you like?" asked Mr. Day.

"It's a new boy. His name is Nathan. He's in my class. Nathan is the biggest third grader I've ever seen. He's a big bully."

"A bully?"

"He's only been going to our school two days," explained Matthew. "So far he's given Stacy a black eye. He tripped Rail twice. Nathan took all my money. He took money from a lot of third graders at recess. Then he stole my Super Squid Master Detective lunch box–before lunch. I had to eat tuna."

"Did anyone tell a teacher?" asked Mr. Day.

"Who wants to be a tattletale? Besides, everyone is afraid of him. I just didn't like him being mean to everyone. Then he came to the baseball game. I was afraid he was going to hurt someone. I really didn't want that someone to be me."

"So, you threw the baseball at his head?" Mr. Day looked worried.

"That's what I'm not sure about," said Matthew. "I just threw it as hard as I could. I keep telling myself I was really trying to throw a strike. But..." Matthew paused.

Mr. Day leaned forward, "But what?"

"I…I was glad I hit him," said Matthew. "Then I saw the pastor being nice to him. I also think Nathan was crying."

Mr. Day patted Matthew on the hand. "All of the sudden, this boy didn't seem so tough. You felt sorry for him. That's called compassion."

"That's right," said Matthew. "I know Nathan deserved to be taught a lesson. All the other boys were happy when Nathan got hit. Yet it didn't feel good to do it. I had imagined all kinds of ways to get even with Nathan. It always seemed right when I thought about it."

"So maybe I did hit him on purpose," said Matthew. "But I wish I had never played baseball, ever…"

Matthew's father knew how Matthew loved to play baseball. "I think it was an accident. But you're feeling guilty because you were happy about it. You're not used to hurting people. I'm glad it bothers you to hurt others. It shows you're a caring person."

"But hurting someone doesn't help. You should try kindness with people like Nathan. If Nathan is being mean to you, he's persecuting you. Being kind to mean people helps them to change," explained Mr. Day.

"I did kindly give Nathan my sixty-four cents. He also kindly helped himself with my lunch. I've been a great blessing to him," explained Matthew. "I even blessed him with my fast ball."

"I'm not sure you understand what true kindness…" Mr. Day started to explain.

"If he learns not to pick on people, won't that help Nathan?" asked Matthew. "Maybe then he could make some friends. That must be why I felt happy about hitting him. I was just being a good person."

Matthew jumped up from the table. He gave his dad a hug.

"Thanks for talking with me. I feel much better. I know I did the right thing now. I'm ready to play some baseball!"

Matthew ran out the door. He almost ran over his mother. She was carrying three sacks of groceries. She was going to ask him to help, but Matthew was too fast. He had grabbed his baseball glove and was running to the park.

"What happened to him?" asked Mrs. Day.

"He was upset. We had a little talk," explained Mr. Day.

"It must have worked. He's not upset now," said Mrs. Day. "Anyway, can you help me unload the car?"

"Sure. I'll even cook lunch," offered Mr. Day.

"I've had your cooking before," said Mrs. Day. "And, I didn't buy any frozen pizzas. So just unloading the groceries is enough. Why would you want to cook lunch?"

"Well," explained Mr. Day, "I told Matthew if someone is being mean to you, you should show kindness to them. And, if you ate my cooking, you would probably feel like I was picking on you. Then you would be kind to me."

Mrs. Day laughed. "First of all, I wouldn't eat your cooking. You would have to take me out to lunch."

"And I would feel picked on when I had to pay for it," added Mr. Day. "I'd have to be kind to you."

Mrs. Day shook her head, "Sometimes you think just like Matthew."

Matthew & Goliath
Part 2

Table of Contents

Chapter		Page
6	The Headless Choir Member	58
7	The Flying Giant	61
8	The Mystery Box	64
9	Citizen of the Month	67

story by Brian Davis
illustrations by Ron Wheeler

Vocabulary Words

frustrated

choir

expressions

expected

attention

recognized

auditorium

assembly

Is the church haunted by a mysterious, headless creature? And, what trap has Nathan set for Rail? The troubles continue for Matthew and his friends, as they learn to deal with the giant bully.

Chapter 6

The Headless Choir Member

Matthew's older sister Rachel was the first one ready for church. She wasn't like other girls who spent hours in the bathroom. That always frustrated Matthew. She was always out in plenty of time for Matthew to take a bath.

"Why can't I have a normal sister?" Matthew grumbled as he headed for the tub.

"Don't make us late," warned Rachel. "We have to sing in the choir this morning."

"I have to take a bath and listen to you sing all in one morning. Now, I know what it's like to be persecuted," answered Matthew. Some mornings he could be pretty grumpy. This was one of them. Then a thought struck him. Persecuted! Sunday would be a day without Nathan. It would be a day without Goliath's persecution. Suddenly, Matthew felt very cheerful.

This was a special day at church. It was the first Sunday for the new pastor. Their last pastor had just retired. He and his wife moved to another state to be near their grandchildren.

The Day family decided to walk to church. It was a beautiful day. It was the kind of day that just made you feel happy inside. Matthew was especially excited. His father told him the pastor had a son his age. Maybe Matthew would meet a new friend.

As soon as they got to church, Matthew and Rachel went to the choir room. The children's choir got to come in a special door. It was at the front of the church. Matthew didn't mind being in the choir.

He thought it was kind of fun. The choir got to come into the service late. Sometimes they missed the first fifteen minutes of church. What Matthew thought was the most fun was sitting at the front of the church.

He could tell who was awake and who was sleeping. He liked the expressions on the faces of the men. Their wives would poke them. The husbands would jump. Then they would pretend they were never asleep. But, at the same time, Matthew's parents could see him giggling. So, he would get in trouble every week the Children's Choir sang.

"Matthew," said Mrs. Clark, the choir director. "Would you take this music out to the piano?"

"Sure," said Matthew. It made him feel important to help Mrs. Clark.

"Good," said Mrs. Clark. "When you get back, we'll practice your solo."

Solo! Matthew had forgotten all about it. He was going to be singing in front of everyone. He would have to sing all alone. Matthew began to feel butterflies in his stomach.

Matthew walked out to the piano. He saw his parents were sitting in their usual spot. They sat three rows back, right in front of the choir. They said it was because they liked to hear Rachel and Matthew sing. Matthew knew it was also so they could keep an eye on him.

He was walking back to the little door on the platform. All of the sudden, his jaw dropped. The new pastor had just walked in. But that's not what surprised him. Right behind the pastor was Nathan Goliath. Nathan had a big black eye.

Matthew ducked down behind some chairs. He crawled back to the door. Matthew pushed it open. Safe in the choir room.

"Did you see that?" Mrs. Jones asked Matthew's mother. She was sitting in the fourth row.

"What?" asked Mrs. Day.

"That door just opened by itself," said Mrs. Jones. "You don't think the church is haunted?"

Mrs. Day laughed. "Sure, it's probably the headless choir member," she teased

Meanwhile, Matthew had made it safely back to the choir room. He didn't think Nathan saw him. He was still crawling along the floor. Mrs. Clark saw him.

"Why are you lying down? Are you not feeling well? Your mother told me you had been sick. Maybe you should go sit with your parents," said Mrs. Clark.

"Maybe you're right," said Matthew as he stood up.

He opened the door. Matthew saw his parents. He also saw Nathan. The giant third grader was sitting on the front row. Mrs. Jones was introducing herself. There was no way Matthew could get to his parents without walking past Nathan.

"I think I'll stay here," said Matthew.

Surely, Nathan wouldn't try to hit him while he was singing. Still, Matthew would have to get out of the church without Nathan catching him. He would have to sneak out. What he needed was a disguise. He looked around the choir room. There wasn't much for disguises. Matthew would have to be creative.

The church service began with everyone singing a song. The Children's Choir waited in back. All the people stood while they sang. Next, the new pastor walked to the front of the church. He stepped up to a microphone. It squealed when he turned it on.

"I'd like to welcome any visitors this morning," said the pastor. "If this is your first time here, I know how you feel. It's my first time here, too." Everyone laughed.

"At least you don't have to preach," he continued. "My wife tells me I better stay awake during the sermon this week. I don't want to make a bad first impression." The people laughed even harder.

"Who's the boy on the front row?" Mr. Day whispered to Mrs. Day.

"That's the pastor's son," Mrs. Day whispered to Mr. Day. "He's in Matthew's class. His name is Nathan."

"That's Nathan?" whispered Mr. Day to his wife. "The Nathan?" he said more loudly.

"Shh…" said Mrs. Day. "The choir is about to sing."

The Children's Choir came out the narrow door. Mrs. Clark led the way. Matthew made sure he was last. He would have stayed in there. On most mornings, he could have gotten away with it. But this morning he had a solo. Suddenly, Matthew had an idea.

The choir sang its first song. Then they sang the first verse of the next song. It had Matthew's solo part in the middle. Matthew slipped through the door. The choir was still standing. He hid behind Rachel.

Soon, the choir would sit down. Matthew would stay standing and sing his solo. At least that was the way it was planned. Just as Matthew opened his mouth, Mrs. Jones screamed.

"The headless choir member!" she shouted right before she fainted.

Matthew had pulled the choir robe above his head. He was just hiding his face from Nathan. But Mrs. Jones was right. Matthew looked just like a headless choir member.

The screaming and fainting caused a great stir in the church. Everyone gathered around Mrs. Jones. Matthew saw his chance. He threw off the robe, ran down the aisle, and out the door.

Chapter 7
The Flying Giant

Matthew looked out the window. His parents and Rachel were coming up the sidewalk. Matthew could tell his parents were upset. He expected them to be upset. They didn't come home from church right away. It seems nobody noticed that Matthew had left. Everyone was paying attention to Mrs. Jones.

Mrs. Clark had ushered all the children off to Sunday school. His parents just thought Matthew was with them. After church, Rachel told them that Matthew had skipped Sunday school. Matthew couldn't imagine how much trouble he was in.

He had thought about it a lot over the last hour. He wanted to run away and hide. But there was no use. Where would he go? Besides, it was almost lunchtime. He was getting hungry.

The door opened. Matthew braced himself to be yelled at. His mother was the first through the door. She was followed by Rachel. Finally, his father came into the house. He looked the most upset.

"Oh good, you're safe," said Mrs. Day. She gave him a little kiss on the forehead. Then she walked off to the kitchen.

"How's my Matty boy holding up?" asked his father. "That was some solo."

He ruffled Matthew's hair as he walked by. He followed Mrs. Day and kept talking to her.

"What a solo! It was *so low* we couldn't even see your head," Rachel said to Matthew. She went up the stairs to change clothes. "And, Mrs. Jones still thinks she saw a headless choir member," she yelled back.

Matthew followed his parents into the kitchen. Matthew's dad pointed at him.

"That's exactly what I mean," said Mr. Day to Mrs. Day. "That big bully has made going to church frightening."

"Who me?" said Matthew. "I didn't mean to frighten anyone."

"Not you," said Mrs. Day. "Nathan Goliath, the pastor's son."

"So, you're upset because he's a big bully?" asked Matthew.

"No, we're upset with his dad," answered Mr. Day.

"Did he pick on you too? Did he take our lunch money? Is that why we're eating at home?" Matthew was starting to get angry.

He could just picture Nathan and his dad with offering plates. He pictured them walking up and down aisles. He imagined frightened old ladies giving them all their money. Nathan and his dad would just smile at all that money.

"No, nothing like that," said Matthew's mother.

"It was his sermon," explained his father.

"Did it keep you awake?" asked Matthew.

Matthew's mother laughed.

"No," answered his father.

"So, you did fall asleep?" asked Matthew.

"I mean no, that's not why I'm upset. I didn't like what he talked about," explained Mr. Day.

"Well, it was from the Bible," said Mrs. Day. "Everything he said was true."

"Yes, but he's the wrong person to talk about it!" answered Mr. Day.

"Talk about what?" asked Matthew.

"Blessing those who persecute you, being nice to people who aren't nice to you," said Matthew's father.

"Isn't that what you told me yesterday?" asked Matthew. "When you explained to me that I was being kind to Nathan when I hit him."

Mrs. Day frowned at Mr. Day.

"I didn't say that. Anyway, I know it's true that we should bless those who persecute us. Yet from Pastor Goliath it sounds like he's saying we should let his son get away with being a bully."

"Maybe he doesn't know his son is a bully," suggested Mrs. Day. "You should call the pastor and talk to him."

"I have a better idea," said Mr. Day. "I'll go right over to the church and talk to the pastor in person."

Mr. Day left the house and walked toward the church. Matthew followed him from a distance. He didn't want his father to see him. Matthew didn't want to be told to stay home.

Matthew was glad he followed. His father needed a witness. Matthew saw it all. In fact, he was the only one who saw what happened. His father was so upset, he wasn't really paying attention.

Mr. Day was walking across the yard to the pastor's house. It was right next to the church. That's when it happened. Matthew couldn't believe his eyes. Nathan Goliath came flying through the air. He tackled Mr. Day. Matthew watched his father fall under the weight of the giant third grader. Mr. Day was stunned.

Nathan ran to his house. Matthew ran to his father. Mr. Day was just trying to stand. Matthew knew he needed to act quickly. He didn't want to be around if Nathan came back.

Matthew helped his dazed father out of the pastor's yard. They walked to the park. Matthew and his father sat down on a park bench. It was behind some tall bushes. Matthew knew Nathan wouldn't be able to see them.

"What happened?" asked Mr. Day.

"Nathan attacked you," said Matthew. "He just flew through the air and knocked you down. It's a good thing I followed you. I knew there might be trouble."

Mr. Day rubbed his jaw. "It feels like he punched me."

"It looked like he punched you," said Matthew.

"Well, let's go home," said Mr. Day.

"You're going to let Nathan get away with this? Like in the sermon?" asked Matthew.

"No," said Mr. Day. "I'll talk to Nathan's parents. Right now, I'm too angry. Sometimes when I'm too upset it's better for me to calm down before acting. I'll call the pastor when we get home. I'll invite him over tomorrow night. Then we'll talk things through."

"Can I stay home from school tomorrow? I'm afraid of what Nathan will do when he sees me," said Matthew.

"No," said Mr. Day.

"Then can I have next week's allowance?" asked Matthew.

"Why?" asked Mr. Day.

"In case I have to bless Nathan to not hit me. One week's allowance just might cover it."

"Paying someone to not pick on you isn't the answer. I'll call the school and let them know about the problems Nathan is causing. By tomorrow night your little bullying problem will be solved. Just leave it to your good ol' dad."

Chapter 8
The Mystery Box

Matthew made it safely to class Monday morning. It didn't even cost him any of his allowance. He didn't even see Nathan until he got to the classroom. Matthew knew his father was going to call the school. The principal must have sent Nathan to the room so the teacher could keep an eye on him.

Matthew sat down. He noticed something on Rail's desk. His friend wasn't in class yet. Yet on his desk was a box. Matthew recognized the box. He had one just like it. It was a Double-Pump Slammers shoe box.

"Where'd the box come from?" Matthew whispered to Buzz.

"I saw Nathan put it there," Buzz whispered back. "What do you think it is?"

"Uh…shoes I guess," said Matthew.

"I thought I was the funny one," said Buzz.

"What do you mean?" asked Matthew.

"It could be anything," said Buzz. "It has to be a joke. I sure hope it doesn't hurt Rail. What would a bully put in a shoe box?"

Matthew was worried. He wasn't just worried that Rail might get scared. He would also be embarrassed. Everyone would laugh at him. Matthew knew that things like that hurt Rail's feelings.

"We've got to get that box," said Matthew.

"But Nathan will get mad if the box is missing," said Buzz.

The two boys thought for a moment. "I've got an idea," said Buzz. "I saw a box just like this one. Mr. Morgan was carrying it. We can sneak into his room. He has hall duty. We'll get his box and switch them."

Matthew smiled. He could just imagine the look on Nathan's face when his trick didn't work. Matthew and Buzz raised their hands. Mrs. Anderson was sitting at her desk.

"Yes boys?" asked Mrs. Anderson.

"Can I go to the restroom?" asked Matthew.

"Yes. Be back before class starts," said Mrs. Anderson.

Matthew and Buzz started to leave. "One at a time in the restroom," said Mrs. Anderson. "You know the rules."

"I don't need to use the restroom," said Buzz. "I need to check the lost and found."

"For what?" asked Mrs. Anderson.

"I'm not sure," said Buzz. "But I'm sure I lost something. I'll know it when I find it."

It wasn't one of Buzz's better excuses. He knew it. That's why he was surprised that Mrs. Anderson still let him go. Buzz was almost out the door when she stopped him.

"Oh, Bradley can you show Nathan to the office? He's this week's helper. You can show him where to turn in the lunch count."

Buzz didn't know what to say. Matthew was standing next to him by the door. Matthew poked him.

"That's perfect," whispered Matthew. "You keep Nathan busy while I switch the boxes."

"Can I go to the restroom for Matthew and let him show Nathan to the office?"

Mrs. Anderson laughed, "Quit joking around and go to the office with Nathan."

Buzz sighed. He glanced at Matthew. Matthew gave him a thumbs-up. Buzz started to shake his head no. It was too late. Nathan was walking to the door.

"It was nice knowing you," Buzz said to Matthew.

Matthew watched them walk down the hall and turn the corner. He then rushed to Mr. Morgan's room. The room was empty. The teacher was still on hall duty.

Matthew saw the Double-Pump Slammers box and grabbed it. He hurried down the hall. Just then he saw Mrs. Anderson. She came out of the room and turned the other way.

Matthew couldn't believe what she was carrying. Tucked under her arm was a Double-Pump Slammers shoe box. Matthew ducked behind other students as he followed her.

She stopped around a corner and talked to another teacher. Matthew crept closer so he could hear.

"I thought it would be best to wait until the assembly," Mrs. Anderson said to the other teacher. "I'm taking the box to the auditorium."

"Oh no!" thought Matthew. Rail would open the box in front of all the students. He was really going to be embarrassed. Matthew had to switch that box.

Matthew stepped into the dark auditorium. There was the box. It was sitting on the stage. Matthew switched it with the one from Mr. Morgan's room. He hid Nathan's box behind the tall curtain.

When he got back to class, Buzz and Nathan were in their seats. The bell rang just as Matthew stepped through the doorway. Buzz saw Matthew. He started to get up. He wanted to tell him something.

"Take your seats, Boys," said Mrs. Anderson. "Class starts with the bell."

"Hey, there's a box on my desk," said Rail. He had just walked in the door.

Matthew turned and looked. He was shocked. The Double Pump Slammer shoebox was still on Rail's desk. There were three Double Pump Slammer boxes in school that day. Mrs. Anderson must have had her own box.

Matthew looked at Nathan. The giant third grader had a huge grin on his face. Rail sat down. Matthew didn't have time to warn him. He saw an open window. Matthew dashed for the box. In one smooth, move he scooped it up and tossed it out the window. At last, Rail was safe.

"Matthew Day!" shouted Mrs. Anderson. "Why on earth would you do such a thing?"

"Uh…" Matthew didn't know how to explain it. "I was afraid it might explode?"

"Explode!" repeated Mrs. Anderson.

"Or bite?"

"Do your Double-Pump Slammers explode and bite?" asked Mrs. Anderson.

"Double-Pump Slammers! Is that what was in the box. How could I know?" Matthew tried to defend himself.

"Well," said Mrs. Anderson, "The box had Double-Pump Slammers printed on it. That might have been a clue. Plus, you did help buy them."

"I bought them?" asked Matthew.

"Yes," said Mrs. Anderson. "Buzz, please go outside and get the shoes. Nathan, will you tell Rail what his friends did for him?"

"Yes, Mrs. Anderson," answered Nathan. "Rail, when you fell Friday I noticed your shoes were torn. That must be why you keep falling down. I was worried that you might get hurt. I asked Mrs. Anderson if I could collect money to buy you some new ones."

"So, at recess Friday everyone chipped in. I was able to buy you Double-Pump Slammers. They're the best, you know. They even have the new sky blue soles. They're from all your friends. Even Matthew helped pay for them. I'm not sure why he threw them out the window."

Buzz came back with the shoes. Rail tried them on. They were perfect. All the students admired them.

"That was very thoughtful of Nathan," said Stacy.

Matthew looked at the girl with the black eye. He couldn't believe she could say something good about Nathan. It was hard to believe Nathan could do anything nice. Yet there was Rail wearing brand-new Double-Pump Slammers. It was all because of Nathan.

"Let's line up for the assembly," said Mrs. Anderson.

Chapter 9
Citizen of the Month

Several of the students wanted to sit next to Nathan at the assembly. Mrs. Anderson made him sit on the front row. Stacy sat next to him. Matthew sat three rows back. Buzz plopped down right next to him.

"So, what happened to Mr. Morgan's box?" asked Buzz.

"Oh no!" said Matthew. He saw the box on the stage. Mrs. Anderson picked it up. Matthew thought about diving for it. Then he remembered the shoes.

"What do you suppose is in it?" asked Buzz.

Mrs. Anderson held a microphone. "Good morning everyone. Welcome to our awards assembly." She motioned to Nathan and Stacy.

"We have an unusual citizen of the month. He's unusual because this student has only been with us three days."

"Nathan!" whispered Matthew. "He stole my lunchbox and he's citizen of the month?"

"Uh…about that," said Buzz.

"When I was at lost and found, guess what I found."

"What?"

"Your Super Squid Master Detective lunchbox. It looks just like Nathan's. Only, it has your name on it… and week old lunch leftovers."

"My lunchbox? Then who's cupcake did I take last Friday?" asked Matthew.

"Nathan Goliath," said Mrs. Anderson. "Our citizen of the month! Stacy Lane was chased by a big dog on her way to school. She tripped and fell. Nathan drove the dog away with a stick. Then he helped her to school. Nathan is a real hero."

All the students clapped. Stacy sat down. Nathan started to follow her. But Mrs. Anderson stopped him.

"Our next award is for perfect attendance. As you know, we have a drawing for a prize. All the students who didn't miss a day for the last quarter can win. I have those names in a shoe box. Nathan will pull out our winner."

Mrs. Anderson held the shoe box above Nathan's head. Matthew covered his eyes. He couldn't watch. Nathan reached inside the box.

"Ahh!" yelled Nathan as he jumped back.

The startled Mrs. Anderson dropped the box. Something furry dashed out. The frightened animal slipped under the seats. Students all over the auditorium hopped up.

"It's a skunk!" someone shouted.

"It's a rat!" another student shouted.

Children were running out the doors. Everyone was panicking. Teachers were trying to keep their classes together. It was no use. The assembly was over.

Matthew wanted to run too. Not away from the animal. He wanted to run and hide. Soon, nobody was left in the auditorium except Matthew.

The door opened. In walked Mr. Morgan. He was looking under the seats. He stopped in one row and started crawling.

"There you are," said Mr. Morgan. He stood up. In his arms was a fluffy little bunny. "Is my baby all right?"

"Your baby?" asked Matthew.

Mr. Morgan jumped. He hadn't seen Matthew. "Uh…my bunny. I think I said my bunny." Then he looked at Matthew. "You wouldn't know how my box ended up in the auditorium, would you?"

"Well…" Matthew had a long story to tell. Mr. Morgan thought it would best be told in the office. The principal and Mr. Morgan listened to the whole thing. Matthew didn't know how much trouble he was in. Yet a few times he could tell that they almost laughed. That was a good sign.

They called Nathan to the office. Matthew told him all about his misunderstandings. Matthew apologized. The giant third grader smiled. He stuck out his great big hand.

"Friends?" asked Nathan.

Matthew smiled, "Friends."

"That's great, Boys," said Mr. Morgan. "Matthew, next time you have a problem at school, tell us. We're here to help you."

"So, I'm not in trouble?" asked Matthew.

"We didn't say that," answered the principal. "We've never quite had a problem like this. Give us some time to think about it."

Matthew sighed. Nathan and Matthew left the office. The door closed behind them. Mr. Morgan and the principal roared with laughter. Nathan smiled.

"Can I sit next to you at lunch?" asked Nathan. "I brought you a cupcake."

"You brought me a cupcake?" asked Matthew. "Why?"

"I try to bless those who persecute me," smiled Nathan.

Matthew, Nathan, Rail, and the rest of the gang played baseball after school. It was a great game. Matthew made sure he didn't hit anyone with the baseball. He even cheered when Nathan hit a home run off his best pitch.

After awhile, a car drove by the ballpark. Its horn honked. Nathan waved. Pastor Goliath waved back.

"Where's your dad going?" asked Matthew.

"Someone in the church asked if he could talk to him tonight."

Suddenly, Matthew remembered his dad. Matthew hadn't talked to his parents about Nathan. They still thought he was a bully. He had only been home long enough to get his baseball gear.

He hopped on his bike and raced home. The pastor's car was in the driveway. Matthew didn't know what he was going to do. He just knew he needed to stop his father.

The pastor was just getting out of the car. Matthew walked him to the door. He talked to the pastor all the way.

"I'm so sorry I hit Nathan with the baseball. And, I'm sorry about the "headless choir member thing.""

"Oh, that was you," said Nathan's dad. "Nathan knows the baseball was an accident. And you did make my first church service here very interesting."

They reached the door. Mr. and Mrs. Day were waiting for them.

"Dad, this is Pastor Goliath. He's the father of the greatest third grader that ever lived."

Matthew's parents were puzzled. Did Nathan have a twin brother? "Uh…the same third grader who tackled me yesterday?" asked Mr. Day as Matthew and Pastor Goliath stepped into the house.

"Oh, that was you," said Pastor Goliath. "I owe you a lot of thanks."

Mr. Day was now very confused. He expected an apology. Saying thanks for letting Nathan tackle him didn't make sense.

"Thanks for what?" asked Mr. Day.

"For catching Nathan when the tree swing broke," said Pastor Goliath. "Nathan thought he broke his arm. It was just a bruise. If you wouldn't have caught him he could have been badly injured. When I came outside to see who helped him, you had left."

"Well, I care about the safety of children," beamed Mr. Day. "I'm always willing to do what I can to help."

"Isn't that the tree swing you were supposed to fix?" Mrs. Day asked Mr. Day.

Mr. Day turned red. "Uh…yes," stammered Mr. Day.

"Well it turned out all right," said Pastor Goliath. "Now, you said on the phone you wanted to talk about my sermon?"

Mr. Day didn't know what to say. Matthew spoke up.

"Dad couldn't stop talking about your sermon Sunday. He had even told me the same thing the day before. Still, we've decided to stop persecuting Nathan and the rest of your family."

"I couldn't agree more," said Mr. Day.

"Thank you, kindly," smiled Pastor Goliath.

"But feel free to be nice to us anyway," added Matthew. "Nathan is welcome to bring me one of those delicious cupcakes anytime he would like!"

The Bobcat Cowboys
Steal the Show
Part 1

Table of Contents

Chapter		Page
1	Summer Snow	71
2	Old Sleds	73
3	The Fowl Players Arrive	75
4	Gold Pants	78

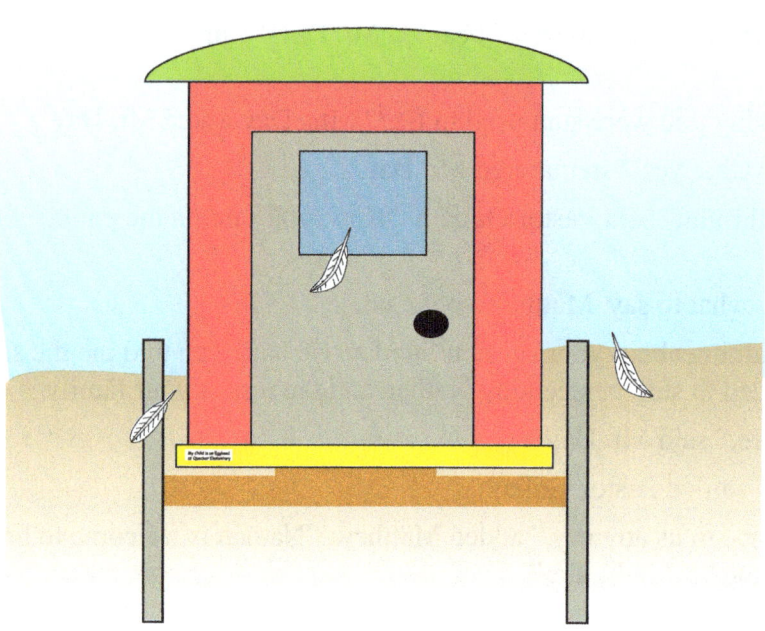

by Brian Davis

Vocabulary Words

brainstorm

decorations

expected

meanwhile

otherwise

tournament

A big event is planned at the Rowdent Gulch Theatre. The Fowl Players are putting on a show for the critters. The bobcat cowboys make their own plan for the town's visitors. Will this mean curtains for the Fowl Players?

Chapter 1
Summer Snow

The brightly painted wagon left a trail of dust and feathers. It was a tall wagon with sides and a roof. In the back was a door. It looked like a little house on wheels. A rat sat on the driver's seat.

The three bobcats hid in the bushes, watching it go by. Billybob Bobcat wondered if the wagons had any gold to steal. Bobbybill Bobcat thought of egg salad sandwiches. His stomach began to growl.

Bubba Bobcat noticed something completely different. He dashed into the road. Bubba picked up a handful of feathers and tossed them in the air. "It's snowing! It's snowing!" he hollered.

"Hush-up, Bubba. It's ninety degrees out here. It's not snowing," snarled Billybob.

"It's the feathers," shouted Bubba. "They're like white, fluffy snow. I love it when it snows, especially when it's so hot out."

"It never snows when it's hot," said Bobbybill.

"That's what makes this so special," said Bubba.

"I wish it would snow," said Bobbybill. "Then we could sell all those sleds we stole in the theatre robbery last week. They're cluttering up our hideout cave."

"We'd be rich!" yahooed Bubba.

"I thought we would be rich when we stole those sleds," sighed Billybob.

"I'm sorry. I thought Mr. Muskrat said he was storing some gold sleds, not old sleds," said Bubba.

"That's why I'm the brains of this outfit," said Billybob.

"But you thought the sleds were gold, too. That's why you had us steal them, remember?" Bobbybill said.

"Hush-up, Bobbybill. I let Bubba do the thinkin' one day and look what happened, a cave full of old sleds," sighed Billybob.

Suddenly, Billybob smiled, "Let me brainstorm on a way to get rid of those sleds."

"A storm? I thought I heard thunder," said Bubba.

"That was my stomach," said Bobbybill. "You can brainstorm on a way to get rid of sleds. I'm going to brainstorm on a way to get rid of my hunger pains.

Bobbybill pointed down the road, "Why don't we chase that wagon and get us some eggs for supper."

"Do you think those birdies would sell us some?" asked Bubba.

"We can't buy eggs," answered Billybob.

"Oh, that's right," said Bubba. "We don't have any money. Maybe we could have a cave sale. We could get all the critters to come to our secret hideout and buy sleds."

"Bubba!" exclaimed Billybob, "We can't let all the rodents know where our cave is. It wouldn't be a secret hideout anymore. Besides, we're famous outlaws. We can't buy eggs. That would be too honest."

"Sometimes it's very hard being an outlaw," said Bobbybill. "Honest folks don't know how good they have it."

"It's a tough job, but someone has to do it," sighed Billybob.

"Otherwise the sheriff would be out of business," added Bubba. "Sheriff Prairie Dog is such a nice sheriff. I'd hate to see him lose his job."

Billybob tapped his chin. He was deep in thought. Suddenly he got a big grin on his face. His pointed bobcat teeth glimmered in the bright sunlight.

"We need a plan to get those eggs," said Billybob, "and I think that brainstorm is rumbling in."

"My brain is kind of cloudy too," said Bubba. Bubba reached out his paw. "I think I just felt a raindrop."

"It's not that kind of a storm. A brainstorm is when you get all kinds of thoughts," explained Bobbybill.

"Then I guess I didn't feel a raindrop. It must have been a braindrop. Why don't you have a snow brainstorm Billybob? That way we could think about riding all those sleds," said Bubba.

"It's not going to snow in my plan," grinned Billybob. "We'll get us some eggs. Billybob nodded. The other two knew that look on their brother's face, "We're going to keep Sheriff Prairie Dog on his toes."

Bubba began to giggle. "Sheriff Prairie Dog sure will look funny walking on his toes. He wears those pointy toed cowboy boots."

"Hush-up, Bubba," said Billybob.

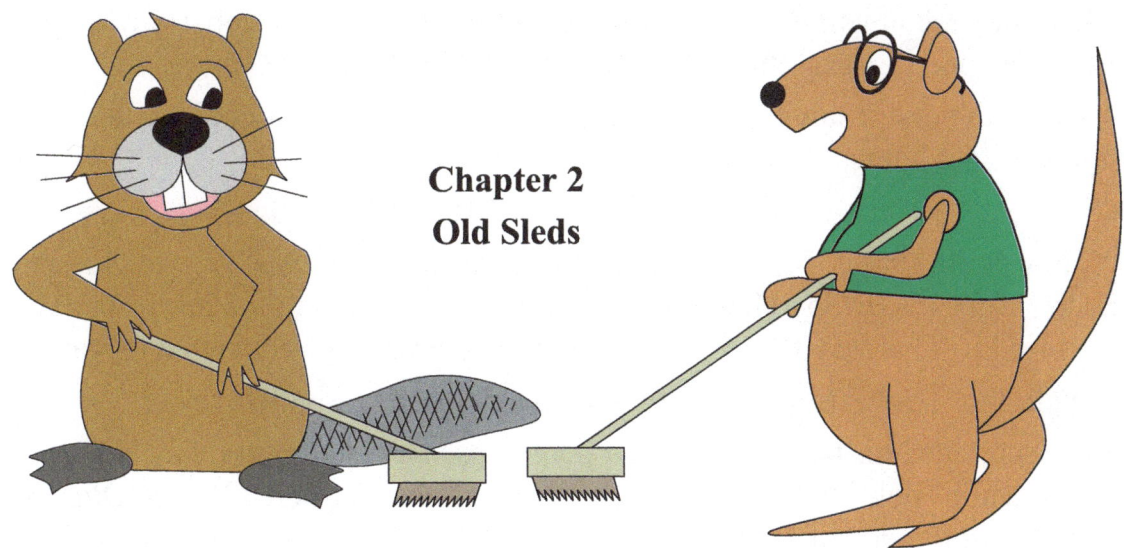

Chapter 2
Old Sleds

Meanwhile, back in Rowdent Gulch, all the critters were getting ready for the town's visitors. Otto Muskrat and Davey Beaver were sweeping up the old theatre. There hadn't been a play in Rowdent Gulch for three years. The old theatre sat empty all that time. Well, it wasn't exactly empty.

Otto Muskrat had kept sleds from his General Store in the theatre. It hadn't snowed in Rowdent Gulch for months, and Otto was tired of storing them.

"How did you get all those sleds anyway?" asked Davey Beaver.

"Remember when I took that trip to Gopher City?" asked Otto.

"That was last fall, right after the big Bobcat Gang trial," answered Davey. "You went to the big city to get those splinters removed."

"Had to, that's where all the best splinter removing doctors live," said Otto, "and I needed to sit down. Anyway, on the way back I fell asleep. After all, I'd been standing for days."

"Why did you stand for days? You could have slept on your belly," Davey suggested.

"Now, you think of that," sighed Otto. "Anyway, I slept right through the Rowdent Gulch stagecoach stop and ended up in Alaska. That's where I got into the big checker tournament.

I thought we were playing for all the marbles. Instead we were playing for all the old sleds. I would have tried to lose if I knew I was playin' for all the old sleds. I thought I'd never get rid of those sleds. They just didn't sell very well in my store once spring came. Who could have expected that?"

"I think all the critters in Rowdent Gulch expected that," said Davey.

"Why am I always the last to find out these things?" grumbled Otto.

"How did you get rid of those old sleds?" asked Davey.

Otto smiled, "I tricked those Bobcats into thinkin' they were gold sleds. They cleared out the whole theatre. We wouldn't even need to be sweeping if I had told them the floor was covered with gold dust."

"Did they take them to their secret hideout cave up on Gooseberry Mountain?" asked Davey, "the one just past the waterfall by the big walnut tree?"

"That's the one. I saw the sleds there the other day. Bubba got lost, and I had to show him how to get home."

"Wow, it's so secret even the bobcats don't know where it is."

"They could find it if they would just read the signs. Sheriff Prairie Dog put 'This Way to Secret Bobcat Cowboy Hideout Cave' signs all over the mountain just so they would be able to find it. That way those low-down, good-for-nothin' bobcats will stay out of town."

"Well, those bobcats are good for stealin' old sleds," said Davey.

Otto scratched his head, "You got a point there Davey. I guess they're low-down, good-for-sled stealin' bobcats. Still, if they would just behave, Sheriff Prairie Dog wouldn't have to leave town to get a little rest."

"He did deserve a vacation. The Prairie Dog Family Reunion came at just the right time. When will he get back?" asked Davey.

"He should get back Saturday in time for the big play," answered Otto.

"Unless he falls asleep on the stage and winds up in Alaska," Davey teased.

"It happens to the best of us," sighed Otto.

"I'm just glad we have Deputy Guinea Pig to protect us," said Davey. "He's the best shot in town. Those Bobcat Cowboys better not try anything."

"I'm just glad Papa Prairie Dog was out of town last Monday. He is one of the two top checker players in town. It's about time I won all the marbles on Monday Night Checkers. I wish you could have been there," said Otto.

"Then why did you have me alphabetize all the soup cans Monday night?" asked Davey.

"It had to be done. I really needed you to be at the store," said Otto.

"Because I'm good at alphabetizing soup?" asked Davey.

"Because you're the second-best checker player in town," answered Otto. "Now, where is that cream of celery soup?"

"In alphabetical order," answered Davey, "right between the tomato soup and the eggplant soup."

"That's T for tomato," mumbled Otto as he studied the shelves, "C for celery and E for eggplant soup. Then B for broccoli soup comes next and P for potato soup..."

"Where did you learn to alphabetize like this?" asked Otto.

"From you," said Davey.

"I thought this system looked familiar," smiled Otto. "Keep up the great work. Now, next Monday night, I'd like you to sort all the gumballs by shape."

"But they're all round," said Davey.

"That's what I like about you," said Otto. "You're so good at sortin'. Now, I need to get Papa Prairie Dog interested in some part-time work. Then I could win the Monday Night Checker match every week."

Chapter 3
The Fowl Players Arrive

The critters of Rowdent Gulch gathered around the brightly painted wagon. It rolled to a stop in front of the old theatre. Saturday night would be the first show in years. The Fowl Players were the biggest chicken, duck, and goose stars in the old west. It was an exciting day for all the critters.

Deputy Guinea Pig was across the street. He hid on top of the post office building. His triple barrel rubber band slingin' shotgun rested on the ledge. The deputy kept his eyes peeled for any sign of trouble. He was remembering what the sheriff had told him, "In Rowdent Gulch trouble is spelled B-o-b-c-a-t C-o-w-b-o-y-s."

"I thought trouble was spelled t-r-u-b-b-l-e," thought Deputy Guinea Pig. He liked to practice spelling words while he was guarding chickens, ducks, and geese.

But this was the first time he had guarded birds in years. "I'd better go ask Otto Muskrat how to spell trouble. He knows everything," thought Deputy Guinea Pig. He climbed off the roof of the building.

Down the alley, the Bobcat Cowboys were sneaking around. Deputy Guinea Pig hopped off the ladder and landed right on Bubba. Both the deputy and the bobcats were surprised. The guinea pig leaped onto a barrel.

"B…b…b…bobcats!" he stammered. "Hold it right there or I'll blast you with my triple barrel rubber band blastin' shotgun!" He lifted his arms and aimed at the bobcats.

"I think you're forgetting something," said Bobbybill.

Billybob laughed, "You forgot your shotgun. How are you supposed to blast us with your scrawny little guinea pig arms?"

The deputy's mouth dropped open. "I forgot it on the roof. Don't move until I get back or I'll blast you." He started to climb back up the ladder. "Wait, I can't shoot you from here. Go stand out in front of the post office. And if you try to run away, don't move. I'm not that good of a shot."

"We'll stand real still if we want to run away," promised Bubba.

"We promise," smiled Billybob and Bobbybill.

The deputy climbed up on the roof. The bobcats watched until the guinea pig was out of sight.

"We'd better go stand where he can blast us if he needs to," said Bubba.

"Hush-up, Bubba. We're getting out of here," said Billybob.

"But we promised the deputy. He'll be mighty disappointed in us," argued Bubba.

"We're lyin', thievin' bobcats. He'll be disappointed in us if we don't break our promise," said Billybob.

"OK, then," said Bubba. "We don't want to disappoint the deputy."

The bobcats hightailed it out of the alley. They ducked into the back door of the theatre. Bubba looked around. He found some feathers on the floor. He picked them up and threw it in the air.

"It's snowing again!"

Billybob smiled. "We're in the right place."

Bobbybill opened a trunk. It was full of brightly colored costumes. He pulled them out one by one. He began to grumble.

"This is the sorriest treasure chest I've ever seen. It's full of fancy lookin' clothes. Where's the gold?"

"This is just what we need. We'll fill this with our own gold," smiled Billybob, "white gold that is!"

The bobcats hid the costumes. Billybob was ready for the next part of his plan. The bobcat opened the lid of the trunk. Billybob pulled out a pocketknife. He cut four holes in the bottom of the trunk. He told Bobbybill and Bubba to get inside. Bobbybill hopped in. His legs stuck out of the holes.

"We can hide in the trunk and walk right out of town," explained Billybob.

"Why are we going to hide?" whispered Bubba. "We're not going to do anything wrong, are we? I don't want to do anything mean to those birdies."

"Uh, no, Bubba," answered Billybob. "We're going to give the birdies a party."

"I didn't know we were going to do that," said Bobbybill. "I thought we were going to kidnap them."

"Now that wouldn't be nice. We're giving them a surprise party," interrupted Billybob. "It's such a big surprise that even I didn't know about until just now. You know me. I can't keep a secret from you two. That's why I didn't even tell myself about it until just now."

"Can I go invite all the rodents?" asked Bubba.

"Uh…that's my job," answered Billybob. "You're in charge of decorations."

"Oh boy, oh boy, oh boy!" shouted Bubba. "I'm going back to the cave right now to get started."

"You do that, Bubba. Bobbybill and I will wait in the trunk for our special guests."

"Wait, how can we have a party at our secret hideout? Nobody will find it," said Bubba.

"We'll give them directions and then ask them to forget how they got there," answered Billybob.

"Wow, Billybob, you thought of everything," said Bubba.

Bubba was so excited. He sneaked out of the backdoor of the theatre. The bobcat headed toward Otto Muskrat's store. He was going to get decorations for the party.

"Won't the rodents get lost after the party?" Bobbybill asked Billybob. "I mean if we ask them to forget how they got there."

"We're not going to invite any rodents to our party," sneered Billybob, "just some pretty little birdies."

"Good, I didn't want to have to lick all those envelopes," sighed Bobbybill. "My fur always gets stuck in the glue."

Chapter 4
Gold Pants

Davey Beaver had just unloaded the wagon in front of Otto Muskrat's General Store. Cans were stacked around the front door. Otto came out the door. He looked all around.

"Where's my order?" he asked Davey.

"It's right here – four cases of gold colored paint," answered Davey.

"Gold colored paint! I ordered four cases of gold colored pants. It's right here on my order form.

Look, pants p-a-i-n-t-s. I wish they had someone who could read at the pant factory."

"What do you want me to do with the cans?" asked Davey.

"We'll move out the paint I got last time I ordered pants. I'll have to figure out some way to get rid of the old paint. I'll stack the old cans in the alley. You take the new cans inside," said Otto.

"Where's that low-down, good-for-nothing bobcat?" Deputy Prairie Dog was coming down the street. He had his triple barrel rubber band slinging shotgun ready to fire. "I saw him headin' this way."

"We haven't seen any bobcats around here," said Davey. "What did they do this time?"

"Davey, you don't even have to ask," said Otto. "In Rowdent Gulch we spell trouble, B-o-b-c-a-t C-o-w-b-o-y-s."

"I guess the sheriff was right," said Deputy Prairie Dog. "Trouble isn't spelled t-r-u-b-b-l-e. If you see any bobcats, have them stand still until I can blast'em."

The deputy continued down the street. Otto started piling old paint cans in the alley. He was trying to decide what to do with them. This was worse than when he had all those old sleds. The theatre was being used. He needed to make space for the new cans.

The muskrat tugged the last can to the alley. That's when he noticed the paw prints in the dusty alley. They were bigger than any of the local rodents. Otto followed the paw prints.

Two bobcat paws were sticking out from under a barrel. Otto started to run for the deputy. Suddenly, he had a brainstorm. He picked up a paint can. Otto walked to the barrel and began talking.

"I hope there aren't any thievin', low-down Bobcat Cowboys around. There's all this valuable old gold paint stacked here. Any bobcat could take it. If there was a bobcat hiding under this barrel here, he could take it. He certainly wouldn't be a very good low-down, good-for-nothin' thievin' bobcat if he just left it here."

"How could he carry all those cans?" asked Bubba from under the barrel.

"Davey Beaver would deliver it right to the Bobcat's secret hideout on Gooseberry Mountain."

"That would be great. I could follow him so I wouldn't get lost," said Bubba.

Soon Davey Beaver was on his way up Gooseberry Mountain. A walking barrel followed him. Actually, the barrel tried to follow him. There were no holes for Bubba to see out of. He kept bumping into things.

Davey got tired of waiting. Finally, he told the barrel to hop onto the wagon. Bubba and the gold paint were dropped off right at the door of the Bobcat's secret hideout.

"Don't forget to forget how you got here," Bubba yelled from inside the barrel. "This is our secret hideout."

"I'll remember to forget," answered Davey.

A few hours later Davey made it back to town.

"Next time I'll remember to forget after I get back in town."

"I'm just glad I got rid of that old paint and that old barrel," said Otto. "I'm especially glad to get rid of that low down, good-for-nothin' bobcat."

"He's good for paint stealin'," Davey Beaver reminded him, "if we deliver it."

"You've got a point there," said Otto. "I guess he is a low down, good-for-paint-stealin' bobcat. But we're not going to deliver anything we don't want those bobcats to steal. Not without charging them a delivery fee that is."

Deputy Guinea Pig came running into the store. He was almost out of breath. "I need a box of rubber band slingin' shotgun rubber bands."

"What happened to the rubber bands on your shotgun?" asked Davey.

"I used them," answered the deputy.

"On a bobcat?" asked Davey.

"Something worse than a bobcat. I used them on a new critter. I think it was a bobturtle."

"A bobturtle? I've never heard of a bobturtle, and I know about everything there is to know," said Otto.

"I saw it with my own eyes up on Gooseberry Mountain," said the deputy. "It had a turtle shell shaped like a barrel. Its footprints looked just like a bobcat's. I shot it with all three rubber bands and they just bounced off," said Deputy Guinea Pig.

"The rubber bands bounce off everything," said Davey Beaver. "That's why we use them. We wouldn't want anyone to get hurt. We wouldn't use them at all, but it is kind of annoying."

"Oh," said the deputy. "I didn't know that. I've never actually hit anything before. I wouldn't have hit the bobturtle either, but I was aiming at a tree."

"Why did you aim at the tree?" asked Otto.

"The tree wasn't moving," said the deputy. "The bobturtle was moving. I thought I had a better chance to hit the tree. Turns out I was wrong."

"What happened to the bobturtle?" asked Davey.

"It hopped on a wagon and rode off," answered the deputy.

"That's pretty scary," said Davey. "I was up on Gooseberry Mountain today. I'm glad that bobturtle didn't hop on my wagon."

"That does it," said Otto. "We're going to charge those bobcats double to deliver the stuff they steal from us. Davey has to risk running into bobturtles. I'll need to make more money. If anything were to happen to Davey, I would have to pay someone twice as much to do his job."

"Thanks Otto," smiled Davey. "Does this mean I'll be getting that bonus?'

"If the bobturtle gets you, we'll talk about it," answered Otto.

"Yahoo!" shouted Davey. He was so excited he took a bite out of Otto's wagon. "Sorry, Otto."

"You should be," said Otto. "There's no eating on the job. Next time wait until our break time.

That reminds me. We haven't had a break in over fifteen minutes."

"I guess it is time for our thirteenth afternoon break," Davey checked his watch. "No wonder I'm so tired."

Otto pulled up a wooden rocking chair for Davey. The hungry beaver ate every last bit of it.

The Bobcat Cowboys
Steal the Show
Part 2

Table of Contents

Chapter		Page
5	The Missing Trunk	82
6	The Bird Trap	85
7	Chicken Out	88
8	A Visit with Mama	91

by Brian Davis

Vocabulary Words

annoyed

autograph

disguised

porridge

posse

A trunk belonging to the Fowl Players is missing. It couldn't have walked off by itself, or could it? Maybe it was taken by the mysterious creature on Gooseberry Mountain. Read the next part of the story to find out.

Chapter 5
The Missing Trunk

A duck, goose, and a chicken walked into the sheriff's office. The Fowl Players looked very worried. Babs Bluejay was the first to notice them. She was a big fan. She liked Golda Goose and Meg Egging the chicken. But Mallard LaQuack was her favorite.

Babs squealed in delight, "Duck!" she shouted as she pointed to Mallard.

Deputy Guinea Pig dove under a bench.

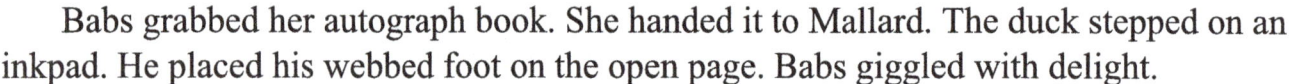

"Where's the deputy?" asked Mallard.

Babs pointed to the bench. The deputy peaked out. He was very embarrassed. Deputy Guinea Pig pointed to Babs.

"She told me to duck," he explained.

Babs grabbed her autograph book. She handed it to Mallard. The duck stepped on an inkpad. He placed his webbed foot on the open page. Babs giggled with delight.

Golda scolded Mallard, "We're not here to meet your fan club."

Meg looked at the deputy. "She's right. We're here because we've been robbed."

"Robbed!" shouted the deputy and Babs.

"Did you see any bobcats?" asked Deputy Guinea Pig.

"We just came back to the theatre and our trunk was gone," explained Golda.

"It had all our beautiful costumes in it," added Meg.

"Sounds like the work of those Bobcat Cowboys," sighed Deputy Guinea Pig.

"Do you have any idea where they would have taken it?" asked Mallard.

"Probably to their secret hideout," answered Babs.

"Secret! Oh, no. We'll never find it!" cried Golda.

"Just follow the signs. You can't miss it," said the deputy.

"Aren't you coming with us?" asked Meg.

"Why would I do that?" asked Deputy Guinea Pig.

"You are the law around here," said Mallard.

"Sorry, I forgot," frowned the deputy. "Uh…maybe your trunk wasn't stolen. It could have been termites. They get mighty hungry this time of year."

"That's not possible," said Babs. "Wilma Woodpecker's family checked out the theatre right after Otto cleaned it. They didn't find enough termites for a good snack. It was rather disappointing for them."

Deputy Guinea Pig let out a heavy sigh. He knew there was only one thing to do. The deputy reached for the triple barrel rubber band slingin' shotgun. He grabbed a full box of rubber bands.

Soon the brightly colored wagon was heading out of town. The deputy rode up front with the Larry the driver. He kept his eyes peeled for any sign of the trunk. The deputy hoped he could find it before they got to Gooseberry Mountain. He would be disappointed.

They didn't see the trunk anywhere in town. The wagon was getting near another small road. It led to the Bobcat Cowboy's secret hideout. The deputy pointed to the sign.

The wagon began to turn. Suddenly it stopped. The deputy flew right off his seat. The driver pointed ahead.

"Would you look at that!" said the surprised rat.

The deputy couldn't believe his eyes. Walking across the road was an unusual critter. It had a body like a trunk. It had legs like a bobcat. It didn't see very well. The critter kept bumping into trees and rocks.

"What is it?" asked Larry the rat.

The deputy whispered, "It's a bobturtle. It's the biggest one I've ever seen."

"How many have you seen?" asked Larry.

"Two."

The deputy reached for his triple barrel rubber band slingin' shotgun. He carefully aimed at a large tree. Boing, boing, boing. The rubber bands zinged past the tree. All three hit the moving object ahead of them.

"They just bounced off," said the driver.

"They always do. But I think that bobturtle is really annoyed," said the deputy.

The birds poked their heads out of a little door behind the driver. They watched the driver and the deputy. The two rodents started walking back to town. The three birds hopped out of the backdoor.

"Where are you going?" asked Meg.

"We just saw a bobturtle," said Larry.

"I'm gonna need a posse. Those bobturtles might be dangerous. Rubber bands just bounce right off them. I'm not going up Gooseberry Mountain with just the five of us. We'll be right back," answered Deputy Guinea Pig.

"Why not drive back to town?" asked Mallard LaQuack.

"I need the wagon to mark the spot," explained the deputy.

"So you can find the trail?" asked Golda.

"No," answered the deputy. "I need to remember where to put the Bobturtle Crossing sign. If a wagon hit a bobturtle it would be a real mess. You three stay here. If any wagons come by, tell them to slow down."

"When can we find our trunk?" asked Meg Egging.

"Let's see," the deputy began to figure. "I'll need to get a help wanted ad in the paper. Then I'll need to hire just the right critters. Then there's the posse training course. I'll have to teach the new workers how to fire a triple barrel rubber band slingin' shotgun. Then I'll teach them all about bobturtle hunting. That won't be easy. Not everyone is a natural shooter like me.

I just hired Larry. So, I'm already starting. I'd say Larry and I will be back in three weeks. Just wait right here. Like I said we'll be right back. Don't wait up for us."

Larry waved goodbye. Mallard rubbed his head. The duck was upset. He began to quack loudly to himself. He flapped his wings and stirred up the dust.

"Your feathers are getting ruffled," honked Golda.

"I didn't get a look at that bobturtle," said Meg, "but it doesn't sound dangerous to me. I think I could outrun a turtle."

"Even if his name is Bob," added Golda. "Let's go up on that mountain and get our costumes!"

"We're birds of a feather," said Mallard, "So let's stick together." He climbed to the bench on the front of the wagon. "Let's go to Gooseberry Mountain."

Chapter 6
The Bird Trap

The duck, goose, and hen sat on the branch of a big walnut tree. They watched the front of the cave. There was no sign of their trunk. The three birds suddenly didn't feel too brave. They had roosted in the tree all night. None of them wanted to walk into a cave full of bobcats. Golda tried to be courageous.

"We didn't come up here for nothing," honked the goose. "We need to get our costumes."

"I do enjoy the view of the waterfall. It's quite relaxing. I think we should continue relaxing back in town. We can wait for the deputy and his posse," said Meg.

"Don't be such a chicken," said Golda.

"But I am a chicken," cackled Meg. "I come from a long line of chickens. I'm proud to be a chicken."

"Ladies, not so loud. I think I hear something," quacked Mallard.

The birds sat quietly and watched. A strange creature walked up to the cave. It didn't have arms. It didn't have a head. The creature kept bumping into the door.

"That must be the bobturtle!" Meg shuddered.

"That's not a bobturtle," said Golda.

"Have you ever seen a bobturtle?" questioned Meg. She was still upset at the goose.

"No," said Golda. "Have you?"

"Ladies," Mallard reminded them. "That creature might hear you. Until we know that it doesn't like birds, I'd prefer to stay hidden."

"But that's not a creature. That's our trunk," argued Golda.

"Our trunk doesn't have bobcat legs," argued Meg.

Mallard wanted to fly off to another tree. The goose and the chicken were making quite a bit of noise. Golda and Meg continued to argue. Wings were flapping. Feathers were flying.

They didn't notice the cave door opening. Bubba had rescued his brothers from the trunk. The birds didn't even notice the lasso. Billybob roped all three birds. With one tug, the goose, hen, and duck were on the ground.

The three bobcats stood over the birds. They were all smiling. The duck glared angrily at the goose and hen. He let out a loud quack. Golda started honking. Then Meg started cackling. The birds were blaming each other for the trouble they were in.

"I'm not ready for the party," said Bubba.

"I don't think they're ready to lay eggs," sighed Bobbybill.

"And, I don't think we want them in our cave," said Billybob. "It echoes too much. It would sound like we had a whole flock of geese, ducks, and chickens."

"What will we do with them?" asked Bobbybill.

"We'll toss them in the trunk," said Billybob.

That's just what the bobcats did. The Billybob and Bobbybill piled some brush on the trunk. They didn't want anyone to see it. The trunk looked like a large quacking, honking, cackling bush.

"Nobody will even notice," smiled Billybob.

"Why are we hiding our guests?" asked Bubba. "They won't have much fun at our party."

"With all their arguing it would ruin the party," Billybob explained. "What would all the other guests think?"

"I'm too tired to think," said Bubba. "Too much thinking gives me headaches. I've been painting for the party."

"Painting?" asked Bobbybill. "What have you been painting?"

"Otto Muskrat asked me to steal his gold paint. He even had it delivered," said Bubba.

"He didn't charge you for delivery, did he?" asked Billybob. "Sometimes I think he's trying to rob us on those delivery charges."

"We're still paying for the sled delivery," added Bobbybill. "He didn't tell us we would have to pay for the sleds we stole."

"There ought to be a law against that," said Billybob. "That low down, good for nothing muskrat."

"He is good for getting robbed of sleds," Bubba reminded Billybob.

"You're right. He's a low down, good for robbing of sleds muskrat," agreed Billybob.

"Did you invite Otto to the party?" asked Bubba.

"We got locked in the trunk. We couldn't even jump out and surprise the birdies," explained Bobbybill. "We walked all the way back. You don't know what it was like. It was like walking in a barrel."

"That had to be a bad feeling," said Bubba.

"Hush-up, you two," growled Billybob. He held up a paw. "Do you hear that?"

The other two bobcats listened. They seemed confused. That wasn't unusual. They seemed even more confused than normal.

"I don't hear anything," said Bubba.

"That's right," said Billybob. "No quacking, no honking, no cackling. I hope those birds didn't escape."

The bobcats ran to the trunk. The lid was still closed. Billybob tapped on the trunk. Thump, thump, thump. A thump, thump answered back. The birds had stopped fighting. The bobcats carried the trunk into the cave. They placed the trunk on two sawhorses.

"What are these sawhorses doing here?" asked Billybob.

"I was painting the decorations," said Bubba.

"What decorations?" asked Billybob.

"For the party," whispered Bubba. He didn't want the birds to hear. "Did you get out the invitations?"

"We were locked in the trunk," said Billybob.

"There wasn't a mailbox in the trunk?" asked Bubba. The bobcat knocked on the trunk. "Is there a mailbox in there?"

"No," quacked Mallard.

"How will we get invitations to everyone? We'll have to go to every house. This will take hours," said Bubba. "Should we just leave the birds in the trunk?"

"You won't have to go all over town," explained Mallard from inside the trunk. "All the critters will be in one place. They'll be waiting to see our play."

"With our costumes," added Golda.

Meg didn't say anything. She was a little chicken. She was shaking out of fear. The little hen didn't like being in a bobcat's cave. The hen shook so much the lasso began to loosen.

"Those critters will be mighty disappointed," said Mallard.

"Oh, no," said Bubba. "Why?"

"There's not going to be a play," quacked Mallard. "All the little critter children will be so sad. They'll be no laughter in Rowdent Gulch tonight."

Tears started rolling down Bubba and Bobbybill's faces. Even Billybob sniffled a little. The duck could tell he was making them cry. The duck expected to be let out of the trunk any second.

"And it will be all your fault!" said Golda Goose. "We're stuck in this trunk."

"I love to disappoint critters, but not that much," said Bobbybill.

"I don't like to disappoint anyone at all," added Bubba.

Billybob rubbed his chin. "It's tough being the only bad guy," said the bobcat. "If you two won't help me be bad, I'll just have to do something good."

Mallard started quacking his cheers. Golda honked with delight. Meg started cackling. She got so excited, she laid an egg.

The birds got quiet again. The trunk was still closed. The birds waited. The birds listened. The cave was silent. The bobcats had left.

Chapter 7
Chicken Out

"Hello. Is anyone there?" honked Golda Goose.

"Just us chickens," giggled Meg.

"I think we're alone," said Mallard. "Now we just need to get this rope off us."

"Just shake a lot," cackled Meg. "It worked for me."

Golda began to shake. "It works."

"It's a good thing I'm such a chicken," cackled Meg.

Mallard shook off the rope. "That solves one problem. We can't open the trunk."

"And our costumes are not here," added Golda.

"Maybe I can open the trunk. Just a second," said Meg.

The other two birds waited in the dark trunk. Soon they heard scratching on the lid. At first, they thought it was bobcat claws. Then they heard pecking.

"I can't get it open," cackled Meg. "It's stuck."

"Meg?" quacked Mallard.

"Yes Mallard," answered Meg.

"How did you get out?" asked Mallard.

"Through one of the holes in the bottom of the trunk," answered Meg.

"Why didn't you tell us?" asked Golda.

"I thought we were trying to open the trunk," said Meg. "I was going to unlatch it. Then you could push it open."

"We were trying to open it to get out. You are such a silly chicken," honked Golda.

"If I'm silly, why am I the only one outside the trunk?" cackled Meg.

"She has a point there," said Mallard.

Meg was now underneath the sawhorses. She poked her head through a hole. "Could you kindly hand me my egg?" the hen asked Mallard.

The other two birds climbed out. Meg cradled her egg. Golda started looking for her costumes. Mallard tried to get the other two birds out the door. He didn't know when the bobcats would be back.

The cave was dark. Golda lit a lantern. Mallard was almost to the door. That's where he stopped. The duck let out a loud quack. Golda honked. Meg cackled. The birds couldn't believe their eyes.

The cave was full of gold sleds. Mallard wasn't in such a hurry to leave now. He began tugging at a sled. The other two birds grabbed another sled. Golda tugged one end. Meg tugged the other. The birds started honking and cackling.

"There's enough for all of us," Mallard reminded them.

"How are we going to get them out of here?" asked Golda.

"We could wait until it snows," suggested Meg. "Winter's only six months away!"

"I think the bobcats might come back by then," answered Mallard.

The birds thought and thought. Finally, they remembered they had a wagon. Mallard brought it up to the cave. The back of the wagon was filled with feathers. There was no room for the sleds.

The birds brought the feathers inside the cave. Next, they loaded the sleds into the back of the wagon. The three birds started down the road. They decided not to go back to Rowdent Gulch. They didn't want any of the critters to find the sleds. Meg looked worried.

"What's wrong," asked Mallard.

"Well, maybe it's just because I'm a chicken," explained Meg, "but won't those bobcats be angry? We stole all their gold."

"It serves them right," said Golda. "They stole our costumes. They locked us in a trunk. They left us in the cave. Those low down, good for nothing bobcats had it coming."

"Won't they come after us?" asked Meg.

"Maybe she's right," said Mallard. "They may come looking for us."

"Not if they're in jail!" honked Golda. "That's where they belong."

"Hmm," said Mallard. "That's the solution for our problem. We've got to make sure those bobcats land in jail."

The birds turned the wagon around. They headed back to Rowdent Gulch. The birds wondered what was happening at the theatre. Sure, all the critters would be disappointed. Then they would be excited to see the birds free. Maybe they would get back in time for the play. The birds promised not to tell anyone about the gold.

The wagon entered town. It was quite different from the first time they came to Rowdent Gulch. No critters were on the streets. All the lanterns were off in the houses. The stores were closed.

The birds thought everyone must be scared. Deputy Guinea Pig and his bobturtle stories sent everyone into hiding. Or maybe, everyone was out looking for them. That must be it, the birds reasoned. The critters must be on Gooseberry Mountain.

The wagon pulled to a stop in front of the theatre. It wasn't the only wagon parked on the road. There were all kinds of wagons in front of the theatre. Larry the rat came up to them.

"You can't leave this wagon here," said Larry.

"You can't tell us where to park," argued Mallard. "I am the star!"

"I thought I was the star," cackled Meg.

"Don't be silly. Everyone knows I am the star," honked Golda

Larry showed them a badge. "I have my own star."

It had the words "Deputy Trainee" carved on it. "Don't make me get a rubber band slingin' shotgun," said Larry. "I don't know how to use it yet."

Mallard was quite upset. "OK, but you're making everyone in that theatre wait."

Mallard shook the reins. They had to go three blocks to find a parking space. The three birds waddled back to the theatre. As they reached the door the birds heard something strange. They heard laughter. They heard a lot of laughter.

Chapter 8
A Visit With Mama

The bobcats realized the whole town would be disappointed. When they left the cave, there was only one thing they could do. They did what any low down, good for nothin' bobcat would do. They ran to their mommy.

Bessybob had just taken a cake in the oven. It had a file in it. She was always thinking of her sons. Mama bobcat looked out her window. The three bobcats were coming down the road. She saw the looks on their faces. It was the same look they always had. Her cubs were in big trouble.

Still, she was always glad to see them. Bessybob was so proud of her cubs. They were very important bobcats. Without them, Sheriff Prairie Dog would have nothing to do. Bessybob liked Sheriff Prairie Dog. She wouldn't want him to lose his job.

The Bobcat Cowboys told their mommy all about the birds. They told her how disappointed all the critter children would be. Mama handed out tissues. All the bobcats dried their eyes. They blew their noses. They were ready to go on.

Bessybob Bobcat walked to a bookshelf. She scanned the neat rows of books. Finally, she found just was she was looking for. The old book was worn from being lovingly read time and again.

Bubba smiled, "You're going to read us a bedtime story!"

Bobbybill grumbled, "I don't want a bedtime story. I'm not sleepy."

"I'm thirsty," whined Billybob. "Can I have a drink of water?"

"You'll leave a light on for us, won't you?" asked Bobbybill.

"Hush-up, bobcats," said Bessybob. "It's not your bedtime. This book is the solution to your problem. We're not going to disappoint the whole town. Remember what I always taught you."

"Disappoint one critter at a time," all three bobcats chimed.

"I know it's much more work. And you boys work very hard. It's just so much more special that way," said Bessybob. "It lets them know you were thinkin' only of them. But tonight, we're not going to disappoint any of the little critters."

She led her sons to the backdoor of the theatre. The bobcats found the costumes they had tossed from the trunk. Bessybob thought the costumes would need a little work. Mama pulled out a needle and thread. She had the bobcats read a story from the book. Then she had her cubs gather up all the feathers they could find.

Critters filed into the theatre. It was packed to the rafters. In fact, Peppy Possum's whole family hung upside down from the rafters. Sheriff Prairie Dog and Papa Prairie Dog made it back just in time. Everyone was so excited to see the famous Fowl Players.

When the curtain went up, the bobcats were ready. Bessybob had done a wonderful job. She hoped nobody would know the difference. The bobcats had disguised themselves. She had reserved the front rows for moles. Moles live underground. They don't have good eyesight, so they wouldn't notice how bobcat-like the birds looked.

Bessybob wasn't just counting on the moles. That's where the feathers came in. The four bobcats were covered in feathers. Then they put on their costumes. They were very strange looking birds.

The bobcats were ready to give their performance. Billybob came out first. He was dressed like a chicken wearing a bear costume. He sat at a table. He picked up a newspaper.

"Good morning, Papa Bear," said Bessybob. She was also wearing a feathered bear costume. She picked up a cookbook.

"Good morning, Mama Bobcat…I mean Bear," said Billybob.

Finally, Bobbybill came in. The bobcat was wearing a feathered bear costume too. He sat in a chair that was way too small for him.

"Good morning, Baby Bear Bobbybill," said Mama Bear.

"What's for breakfast?" asked Baby Bear Bobbybill.

"Porridge," answered Mama Bear.

"Yum, yum," said Baby Bear Bobbybill.

Just then, Baby Bear's chair collapsed. Mama Bear jumped up. That flipped the table over. The porridge bowls shattered on the stage floor. All the critters started laughing.

Papa Bear put down his newspaper. "It looks like we'll have to eat breakfast out."

"You can go get some of Bubba's Marshmallow Pineapple Burgers," suggested a voice offstage. It sounded a lot like Bubba.

"I have an idea," said Papa Bear. "Let's go get some of Bubba's Marshmallow Pineapple Burgers. Then we can go to a cave sale. Those Bobcat Cowboys are selling some really nice sleds."

"I'd rather have egg salad," grumbled Baby Bear.

All the critters were laughing and clapping. The Fowl Players were much sillier than anyone had expected. They laughed even harder at the next part.

In came Bubba. He too was disguised as a bird. But he did not have on a bear costume. Bubba was wearing a frilly blue dress. He had a blond wig on his head. Bubba Bobcat was playing the role of Goldilocks.

The porridge bowls were gone. Bubba had to pretend he was eating from Papa's bowl.

"This porridge is too hot. It's also too invisible."

The coyotes on the back row howled with laughter. So did the other critters.

Next, Goldilocks tried Mama Bear's invisible bowl.

"This porridge is too cold. It's invisible too."

Finally, Goldilocks went to Baby Bear's seat.

"I thought I was supposed to break the chair," Bubba yelled off stage.

Deputy Guinea Pig laughed so hard his triple barrel rubber band blastin' shotgun went off. The rubber bands bounced off three opossums. Their tails uncurled. The opossums landed right onto Davey Beaver's lap. Davey jumped and took a bite out of the bench in front of him. Just then, Otto came back with a tub of popcorn.

There was a hole in the seat. Davey tried to warn Otto. The laughter was too loud. Otto sat down. He quickly jumped up. The popcorn tub flew in the air. It landed on the stage.

The Bobcat Cowboys
Steal the Show
Part 3

Table of Contents

Chapter		Page
9	Bobcats on Trial	95
10	A Fowl Crime	99

by Brian Davis

Once again, the Bobcat Cowboys find themselves on trial. Birdnapping and trunk stealin' are serious crimes in Rowdent Gulch. Will Judge Polecat decide to throw the book at them? Read the exciting conclusion to the Bobcat Cowboys Steal the Show.

Chapter 9
Bobcats on Trial

The courtroom was packed. This was the biggest trial since the last time the bobcats were in trouble. The three birds sat with Alice McHoot. The owl was the prosecuting attorney. The bobcats had their favorite lawyer. Frazzle O'Hare was not nearly as afraid of the bobcats this time. He still wasn't sure about the owl, Alice.

Both Alice and Frazzle agreed about the jury. Animals that ate only vegetables were allowed this time. In fact, wolves, coyotes and other scary animals weren't allowed in the courtroom. The judge didn't want anyone to get eaten.

Papa Prairie Dog couldn't make it. He had started a new job. Otto Muskrat had hired him to work on Mondays. Papa was sorting jellybeans by color. He was hoping to be finished in time for the evening checker match.

Otto was in the courtroom. He had to stand up. The poor muskrat had another splinter. It wasn't so bad. Otto wanted to go back to the big city for a few days. He would leave Tuesday. Otto planned on winning at checkers before leaving.

He wanted to be Monday Night Checker Champ two weeks in a row. It might mean paying Papa Prairie Dog to work all night. He planned on having his new help weigh and measure each jellybean.

It was worth the ten cents an hour he was paying Papa Prairie Dog.

"That should take Papa about four hours," thought Otto. "Four hours times ten cents an hour equals..." Otto squinted. It helped him think harder. "Fifty-seven cents. It costs a lot of money to be a checker champ."

Judge Polecat took the stand. He asked Bailiff Mouse to read the charges. The bobcats were accused of birdnapping, trunk stealing, and wearing feathers without a permit. Alice McHoot called Golda Goose to the stand.

"What happened to your trunk?" asked Alice.

"Those low-down, good for nothing bobcats stole it," honked Golda.

"What happened to you yesterday?" asked Alice.

"My friends and I were birdnapped," honked Golda.

"By whom?" asked Alice.

"Those low-down, good-for-nothing bobcats."

"They're good for sled stealin'" said Otto from the back of the courtroom.

The judge hammered his gavel. "Mr. Muskrat, do I need to have you sit down?"

"No sir," said Otto. He thought of those new splinters. The muskrat winced.

Alice turned back to her witness. "What did you see the bobcats do Saturday night?"

"They were wearing feathers," honked Golda. "They looked like bobchickens! It was a disgrace."

"They looked more like bobgeese," cackled Meg.

"I object," said Frazzle. "They looked like the three bears with feathers."

"Objection sustained," said the judge. "They looked like feathery bobturtles without their shells."

"I have no more questions for Miss Goose," sighed Alice McHoot.

"Your witness," said the judge to Frazzle.

Frazzle hopped to Golda Goose. "What happened to you when the bobcats saw you?"

"They locked us in our trunk!" honked Golda.

"So as soon as they saw you, they gave it back to you?" asked Frazzle.

Golda looked confused. The bobcats smiled.

"Did they really mean to steal it? They brought it right to you," added Frazzle.

"He's such a fine bunny," Bessybob whispered to Bubba.

"But they did lock us up!" honked Golda. "That's birdnapping!"

"How did you get out?" asked Frazzle.

"There were holes in the bottom of the trunk," sighed Golda.

"Did the bobcats know there were holes in the trunk?" asked Frazzle.

Golda looked angry, "They made the holes in the trunk!"

"Was the trunk on the ground?" asked Frazzle.

"It was at first," answered Golda. "Then they put it on sawhorses."

"If they put it on sawhorses you could get out anytime you wanted. That doesn't sound like birdnapping to me. Why would they put you in a trunk with big holes in it? Just how dumb do you think the bobcats are?" asked Frazzle.

"Do you really want me to answer that?" asked Golda.

Frazzle thought for a moment. "I guess not." The rabbit hopped to the jury. "This witness said the Bobcats gave them the trunk. Then the bobcats put the trunk on sawhorses. The birds were free to go at any time. The trunk wasn't stolen. The birds weren't birdnapped."

The jury left the courtroom. A few minutes later they came back. A red squirrel was the jury foreman. "We find the bobcats not guilty of birdnapping. We find the bobcats not guilty of trunk stealing."

The birds were very upset. They started quacking, honking, and cackling. Meg was so upset she laid an egg. Billybob licked his lips. He really wanted an egg salad sandwich.

"We find the bobcats guilty of wearing feathers without a permit," said the jury foreman.

"I never thought that law was fair," Babs Bluejay said to Willie Woodpecker.

"We can't have just any critter wearing feathers," said the judge. "Next thing you know sparrows will be wearing fur." The judge looked at the bobcats. He was not happy. "I'm tired of you bobcats stirring things up around here. I'm going to have to throw the book at you."

He picked up Bessybob's bedtime storybook.

Bessybob gasped, "No your honor. Please have mercy."

The bobcat cowboys smiled. They could always count on their mama. She wouldn't let anything bad happen to them. She would tell the judge how sweet they were.

"Please don't throw that book," said Bessybob. "It's rather old. It's also special to me. I wouldn't want to see anything bad happen to my book."

The judge was moved. "I'll reduce the sentence. I won't throw the book at them. I'll have Bailiff Mouse hand it to them."

The judge handed the book to the bailiff. Unfortunately, the book was bigger than the bailiff.

It covered the mouse completely. The mouse struggled to stand up.

"I want you to read that book. You'll learn every story. I sentence you to read every sentence. Then you will put on a new play every Saturday night.

"Is that like a book report?" asked Bubba.

"No," said the judge. "You bobcats were so funny. I just want to see more plays. Bubba might consider putting in a concession stand. You could sell marshmallow pineapple burgers."

"Yum, yum," said the rodents in the courtroom.

Mallard started quacking, "Aren't you going to punish them? What kind of judge are you?"

The judge smacked his gavel. It landed on the bedtime storybook. "Bailiff, remove that duck from the courtroom. Bailiff? Where's that bailiff?"

Sheriff Prairie Dog pointed to the book. A muffled cry came from underneath. The judge lifted the book.

"Oops," said the judge.

After the trial the bobcats were very happy. Bessybob thought Frazzle O'Hare was brilliant. She wanted to thank him. Her cubs had the best bunny lawyer they had ever had.

"Mr. O'Hare," Bessybob shook Frazzle's paw. "Thank you very much. You looked so good today. Would you join us for lunch?'

"We're very hungry," said Bubba.

The bunny jumped back. "N...n...no."

He quickly gathered his papers. They were sticking out of his briefcase. "I've got a very important meeting. I can't be lunch today. I mean I can't have lunch today."

The bunny hopped out of the courthouse.

"Maybe some other time," Bessybob called after him. "Bring the whole family."

"He's a great lawyer," Bessybob said to her cubs. "But he's kind of hard to get to know."

Chapter 10
A Fowl Crime

The following Monday the bobcats were just coming to the theatre. Each one carried a huge bag. They had to get ready for their next play. The three brothers stopped beside the wagon. They looked at the brightly colored pictures.

It showed the three Fowl Players. Golda was wearing a blue dress. It was a picture of the one Bubba wore in the play. Billybob laughed and pointed.

"She looks a lot prettier in it than you."

Bobbybill chuckled, "I'm glad you think so. We can't afford to steal you some glasses. We can only pay for one crime at a time."

Larry the Rat was so happy this morning. It was his first time to carry the triple barrel rubber band slinging shotgun. Deputy Guinea Pig even let him put one rubber band on it. The sun was in his eyes as he walked toward the theatre.

The rat didn't see the bobcats behind the wagon. Well, he didn't see all of the bobcats behind the wagon. He did see their legs. The wagon looked like a turtle shell.

"A six-legged bobturtle!" Larry yelled. "It's the biggest one yet."

He raised the shotgun and fired. The rubber band hit the latch on the backdoor. The wagon's door squeaked open. Out fell a stack of gold painted sleds. It made a loud noise.

Sheriff Prairie Dog came running. Deputy Prairie Dog was right behind him.

The bobcats peaked around the corner. More and more critters came to see what was happening. Larry the rat pointed to the bobcats.

"Did we do that?" asked Bubba.

Larry the rat nodded yes. The Fowl Players dashed out of the theatre. The three birds pushed to the front of the crowd. Golda and Meg spread their wings to block the view. Mallard tried to stuff the sleds back into the wagon. They didn't want anyone to grab their treasure.

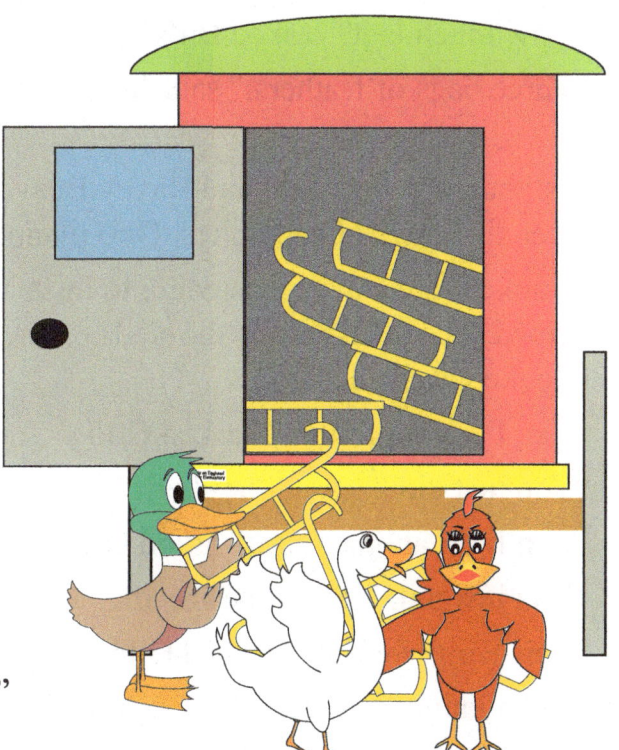

"Our sleds," said Bubba. "They took our sleds!"

"We're not paying them any delivery fees," grumbled Billybob.

Judge Polecat came up, "What's the big stink? Did those bobcats commit another crime?"

"It looks like they were the victims of the crime," said the sheriff. "I think the Fowl Players robbed them."

All the critters applauded. The bobcats got a taste of their own medicine. The birds took a bow. Meg was so happy she laid an egg.

"There's nothing to celebrate. A crime is a crime," the judge scolded the crowd. "Who caught them?"

"It was…" the sheriff started to point to the bobcats.

"Me," said Larry the rat. "I shot the latch off the wagon. I knew something didn't look right."

"I trained him myself," said Deputy Guinea Pig. "I taught him everything I know. It took almost an hour."

"Do you think we should see what the bobcats have in the bags?" asked the rat.

"Good idea," said the deputy.

"It's just feathers," said Bubba. "The birdies left them at our cave. I thought they might have forgotten them."

"Do you have a permit to carry those feathers?" asked the deputy. "You need a permit to carry feathers in Rowdent Gulch on a Monday."

"I never liked that law," Babs Bluejay whispered to Sylvia Sparrow.

"I didn't know we needed a permit," said Bobbybill. "That's a silly law."

"Ignorant laws are no excuse," argued the deputy. "You'll have to pay the fine."

"How much is it?" asked Billybob.

"Three bags of feathers," said Judge Polecat. "The fines go to the sheriff's retirement fund."

Just then Otto Muskrat and Davey Beaver came up. They had just finished hooking together six crates of paperclips. Otto planned on having Davey unhook them that night.

It looked like Davey was going to miss Monday Night Checkers again. Otto looked at the crowd. The muskrat saw the sleds on the street. He saw three very guilty looking birds. Otto looked at the bobcats.

"Can I ask a question?" asked Otto.

"You just did," teased the sheriff.

"Can I ask another one?" asked Otto.

"You just did," teased the sheriff.

"This isn't working," sighed Otto. "Bubba, where did you get those gold pants?"

Bubba laughed, "These aren't gold. They're blue."

"They look gold to me," said Otto.

"They're blue," said Bubba. "The paint on the blue pants is gold."

Otto rubbed his chin, "You just painted the pants gold. I've been trying to get gold pants for months. That's it. All I need to do is paint them."

"I wasn't painting my pants," correct Bubba. "I was painting those old sleds." Bubba pointed to the sleds on the street.

"The low-down, good for nothin' sleds you stole from me?" asked Otto.

"Yep," answered Bubba.

"They're painted?" asked Golda.

"They're worthless?" asked Mallard.

"They make nice decorations for surprise parties," said Bubba.

The sheriff pointed to the sleds, "You can take your sleds back, Otto."

"Do I have to?" asked Otto.

"They're your sleds," answered the sheriff.

Suddenly Otto had an idea. He turned to Davey.

"I've been promising you a bonus," said Otto. "The sleds are yours."

"Do I have to pay to deliver them to myself?" asked Davey.

"Yes, but I'll give you a discount," said Otto. "You'll have to use your own wagon. Just do it in your free time."

"Yahoo!" yipped Davey. "The worthless sleds are all mine!" He was so excited he took a bite out of the wagon.

"That worked out nicely," quacked Mallard.

The three birds decided it was time to leave. They tried to slip into the crowd. The Fowl Players almost got away. Then they bumped into a wall of black and white fur.

"Not so fast," said Judge Polecat. "A crime is a crime. You stole those sleds. Try to get away and you'll be jailbirds."

"Can we have a sentence like the bobcats?" cackled Meg.

"Yes," honked Golda. "We could work in the theatre."

"That's a fine idea," said the judge. "You can work in the theatre."

And that's just what they Fowl Players did. The judge had them work in the concession stand. The birds worked very hard. All the critters loved the marshmallow pineapple burgers. The theatre was packed every night. Critters from all around came to see the bobcat cowboy's silly plays.

The birds decided never to steal again. Plus, they always had all the right feather wearing permits. The fowl players learned their lesson. They weren't the only ones. Otto learned a lesson as well.

Papa Prairie Dog was the only retired sheriff in town. He got the three bags of feathers the bobcats were fined. Papa liked tossing them in the air. He pretended it was snowing. A pile of feathers is slippery like snow. Papa liked to call his feathers "summer snow."

That gave Davey Beaver an idea. He had a wagonload of sleds. Papa had "summer snow." Together they opened a sled run on Gooseberry Mountain. It became very popular. They both quit working at Otto's store. They were now free every Monday night.

Otto missed being Monday Night Checker Champ. But he missed Davey even more. Otto learned that it was wrong to treat his friends unfairly. It was also cheating to keep them away from checker matches. Winning wasn't as much fun as just playing with his friends.

Yet there were still some lessons Otto didn't learn. Three weeks later a wagonload of crates was dropped off at his store. The muskrat opened them up. It was not what he expected. Half were filled with gold pants. The other half was filled with blue paint.

"I ordered gold paints and blue pants," he grumbled. "Gold Paints P-a-n-t-s, paint. Blue pants, p-a-i-n-t-s, pants. I wish those critters at the warehouse would learn to read!"

The King is Coming

Table of Contents

Chapter		Page
1	King Josiah's Problem	104
2	The Beggar King	107
3	The King Cobbler	109
4	The New King	112

Vocabulary Words

carriage

cobbler

guard

noblemen

tailor

by Brian Davis

King Josiah wants to find someone to be the next king. The evil Lord Lester wants to rule the kingdom. He has a plan. King Josiah must find a way to save his kingdom from Lord Lester's rule.

Chapter 1
King Josiah's Problem

On the hill above the village stood a huge castle. It was the home of King Josiah. He was known as a good and kind king. He had one big problem.

King Josiah had no wife. He also had no children. He was quite lonely, but that wasn't his biggest problem. King Josiah cared about the village and the people in it. They needed a king.

He had been sick all winter. The king almost died. As he lay in bed, he had lots of time to think. He must find someone who could someday take his place.

There was someone else who lived in the castle. Lord Lester was as evil as Josiah was good. Lord Lester had his own plans. He wanted to be the next king.

He wanted to tax the people more. Lord Lester wanted to be rich and powerful. The people in the village would have to work harder than ever. He thought King Josiah had been too kind to the people.

The king did not know of Lord Lester's evil plans. Lord Lester acted very nice to the king. He wanted the king to trust him. Each day Lord Lester brought a hot cup of medicine to the king.

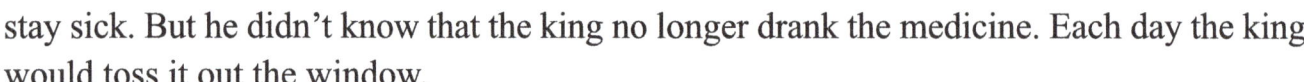

At least that's what he wanted the king to think. Lord Lester was actually giving the king poison. He wanted the king to stay sick. But he didn't know that the king no longer drank the medicine. Each day the king would toss it out the window.

The king soon began to feel better and stronger. He told Lord Lester of his plan to find a new king.

"I will search the village for someone worthy to be king," said Josiah. "Tell the people of the village that I will begin my search the first day of spring."

"We don't know if you'll be well by then," said Lord Lester. "I wouldn't want your health to fail. I will give you stronger medicine."

Now, Lord Lester didn't want the king to get well. If the king was too weak to find a replacement, he knew he would be king. So, Lord Lester decided to give the king stronger poison.

The king still tossed it out the window. On the first day of spring, the king was ready to go to the village. The bright sun poured through the window in the castle wall. The king lifted his legs over the edge of his bed. His feet shuffled to the window. It had been a long time since he had walked outside.

King Josiah had been sick much of the winter. His body was weak, but his spirit felt strong. He wanted to leave the dark castle. The green trees and colorful flowers made him feel alive again.

The last three days he had left his room. Each day he was greeted by Lord Lester. The tall, thin man had a curly black mustache. A long thin nose sat right between his beady eyes. In his hand was a cup of steaming liquid.

"It's time for your medicine," Lord Lester would say. "You must stay in bed until you are well. You will need your strength. The big announcement is only a few days away."

King Josiah would then shuffle back to bed. Today was no different. King Josiah stepped into the hall. Lord Lester was right there. The king was beginning to get upset. He wanted to enjoy the great weather. He was sure that would be better than the hot medicine.

"Don't stop me," said King Josiah. "I must get some fresh air."

"The air is not fresh," said Lord Lester. "It's cold and damp. It's just the thing to ruin your health. You must stay in your room. I will put a guard by your room to make sure no one bothers you."

The King sighed. Lord Lester had not let anyone near him for months. He was not only tired of being in the castle. King Josiah was also lonely. He was beginning to wonder if Lord Lester really wanted him to get better.

Josiah went back to his room. He sat on his bed and sighed. Did Lester really want him to get well? King Josiah felt like a prisoner in his own castle.

The king's thoughts were interrupted by a sound outside the window. A wet rag slapped against the glass. The king walked to the window. He tapped lightly. The man washing the window almost jumped off the ladder. The king swung open the glass.

"I'm sorry, King Josiah. I didn't mean to wake you. I just thought the view of the garden would be nicer through clean glass."

"Thank you for your thoughtfulness, Bradley" said King Josiah.

He was about to ask Bradley to come back later. Then he noticed the man was about his size.

Suddenly, the king had a plan. He reached out and tugged Bradley's arm.

"Come in. I have something else I'd like for you to do for me."

"Anything, your majesty," said the servant.

The king dressed the servant in his finest robe. King Josiah then put on the servant's old, torn clothes. He gave some instructions.

"Remember, go out the door and don't stop for anyone."

The servant did as he was told. The king heard the guard yelling after the servant in the hall.

"King Josiah. Stop. I have instructions from Lord Lester."

The guard was falling for it. King Josiah peeked into the hallway. The guard was following the servant. He was pleading with the servant to stop. King Josiah had tricked the guard.

King Josiah pulled the hood of the servant's robe over his head. He walked out into the hallway. Down the back steps he went. Soon he was out in the fresh air.

Chapter 2
The Beggar King

The king drank in the sunshine. He took a deep breath. The scent of roses filled the air. King Josiah started walking to the flower garden.

"Stop," said a guard. "You can't go into the king's garden."

King Josiah chuckled. He realized he was still wearing the old robe. "I am the king," said Josiah as he kept walking.

He did not expect what happened next. The guard picked up the king. He put him over his shoulder. The guard carried him outside the castle wall.

"Now stay here with the other beggars. I don't want to have to hurt you," said the guard.

"I am the king!" yelled Josiah. "Bring Lord Lester here now!"

"He's in the village," said the guard. "Besides, I wouldn't waste his time with an old beggar. He's getting ready to be the next king."

"I have not said he would be king," said Josiah.

"Beggars do not choose kings. King Josiah has chosen Lord Lester to be the next king."

The guard slammed the gate shut. King Josiah was trapped outside the castle. At first the king was angry. He was locked out of his own castle. All he had was the old robe. King Josiah didn't even have a pair of shoes to wear.

He took a deep breath. The air tasted fresh. It felt good to be in the daylight.

Nobody seemed to notice him. That was a different feeling too. All his life, people stopped and bowed. Everyone was too afraid to speak to him. People never acted the way they really were.

"This may be the best way to find the next king," thought King Josiah. "I will become a beggar."

The king walked down the street. He stopped people and asked for money. One man tossed him a coin. Just as Josiah reached for it, another beggar pushed him.

107

Josiah landed in a puddle of mud. The other beggar took the coin. The man who tossed the coin laughed at Josiah. He stomped in the puddle and splashed Josiah again.

Mud landed in Josiah's eyes. He couldn't see. Suddenly, someone jerked on his arm. He was dragged from the mud puddle.

"We can't have beggars on the street today," said the sheriff. "Lord Lester is coming. He's going to be the next king. We can't have people like you making the streets look dirty. Lord Lester will think I'm not doing my job. Go on, before I put you in jail."

King Josiah wiped his eyes. It was still hard for him to see. He stumbled down the street. He decided to rest outside a shop.

The smell from inside made him hungry. The king wasn't used to walking. He was hungry and tired. Through the window, Josiah could see loaves of fresh baked bread. He licked his lips.

King Josiah went inside the bakery. "You have so many fine loaves of bread. I would like to buy a loaf."

The baker looked at Josiah. "Do you have any money?"

King Josiah smiled, "I have lots of money. I just don't have any with me. If you could be so kind, I would pay you back."

The baker picked up a broom. He poked it at Josiah. "Get out and stay out, you old beggar! This bread is for the king. He is having a party for Lord Lester."

King Josiah scooted out the door. He was now even more hungry and tired. He began to look around for a place to take a nap. He found a nice bench, but the sheriff was watching him.

Josiah quickly walked away. He walked and walked. Finally, he came to the edge of the village. The last building was a little barn. It was right behind the shoe store.

King Josiah found an old blanket. He snuggled into some hay. Soon, the king was fast asleep.

Chapter 3

The Kind Cobbler

The king was startled the next morning. He looked up. A goat was munching on his bed of hay. Josiah could see the morning sun coming through the boards of the barn.

The gnawing feeling in his stomach was stronger. The king hadn't eaten in a day. That was a long time for a king not to eat. He was used to having anything at anytime.

Then he remembered he was on an adventure. The tattered robe reminded him he was playing the part of a beggar. He rubbed his eyes. Mud flaked off.

He thought about how cruel everyone had been to him. He wondered if all beggars were treated so poorly. He looked around the barn. That's when he first noticed the basket.

A loaf of bread, cheese, milk, and fresh fruit was waiting for him. Josiah enjoyed every bit of food. He felt stronger and happier with every bite. The door to the barn opened just as he finished.

"Did you enjoy your breakfast?" asked a young man.

"It was a meal fit for a king," smiled Josiah. "You must let me pay you back."

"No," said the young man. "I won't have a guest paying me back. I'm just sorry for this poor barn. You must stay in my house tonight. I did not discover you until this morning."

"You are the first person to show me kindness," said King Josiah. "What is your name?"

"My name is John. I am the village cobbler."

Just then, a bell began to ring.

"I have a customer," said John. "Please don't leave. You look like you could use some help."

John quickly ran to his little shoe shop. Josiah watched him from the barn door. A fine carriage was waiting out front. Josiah walked slowly to the edge of the building.

He could hear John talking to the customer. King Josiah recognized the man. It was Lord Lester. King Josiah thought he would surprise Lord Lester.

"How he must be worried about me," thought King Josiah. "He's probably searched every store in the village."

Josiah pulled the hood over his head. He sat on the bench in front of the shoe store. He listened to Lord Lester as he waited. What he heard surprised him.

"I hardly think these shoes are worthy of a king. I'll pay you half the price for them," said Lord Lester.

"These are the finest shoes in the kingdom," said John. "I won't sell them for less."

"Young man, you do not know who you are speaking to. I will soon be king. I expect you to treat me with honor due a king. If I say the shoes are no good, you are not to question me. Only I can decide what is fit for a king."

"Finish the shoes. I will be back tomorrow. I will pay you one-fourth of what you ask."

"That's not fair," said John. "I won't sell them for that."

"Very well," said Lord Lester. "Then I shall take them for free."

Lord Lester turned to leave. King Josiah turned to stop him. Lord Lester gave him a shove. Josiah landed on the bench.

"Stay out of my way, Old Beggar," said Lord Lester.

"King Josiah will hear of this!" said John. "He will not stand for this. He is a good and fair king!"

"King Josiah will soon be gone," said Lord Lester. "Then I will be king."

Just then, one of Lord Lester's servants came up to him. "I have the poison," said the servant.

"Good," said Lord Lester. "I have one last treatment for King Josiah."

Josiah watched the carriage pull away. John came outside the store. He picked Josiah off the bench.

"Are you all right?" asked John. "I saw him hit you."

"Is he this mean to everyone?" asked Josiah.

"That was about as nice as he gets," said John. "If he becomes king, this will be a very sad place. Someone should warn King Josiah."

Josiah rubbed his chin. He was getting an idea. "Why don't you tell the king?"

"Lord Lester won't let the people of the village near the king. Only his rich friends can get into the castle."

"Then we shall be rich," said Josiah. "I will need a bath, a carriage, and a fine robe."

"I have a pair of shoes fit for a king," said the cobbler. "The tailor can loan us some clothes. But what do you know about acting like a nobleman?"

"More than you might think," said Josiah. "The king has a servant named Bradley. Can you find him for me?"

"I know right where he lives. Do you know him?" asked John.

"Yes," said Josiah, "and I think he is just the right person for what I have in mind."

Chapter 4
The New King

Bradley waited in the shadows of the carriage house. It was the place the king kept his gold carriage and his fine horses. A little lantern was the only light in the dark barn. The guard's shadow passed by the hiding servant.

It was midnight. No one would check the horses again until morning. Bradley had played in the carriage house ever since he was a little boy. His friends would play hide-and-seek. It was even more fun in the dark.

The servant wasn't here to play tonight. He had to be very careful. He knew what Lord Lester would do to a thief. Bradley wasn't really stealing, but he knew Lord Lester wouldn't believe him.

Bradley slipped on the uniform he had borrowed. The carriage driver had been asleep when Bradley took the fine jacket and hat with the tall peacock feather. Bradley had always thought the hat looked silly.

His hands shook as he buttoned the fancy gold buttons. The jacket was almost too small for him. Bradley took a deep breath. He buttoned the last button.

It was tricky for one person to hitch the horses to the carriage. The darkness made it even harder. But Bradley knew what to do. He had watched his father do it hundreds of times. Bradley was a little boy then, but he remembered all the steps.

Bradley opened the huge doors of the carriage house. He winced as the doors creaked. Had a guard heard the sound? Bradley looked around. Everything was quiet around the castle.

Climbing up onto the driver's seat, Bradley grabbed the reins. He gently shook the leather straps. The horses grunted softly. The chains rattled quietly. The carriage pulled away from the carriage house.

The guard at the gate looked surprise. He was about to yell at Bradley. Then the guard stopped. There was a reason the guard didn't yell. John, the cobbler, poked the guard in the back with a sword.

"Open the gate," John told the guard.

The guard obeyed John. "You have to come with us," said John.

He whistled softly. Someone in the dark shadows stepped forward. The person had a rope. They tied the guard up. The guard was then blindfolded and put into the carriage.

Back at the castle, Lord Lester walked into the king's room. The empty cup that had held the poison was on the floor. A lifeless hand stuck out from under the blankets.

Lord Lester listened. He couldn't hear the king breathing. He poked the lump under the blankets. It was cold and hard.

Lord Lester's face had an evil grin on it, "finally, I am king!"

"Guards!" Lord Lester left the room. "The king is dead. It was King Josiah's dying wish that I would be the next king. We must prepare a grand party. Tomorrow the people will celebrate with their new king! You must tell all the noblemen in the kingdom to be here. Won't they be surprised to learn that I am the new king?"

"Shouldn't we bury King Josiah first?" asked the guard.

"We can do that later. This is a time for happiness, not sadness," said Lord Lester. He had waited a long time to be king. Lord Lester could wait no longer.

It was a good thing, too. If the guard had tried to bury the king, he would have been surprised. The arm was only one of the king's shirts stuffed with straw. One of Bradley's gloves was the hand.

The cold body in the bed was only a sack of oats. King Josiah's plans were working. Lord Lester had been tricked.

The carriage stopped in some woods. They were now far away from the village. "This is the place," said the man who had tied up the guard.

He was John's best friend. He was also a tailor. His name was Robert. Kings from many kingdoms bought Robert's royal robes. A woman rode a horse out of the dark woods.

"I brought the clothes," said the woman to Robert. She was Robert's wife. "Our friend is waiting behind that rock. He wants to talk to you and the guard. John will watch the carriage."

She then handed John a bundle of cloth. "Put this on."

John and the guard walked behind the large rock. King Josiah was sitting on a log. He was now wearing a robe that Robert's wife had brought him. King Josiah looked at the guard. He remembered him.

"Remove the blindfold," said King Josiah.

The guard looked shocked. "Your Majesty what are you doing here? Your illness will get much worse. How did you get out of the castle?"

"You pushed me out," said Josiah. "I believe you called me an old beggar."

The guard almost fainted. He fell to his knees and began to beg. "Can you ever forgive me?" he cried.

"Who's the beggar now?" asked King Josiah. He smiled, "I forgive you. I need your help. I fear that Lord Lester has evil plans for the kingdom. He must be stopped."

"John still thinks you're a beggar," said Robert. "Isn't it time to tell him the truth?"

"Not yet," said King Josiah.

The next morning, Lord Lester was angry. Bradley was in the courtyard. He could hear Lord Lester yelling at the captain of the guards.

"First my carriage is stolen. Now, Josiah's body is missing? All the noblemen must see the body."

Bradley smiled. He had sneaked back into the castle in the early morning. Bradley had walked right by Lord Lester. The bag of oats was on Bradley's shoulders.

"How will they know that I am now King. They may think that King Josiah is just on a trip," Lord Lester yelled louder.

"Why would they think that? They will believe you," said the captain.

"His carriage is gone, and he is gone," said Lord Lester. "What else could they think?"

"The noblemen are arriving," said a servant who just stepped into the room.

Bradley hurried back to John's barn. The carriage almost filled it. King Josiah was waiting. He was adjusting the robe on John's back.

"You look just like royalty," said King Josiah.

"I'm not so sure about this," said John. "If I didn't know you were a beggar, I would think you were King Josiah himself. But what do I know about being a prince?"

"You'll make a great prince," said Josiah. He looked at Bradley, Robert, and the guard. He gave them a wink. The three men smiled back.

"Let's go," said Bradley as he buttoned up the uniform he had borrowed.

Soon, the carriage was rolling through the streets of the village. Bradley and the guard sat atop the carriage. Josiah, John, and Robert rode inside.

Lord Lester was in the castle courtyard. He was greeting the noblemen and their wives. He was the first to see Josiah's golden painted carriage come through the castle gates.

He was very relieved. If the carriage hadn't been found, he didn't know what he would tell the noblemen. It would seem wrong to throw a party while the King was away. Lord Lester ran to the carriage. He saw the guard.

"You found it," laughed Lord Lester. "You will be rewarded handsomely. Did you find King Josiah's body also?"

"Yes," said the guard. "It is inside the carriage."

"I must tell the noblemen at once," said Lord Lester.

He had the captain of the guards gather all the noblemen. They stood around the carriage. They all looked curious. Lord Lester tried to look sad. Inside he was very happy. In a few minutes, he would be the new king.

"Remove the body," commanded Lord Lester.

Just then the carriage door opened.

"I am quite capable of removing my own body," said King Josiah.

Now, Lord Lester really did feel sad. He tried to look happy. His voice quivered, "King Josiah, you are looking quite well."

King Josiah smiled, "Lord Lester, you look quite pale. Have you been taking the medicine you gave me?"

King Josiah then looked at all the noblemen. "You are gathered here today for a reason. Today I will appoint someone to be king when I die." He put his hand on Lord Lester's shoulder.

Lord Lester began to smile again. But then the king turned toward the carriage. "Come out," said Josiah.

John looked at Josiah. "Are you completely out of your mind?" whispered John. He was still hiding in the carriage. "Let's get out of here before the real king comes."

King Josiah laughed. "I was not a real beggar. I am the real king. Now, John, please come out of that carriage."

Josiah once more spoke to the noblemen. "This is John the cobbler. Today, I will adopt him as my son. He is the kindest man in the kingdom. King John will be even a greater king than I."

All the noblemen cheered. They had feared that Lord Lester would be the next king. Robert and Bradley caught John just as he fainted.

"As for you, Lord Lester," said King Josiah. "You shall also have a new title. From now on, you will be the royal food tester. If anyone tries to poison the king, you will be the first to know."

So, that day John the cobbler became Prince John. He later became a kind and fair king. Lord Robert and Lord Bradley were also greatly loved by the people of the kingdom. Lord Lester became Lester the Food Tester. He never again tried to poison a king.

Big Tom's Café

Table of Contents

Chapter		Page
1	Riding in the Back	118
2	The Moving Closet	120
3	My New Job	122
4	The Grand Opening	124
5	Our New Menu	126

by Brian Davis

Vocabulary Words

cafe`

constantly

customer

impression

restaurant

A lot of new things are happening in Gracie's family. When her parents take them to a new town, she discovers a big surprise.

Chapter 1
Riding in the Back

"Buddy and I always have to sit in the back," I complained to my parents.

"I thought you liked sitting in the back of the station wagon, Gracie," answered my dad.

Buddy is my twin brother. We're both eight years old. I have an eleven-year-old sister named Tracy. Then there's my other brother, Mark. He's fifteen. Sometimes I think he believes he's fifty.

He's constantly telling everyone he's too old. He's too old to sit in the back of a station wagon. He's too old to be told what to do. Last night he said he was too old to do dishes with us kids.

Mom said she agreed. She made him wash the dishes all by himself. My parents are great with Mark. Sometimes they could use some improvement on how they treat me. I try to tell them I'm too young to do chores. They just don't believe me.

It's not easy being the youngest. I get Tracy's old clothes. I go to bed early. Everyone always calls me names, like "Squirt" or "Tiny Tot." The worst is 'Baby Girl." That seems to be Dad's favorite.

Even Buddy has it better than me. He doesn't get called names. Mom says it's because "Buddy" is already a nickname. Buddy's real name is Morris. He was named after my grandfather.

Buddy doesn't have to wear Mark's old clothes. That's because Mark always wore his clothes out. I asked if Buddy could have Tracy's clothes. Then maybe I could get something new. Nobody thought that was a good idea.

Buddy and I climbed in the back of the station wagon. The youngest always sits in the back. That's the rule. I think Mark and Tracy made up that rule.

It really wasn't so bad. Buddy and I could play "I spy." We took turns saying things like, "I spy something furry." The other person had to guess what it was. Plus, we enjoyed seeing where we had just been. The back seat of the wagon faced the back window.

Today, I just wanted to feel older. Not old enough to do chores, of course, just old enough to sit in a seat that faces forward. Buddy never seems to mind being a little kid. I guess I'm just the opposite. I'm eight years old now. It's time for me to grow up. Grown-ups don't sit in the back of the wagon.

"I want to sit in the middle seat," I said.

"But what if something falls off the car? Who's going to watch for me?" said my dad. "What if a speeding fire truck needs to pass us? Who will tell us? You and Buddy have the most important jobs. I need you back there. The whole family needs you. You're just the right size for that seat, too."

I sighed and said, "Well, I don't want to cause a problem. I guess I could ride in the back today."

"We are forever grateful," said my dad.

"I don't want to sit in back," said Buddy. "It's my turn to drive!"

"Your turn doesn't come for another eight years," said my mom.

"That makes me forever grateful," said Tracy.

"By the end of the day," said my dad, "I think we'll all be very grateful!"

Mom and Dad had been acting very funny lately. They had been leaving Tracy, Buddy, and me with a babysitter. This happened three Saturdays in a row. Mark went to a friend's house. He said he was too old to need a babysitter. That was fine with me. It got him out of our way.

This weekend was different. The whole family was going together this time. Buddy, Tracy, Mark, and I still didn't know where we were going. We didn't know why we were going. Wherever it was, Buddy and I would make sure we got there safely.

We rode for quite awhile. I didn't recognize the scenery. Tracy kept asking where we were going. My parents just said it was a surprise. I hoped we were going on a picnic, but we didn't bring food. I wish we had brought food. I was getting hungry.

"I spy something with horns," said Buddy.

"A cow," I answered. "I already did that one."

"Not a cow," said Buddy.

I looked out the back window. There were small farms and pastures along the road. It had been like that for some while. We were far from the city. We were far from our home, or so I thought.

"I see it," I answered Buddy. "It's a goat."

"Right, but I tricked you at first," answered Buddy.

"I'm getting hungry," I yelled to the front of the station wagon.

"Look, there's a restaurant up ahead," said my dad.

We were just pulling into the edge of a small town. I could see some more buildings down the road. Dad pulled the station wagon into an empty parking lot. The restaurant had a closed sign in the window. A freshly painted sign on the door read "Big Tom's Café Coming Soon." My dad hopped out of the car. Mark was right behind him.

"This restaurant isn't open yet. My hunger is already here. This place won't be open soon enough," complained Mark.

"Oh yes it will," said my dad.

He pulled some keys from his pocket. Dad reached for the door and unlocked it. He gave Mom a big hug and a little kiss on the cheek. Mark's stomach growled.

"Baby Girl, would you like to be our first customer?" my dad asked me. I hate it when he calls me his baby girl.

"Your first customer?" asked Tracy. "You mean this is your restaurant?"

"Not exactly," said my dad. "It's our restaurant. It belongs to all of us. That's why it's called Big Tom's."

"I don't get it," said Tracy.

"B-I-G T-O-M. B was for Buddy, I for Irene, G for Gracie, T for Tracy, O for Oliver, M for Mark. It's named after all of us." Irene is my mom's name. Oliver is my dad's name.

"Why can't it be M for Morris? Then it would be named after me twice," suggested Buddy.

Inside the restaurant was a high counter. Stools were fastened to the floor. Buddy hopped up on one and started spinning. There were booths to sit in with red plastic covers. There were also tables and chairs.

I was amazed-my own restaurant. Then I realized something. We had driven a long way from home. It was too far to drive every day.

"How will we get here from home?" I asked.

"We'll walk," said my mother.

"It's too far to walk," said Buddy.

My dad strolled over to what I thought was a closet. He opened the door. It looked like a closet. There was one difference. Two huge ropes hung from the side and two smaller ropes.

"Here we go," said my dad.

"That's our new home?" asked Tracy as she wrinkled up her nose.

"No," said my dad. "This is our ride home."

Chapter 2
The Moving Closet

The closet wasn't a closet at all. It was really an elevator. It was unlike any elevator I had ever ridden in. First of all, the floor moved, but the walls didn't. It didn't have a motor. It had to be pulled up and down.

That's what the big ropes were for. There was only one big rope. It just made a loop. You could look up and see the pulley turning big gears as the elevator moved.

It didn't just stop at the different floors. It had brakes. Two smaller ropes worked the brakes. The elevator made a loud squeal when the braking ropes were pulled.

Our whole family got on the elevator. Mark released the brakes. The elevator started dropping down by itself. Dad grabbed the big rope and started pulling on it. The elevator began to rise again.

"We don't need to go to the basement right now," said my dad as he pulled.

Buddy grabbed the rope too and started helping. We passed the restaurant on the ground floor. Dad kept pulling. We kept going up and up.

"Second floor, kitchen, living room, bathroom and a few other rooms," said my dad.

Mark stopped the elevator at a door. We all got off the wooden platform. We stepped right into a large kitchen. All the cabinets were open and empty. There were no tables or chairs. There was not even a refrigerator. There was an old stove and a dishwasher.

"Well, at least it has a dishwasher," said Tracy. "It looks like I'm out of a job," she smiled.

"There will be plenty of pots and pans for you to wash in the restaurant," said my mom.

We looked through the other rooms. They were all empty. There was a dining room, a living room, bathroom, laundry room, and one extra room.

"This will be our school room," said my mom.

Tracy looked mad.

"What's wrong?" asked my mom.

"I just don't like it here," said Tracy. "Why do we have to move? Why do we have to own a restaurant? Why do we have to live in this old building? I don't like any of it. I wish we could just go home and stay there."

Buddy had wandered off by himself. He opened another door. "There's stairs out here," he yelled.

"Well," said my dad. "You don't always have to take the elevator. It's just more fun."

"Yes," said Buddy, "but there's stairs going up and down."

"Of course," said my dad. "We have to sleep somewhere. There's one more floor. Everyone hop on the elevator. We'll finish the tour."

"I'll race you," said Buddy as he ran up the steps.

Tracy sighed as she got on the elevator. I could tell she was in a bad mood. Dad pulled us up one more floor. He opened the door of the elevator shaft. Buddy was waiting for us.

"Beat ya," he said with a big grin on his face.

"These were once little apartments," said my mom as we walked down the hallway. "Now, they're all ours."

She pointed out my mom and dad's room. Next, we saw Mark's room. Tracy's room came next.

"My own bedroom!" said Tracy. "And it has my own bathroom. I don't have to share it with anyone. I love it here!"

Dad smiled, "I thought you didn't want to move here?"

"Are you crazy," said Tracy. "My own bedroom and bathroom, wow!"

Tracy didn't leave her room, but I was ready to see my room. There were two doors at the end of the hall.

"Gracie and Buddy, you have your own rooms too," smiled mom. "You're growing up, Gracie. You'll need your own space."

I was amazed. Mom realized I was growing up. My room had its own bathroom, too. In fact, all the bedrooms had bathrooms. It didn't excite me as much as it did Tracy. Buddy seemed kind of disappointed in having his own bathroom.

"Does this mean I have to take more baths?" asked Buddy.

"It means you'll have to hang up your own towels now," said Mark.

I wandered over to the window in Buddy's room. I looked out into the back of the building. Below was a roof of another building. It sagged a little. There was also a hole in the roof.

"What's that down there?" I asked.

My dad looked out the window. "That's the old trading post. It's part of our property." He pointed a finger at Buddy and me. "Don't go in there. The floor is rotting out. The roof looks like it could fall in at any time. It's dangerous. That's why there is a wooden fence around it. We'll fix it up and use it for storage."

"Well," said my mom. "Now that we're done exploring our new building, let's explore the local grocery store."

There wasn't any food at the restaurant yet. Our family hopped back in the station wagon. Buddy and I had to sit in the back again. We drove to a grocery store. My parents bought some bread, chips, cheese, and some sliced meat, plus some other things to make sandwiches.

We went back to the restaurant. My parents told us to sit anywhere we wanted. Buddy and I shared our own booth. It was like going out to a restaurant all by ourselves. My mom came over to our table. She had a little pad in her hand.

"May I take your order?" she asked me.

"I would like a sandwich and some chips," I answered. "And what can I have to drink?"

"We forgot to buy something to drink," said Buddy.

"Our soft drink machine is filled and ready to go," said my mom.

"Wow! Our own soft drink machine," I said. "Now we can have all we want."

"Not exactly," said my mom. "You can have some, but you'll need to ask first. You should drink other things that are good for you. Plus, you'll drink up all our profits."

Then mom turned to Buddy, "And you Sir, what would you like today?"

"I'll just have desert," said Buddy, "an ice cream sundae, then some chocolate cake."

Mom wrote something on the pad. Then she read it back, "Okay, the young lady will have a sandwich and some chips. The young man will have a sandwich and chips, too. And, if he eats all of that, then he may have some ice cream and cake." My mom smiled at Buddy and then walked to Mark and Tracy's table.

"Mom isn't a very good waitress," said Buddy.

"Why do you say that?" I asked. After all, mom had called me a young lady. That seemed to be what a good waitress would do.

"She got my order all wrong," answered Buddy.

Chapter 3
My New Job

The next three weeks were very busy. The restaurant still wasn't opened. We were busy packing. Our old house was filled with boxes.

Buddy offered to pack his school books the first day. Mom said no way. We kept working on school. Mom said she wanted us to get ahead a little. That way we could take a little break after we moved.

Dad left a week earlier. He was ordering things for Big Tom's. He needed to be at the restaurant when delivery trucks came. The Grand Opening was just over a week away.

At the end of the week, my dad came home. We were very excited to see him and start the big move. He rented a moving truck. Some friends from our church helped us load up.

I felt a lot of different things that day. It was sad to leave our old house and our old friends. I would miss them a lot. Saying good-bye made me want to cry. Still it was exciting to move. Mom said we would make lots of new friends. That really didn't help much. In fact, it sounded a little scary.

"What if they don't like me? What if I don't like them?" I asked.

"Then I guess they won't be your friends," answered Mark.

Dad patted my head, "What's not to like about you, Baby Girl?"

I really don't like being called "Baby Girl." After all, I was getting my own room. I wouldn't have to share with Tracy anymore. I was growing up. That was exciting.

It was also another one of those scary things. I've never been all alone at night. Once in a while, Tracy spent the night at a friend's house. I would sleep in a sleeping bag in my parent's room. Darkness can be kind of spooky. Mom said she would buy me a nightlight.

Then of course, there was the restaurant. I was getting my first job. Mom said that I would even get paid. I was going to be the hostess. My job would be to help people find seats. I would also help Buddy clear the tables after customers left.

I would get to fill salt and pepper shakers. Part of my job would be to replace empty ketchup bottles. Plus, my mom said there would be lots of other important jobs for me. Running a restaurant is a lot of work. Dad said he really needed me.

That was the truth. Mom and Dad were about to find out how much they needed me. Everything was going very well. We got all our things moved. When we weren't unpacking, we were working on the restaurant. It was lots of fun. It was also lots of work. Suddenly chores didn't seem so bad. I even got paid my first allowance.

Soon the grand opening of Big Tom's was one day away. Mom sliced all kinds of meats. Mark sliced onions, peppers, lettuce, and other vegetables. Dad baked lots of sandwich buns. We would have hot sandwiches and cold sandwiches. Everything was in place.

The next day, Big Tom's was supposed to be open for the first time. The people in town seemed excited. There was no other restaurant around. Cars had been driving in all week. But we kept the front door locked. The sign on our door read, "Grand Opening this Saturday."

I practiced being a hostess. "Welcome to Big Tom's," I would say to my pretend customer. It was actually a coat rack. "Thank you for dining with us today. Please walk this way."

I then led the pretend customer to a table. Of course, the coat rack had a hard time walking. So, then I had to pretend the coat rack was following me. It was hard work being a hostess to invisible customers. There was just so much pretending that had to be done.

"Would you stop playing and help?" complained Tracy. She was filling pepper shakers. "Achoo…"

"I'm not playing," I defended myself. "I was practicing being a hostess. It is a very important job. We want to make a good first impression."

"You have made a very good impression on that coat rack," said Tracy. "I'm sure it will never eat at another restaurant. Now, will you fill the salt shakers?"

"You just don't understand how difficult it is to be a hostess," I told her. "It takes a lot of work. Filling salt shakers is the easy part. You should be grateful that I am the hostess. All you have to do is take orders and bring food to tables."

"All you have to do is show people to the tables," said Tracy. "Being a waitress is much harder."

"You wouldn't have any customers to wait on if it wasn't for me," I said. "They would all be standing at the door. They wouldn't know where to sit. Then they would all go home and be hungry. That would be just terrible."

"You're the hostess because you're too little to be a waitress," said Tracy.

I thought that was a very mean thing to say. I thought it was so mean that I started to cry. I just sat down at a booth and put my head down. Mom had heard what Tracy said. She came and sat next to me.

"You are very important," said my mom. "Not because you are a hostess, but because you are my little girl." She motioned for Tracy to come over.

"Every job here is important. We all need each other. We all have different jobs, but that doesn't mean one is better than the other. Now, we're all getting a little tired. We're all getting a little cranky."

"Why don't the two of you say you're sorry."

"I'm sorry," I said to Tracy. I've found it's always better to be the first one to say I'm sorry.

"I'm sorry, too," said Tracy. "Would you please help me fill the salt shakers? I really need your help."

"Okay," I said.

"I'll help too," said Buddy. "I like pouring salt. I pretend the salt box is a dump truck."

"So, what are the salt shakers?" asked Tracy.

"I pretend they are giant salt shakers. It takes a whole dump truck to fill them," answered Buddy.

Tracy rolled her eyes, "I had to ask. Oh well, I could use your help. You'll have to get your own box of salt."

"No problem," said Buddy. "I already have it loaded."

"What do you mean you have it loaded?" asked my mom.

Buddy pulled out a remote control. He pushed some buttons. His remote-control toy dump truck came out of the kitchen. A box of salt was in the back of it. Buddy drove it right up to the table.

"See, a whole truck load of salt!" said Buddy.

We all started laughing.

Chapter 4
The Grand Opening

Finally, the morning of the Grand Opening of Big Tom's had arrived. I thought I would be the last one out of bed. I kept listening for my mom and dad. I expected them to knock on my door at any time. That's what they had done all week.

The knock didn't come. I looked at my clock. It was 10:30 am. This was very unusual. Then a frightening thought struck me. I realized I had overslept. Maybe everyone else was already downstairs.

At first I thought I had to hurry. Then I remembered I was the hostess. I really shouldn't have to work until the customers came. The plan was to unlock the doors at 11:00. I had a whole half hour to get to work. I could get there in a few seconds on the elevator.

In a few weeks, we would also serve breakfast. Then I would have to get up really early. Dad said we would be tired enough serving two meals for now. Lunch and supper would give us practice running a restaurant. It would also give us more time to hire some extra help.

I stepped out into the hallway. As I walked by my parent's room I heard a noise. I knocked softly on the door.

"Come in," answered my mom.

I opened the door. I was surprised to see my parents still in their pajamas.

"This is the big day!" I said. "We've got to get ready."

"The big day will have to wait," answered my dad. He didn't sound too well.

"Your dad and I aren't feeling well," explained my mom. "We think it was something we ate. Are you feeling okay, Gracie?"

"I'm a little sad that the café isn't opening," I answered "And that you're not feeling well," I added. I didn't want my parents to think I didn't care about them.

"What did we eat that she didn't eat?" my dad asked.

"The chicken salad," answered my mom. "Remember, Gracie and Buddy ate hot dogs."

"Oh no," groaned my dad. "Tracy and Mark ate the chicken salad, too."

"I'll check on them," said my mom.

I followed her down the hall. Sure enough, Mark and Tracy were sick, too. Buddy's room was empty. I knew where to find him, second floor, in front of the TV. It was Saturday morning after all.

I followed Mom back to her room. "Can you do something for us?" asked my mom.

It's no fun when your family is sick. I wanted to do anything I could to help. "Sure," I answered.

"First, check on Buddy. Make sure he's not sick. Then put a sign on the restaurant door saying we won't open until Monday."

"Should I say it's because the food made everyone sick?" I asked. Dad seemed to turn a little pale.

"No, Baby Girl," he said. "That would be bad advertising. Besides, I bought the chicken salad at the store. We didn't make it here."

"It will be nice when Big Tom's opens," I said. "Then you won't get sick eating someone else's cooking. If we get sick, it will be our fault!"

I could see Mom and Dad wanted to rest. I gently closed the door. The elevator was a little hard for me to work by myself, so I went down the stairs. Sure enough, Buddy was right where I thought he would be. He was sitting in front of the TV eating a peanut butter and jelly sandwich.

"I've got bad news," I told Buddy. "Everyone else in the family is sick. Big Tom's isn't going to open today."

Buddy looked at me, "It's got to open. It's the Grand Opening. We can't be closed for our Grand Opening."

"Come on. I've got to put a sign on the door. I don't want to be all alone in the café."

Buddy turned off the TV and followed me. That was quite a surprise. I thought he would tell me to do it myself. Buddy saw the surprised look on my face.

"I have this cartoon on video. I can watch it later. Besides, I left my dump truck down there last night. I didn't want to go down there alone either."

That's the Buddy I knew. We walked down the stairs to the café. It was almost 11:00. It was time for Big Tom's not-so-grand-after-all opening. I found a marker and some paper in the kitchen and started to make a sign.

Then I started hearing the voices of some adults. Someone was in the dining room. I was scared at first. Then I heard Buddy's voice. He must have opened the door. Buddy came back to the kitchen. He was very excited.

"We have our first customers!" Buddy was one big smile.

"Customers! We can't have customers. Mom and Dad are sick," I explained.

"And these people are hungry," Buddy explained. "They said they have waited three weeks for the café to open. Wouldn't you be hungry if you hadn't eaten for three weeks?"

He pointed to the opening in the kitchen wall that gave a view of the dining room. A gray-haired couple sat in a booth waiting to eat. They looked like very nice people. Nevertheless, they didn't look like they were starving.

"I don't think they meant they haven't eaten in three weeks. I think they meant they found out about the café three weeks ago, and they were excited about eating here," I explained to Bubby.

"Oh," said Buddy. "Then I guess I'd better go take their order."

Buddy picked up an order pad and walked to the table. "Welcome to Big Tom's Café. Can I take your order?"

"I'd like a hamburger and fries," said the man as he looked over the menu.

"I'll have a cheeseburger and tots," said the woman.

"Actually," Buddy explained, "the cooks are sick today. We can only serve things we don't need to cook."

"That's an interesting idea for a café," smiled the man. "Serving food that doesn't need to be cooked." He looked behind the counter. The man spotted the chocolate cake Mom had baked last night.

"I think we'll just have some of that delicious looking chocolate cake and a scoop of ice cream."

The woman nodded in agreement. Buddy wrote on the pad. When he finished, he read back what he had written.

"That will be two peanut butter and jelly sandwiches and some chips. If you eat all of that, then you can have some ice cream and cake."

"Who taught you to take orders?" asked the man.

"My mom," answered Buddy.

The couple began laughing as Buddy came back to the kitchen. He tore the sheet off the pad and handed it to me.

"Two peanut butter and jelly sandwiches and chips," ordered Buddy.

Chapter 5
Our New Menu

Buddy then began filling some glasses with ice water. I was amazed at my brother. He was a natural at this. He served the couple the water and asked if there was anything else they needed while they waited.

I couldn't find bread for sandwiches, but I found the buns Dad had baked. We also had a big jar of homemade strawberry jelly. I made the two sandwiches and added chips and a few chopped-up vegetables on the plate.

The hungry couple began eating just as more customers walked in. Buddy showed them to different booths and took more orders. Everyone ordered the same thing. Actually, everyone ordered different things, but Buddy wrote down the only thing we served, peanut butter and jelly and chips. I always added the vegetables. Mom would be so proud of me!

The first couple finished their sandwiches, chips, and even the vegetables. Buddy picked up the empty plates.

"Wow!" said Buddy. "You cleaned your plate. I didn't expect you to eat your vegetables. That was my sister's idea. I guess you're ready for cake and ice cream."

Buddy rewarded the first two customers with a slice of cake and two scoops of ice cream. I watched their faces as they bit into the cake. You could tell they were happy. A smile came on their faces. That was followed by a delighted "mmmm." It was what everyone does when they first try my mom's cake.

The couple finished their desert. I watched the man walk to the cash register. Buddy was taking the next customer's order. I walked to the register. I guess I was also the cashier today. The man handed me the ticket Buddy had written.

"Your brother didn't put in prices on our ticket. I didn't see peanut butter sandwiches on the menu. What do we owe you?" The man smiled and seemed very kind.

His wife joined him, "It was all very delicious," said the woman. "That was the best peanut butter and jelly sandwich I've had in years. And the cake was out of this world!"

"Now, how much do we owe you?" asked the man again as he pulled out his wallet.

I was just so relieved that our first customers were happy. "It's all free," I said without really thinking.

"Free!" said the man. "No, no, no. A worker is worthy of his or her wages."

"What?" I asked.

"You served us good food and you deserve a fair price," explained the man as he pulled a five dollar bill and a ten dollar bill from his wallet and handed it to me.

"Uh, I'll give you some change. How much do you want?" I asked as I opened the cash register.

"None," said the man. "It's worth every penny to see youngsters helping out your family like you two are doing."

"Thank you," I smiled.

"Thank you," said the woman. "We'll be back soon and try some of the things that need to be cooked."

The couple must have told all their friends about Big Tom's. Soon the dining room was packed. I was making peanut butter and jelly sandwiches as fast as I could. Buddy kept piling up the orders.

"I need help," I said to Buddy when he brought a new stack of orders.

"Well, I about have everyone's order taken," said Buddy. "I can help."

"But you're too busy taking food to the customers," I pointed out.

"I have that all worked out," said Buddy.

He picked up a plate and placed it on top of his remote-control dump truck. Next, he blew a whistle. Everyone in the dining room look at him. Buddy waved to some customers in a booth. The dump truck began moving to the table.

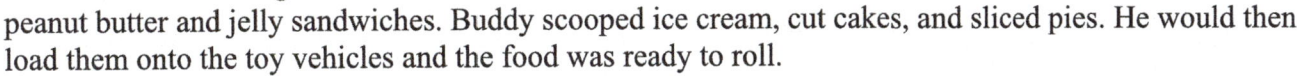

One of the customers had the remote control. They were driving their own food to the table. Somehow Buddy had found the time to gather up his other remote control vehicles. He even had a few of Mark's radio control trucks.

Soon, a whole fleet of remote control "waiters" were serving food. I made peanut butter and jelly sandwiches. Buddy scooped ice cream, cut cakes, and sliced pies. He would then load them onto the toy vehicles and the food was ready to roll.

The customers liked driving the toys full of food. There were a few near collisions, but most of the customers were careful drivers. Buddy used a shiny red sports car to lead customers to tables.

I still didn't know what to charge for the food. I found a big mixing bowl in the kitchen. I placed it next to the cash register. I put a sign on the bowl asking people to pay what they wanted to pay.

Buddy and I worked all day feeding the customers of Big Tom's Café. Everyone seemed very happy with the food. I could tell by how much money piled up in the bowl by the cash register. We locked the doors after the last customer left.

We were too tired to count the money, so we decided to hide the bowl in case any thieves were to break in. I found a place in the refrigerator for the bowl. It was hidden behind the sickening chicken salad leftovers. It would serve a thief right if he stole both the money and the chicken salad.

Buddy and I finished off the last two pieces of cake. My brother looked tired. I watched as he struggled to keep his eyes open. Then I began to yawn.

The next thing I knew, the sunlight was pouring into the café. The loud sound on the stairs woke me up. It sounded like a cattle stampede.

Buddy popped up too. "What's that!"

A door opened and in rushed my parents. They were followed by Tracy and Mark. They looked a little upset.

"We've been looking all over for you," said my Mom. "Your beds haven't even been slept in. Did you sleep down here all night?"

Mark was behind the counter. "It looks like they ate all night."

"Wow!" cried Tracy. "The little pigs at all the cakes and pies."

"Our food is in the kitchen upstairs. This was the food we sell," my father began to explain. "I realize we were too sick to cook for you, but…"

He was interrupted by a knock on the door. It was Big Tom's first customers from the day before. My father opened the door and started to explain that we weren't open, yet.

"We're not here to eat," explained the woman. "I think I left my purse here after lunch yesterday."

"That's not possible…" my mom answered. But the woman wasn't listening. The lady walked to a booth and reached under the seat.

"Here it is!" she smiled as she pulled out a small black handbag. "Thanks for opening up especially for us."

"Two days in a row," added the man. Then he looked at my parents. "I'm sure you'll do really well in this town. Everybody's already talking about how delicious the food is here."

"And the adorable toy waiters," commented the woman as the couple walked out the door.

My parents started looking around the dining room. A few plates were left scattered. A few crumbs were on the table. Many tables had a remote control for a toy car or truck sitting on them.

"You gave away the cakes and pies?" asked my mom.

"We sold them," I said.

"Don't worry Mom," said Buddy. "We made everyone eat a good meal before they got dessert."

"Peanut butter and jelly, chips, and even some vegetables," I explained.

Tracy came out of the kitchen. "I threw out the bad chicken salad and look what I found!"

She dumped the bowl full of cash on the table. Mark and my parents each picked up a hand full of money.

"There's hundreds of dollars here," said my dad.

"We're rich!" said Mark.

"You two made all this money?" asked my mom.

"No," answered Buddy. "We made all this money, plus the bowl of tips. I hid that bowl in the oven."

Dad and Mom gave us hugs. They thanked us and told us how proud they were of us. Then they told us how grown-up we were.

"You can have all the money," I said to my parents.

"Can we keep the tips?" asked Buddy. "There's something I need to buy."

"What's that?" asked my dad.

"Just look at this mess," Buddy pointed around the dining room. "I need a remote-control garbage truck."

Pigs in the Pancakes

Table of Contents

Chapter		Page
1	Open For Breakfast	130
2	Tips for Pets	132
3	Pig Tom's	134
4	The Pig Palace	136
5	The County Fair	138

by Brian Davis

Vocabulary Words

combination

dickering

inspector

invested

livestock

professional

A customer of Big Tom's Café believes every child should have his favorite animal as a pet. When Buddy buys two pigs from him, there are some very interesting problems at the café.

Chapter 1
Open For Breakfast

I sat at a booth at Big Tom's. My markers were spread out on the table. I was just finishing a big project. The future of Big Tom's Café rested on my shoulders.

"That looks lovely, Gracie," said my mom as she admired my work.

Dad walked in with a case of supplies. He passed by the booth, too. "It looks like we hired a professional artist!"

I smiled, "Maybe I should hang this in an art museum."

Dad rubbed his chin, "You would have to give it some fancy name, like the Mona Lisa. No, that one's already taken."

I giggled. Sometimes my dad can be so silly.

"I know," said my dad. "You can call it, 'Open For Breakfast!'"

"How did you ever think of that?" teased my mom. "You're a genius."

"There's just something about it that says, Open For Breakfast," explained my dad.

"Maybe it's the words I wrote on it?" I said.

"Could be," nodded Dad.

I finished coloring in the last egg yolk. Big Tom's great announcement was now finished. Starting tomorrow, our café was open for breakfast. I grabbed the tape and looked for just the right place for the poster.

Mom and I had hired a cook to help us at breakfast. The cook's name was Natalie. She was about the same age as my grandmother. She had some experience with Big Tom's Café. Her husband and she were our very first customers.

Natalie lives on a farm with her husband, Rockwell. Everyone calls him "Rocky." I learned that in her interview. Maybe you think an eight-year-old shouldn't be interviewing an adult for a job. But Mom has always said I am a good judge of character. Besides, I was filling salt shakers while Mom talked to her.

My other brothers and sister were doing schoolwork. I'm usually the first one done with my work. It just comes easy for me. When I finish, I like to hang around the café. You meet lots of interesting people, like Natalie.

She has five children. All of them are grown up. She likes to cook, but her youngest son just left for college. Now, it's just her and Rocky. Her husband likes to eat at Big Tom's for lunch. It isn't just the food. It's also a time to relax and talk to friends.

Natalie said she wanted the job to keep an eye on Rocky. I knew she was just teasing. Taking the job was Rocky's idea. He patted his round stomach and gave his wife all the credit. When he heard we were looking for a breakfast cook, he knew his wife would be perfect.

It was also the perfect job for her. She missed cooking for all her children. Plus, her farm was very close to the café. In fact, one of their pastures was a short walk from our backdoor. So, I guess you could say we were neighbors.

I'm glad we hired Natalie. She has a nice smile and a cheerful laugh. Yesterday morning, she came in for training. We didn't train her. She trained us.

Natalie isn't the bossy type, until she gets into the kitchen. She looked over the supply room and made a list of everything she would need. Natalie and Rocky raised hogs, as well as other animals. She insisted we use meat from her farm.

Dad wasn't too sure about that at first. He called it a conflict of interest. I'm not sure what that meant. But after he tried some of the fresh sausage, smoked ham, and hickory bacon, he was very interested. There was no conflict at all.

"Rocky is bringing up my sausage grinder. We'll put it here," she pointed to the things she wanted my father to move.

Next, she grabbed a big can of baking powder. "This will never do," she said. "We need to keep this in the freezer."

"The freezer?" asked Dad. "I don't think it's going to melt."

"I don't want my baking powder to lose its bounce. We'll only serve flaky biscuits and fluffy pancakes here," she answered.

Natalie was still giving orders when Rocky walked in the door. He watched for awhile and smiled. "I have the sausage grinder," he finally announced. "Maybe you could give me a hand, Oliver."

My dad nodded. He considered it a break. Rocky laughed as he walked to his pick-up truck.

"What's so funny?" asked my dad.

"The look on your face," answered Rocky.

"My guess is you've seen that look before," said Dad.

"Sometimes when I look in the mirror," said Rocky. "I know exactly what you're thinking. You give Natalie a job. Now, you're wondering who hired who."

Dad sighed, "Exactly."

Rocky patted Dad on the back. "It will be all right. Once she's settled in, she'll do all she can to make Big Tom's a big success. Why do you think she wants everything perfectly organized?"

Dad looked puzzled, "To wear me out?"

Rocky laughed, "No. She knows she's going to be busy. By the time she's done with the kitchen, she'll be able to do the work of three cooks."

That sounded exciting to me. It was like a second grand opening. Only, this time I hoped I didn't have to do the cooking. I already had a job for the breakfast time. I was going to be a waitress.

Mom had the schedule all worked out. I would have to get up extra early. Mom would teach Mark and Tracy first thing in the morning. Buddy and I would help at Big Tom's. When Mark and Tracy finished, Mom would teach Buddy and me. After the breakfast crowd left, we would all work on assignments.

Homeschool had been fun so far at Big Tom's the last few weeks. We'd sit in the booths. Mark and Tracy even helped teach Buddy and me sometimes. Mom and Dad were always around if we had any questions. Sometimes, I helped Mark and Tracy study for tests. I held flashcards or quizzed them from Mom's teacher's manuals. It was fun being the teacher, only Mark wouldn't sit in the corner when he didn't do what I asked.

"Baby Girl, hold the door open for us," said Dad. Rocky and my dad were carrying the sausage grinder.

"Baby Girl!" I thought. I'm a waitress and a teacher. I can't believe he called me "Baby Girl."

Chapter 2
Tips for Pets

I liked being a waitress. It was fun helping people. It felt great to help my parents. Then of course there were tips.

Sometimes it would be a few dimes. Lots of times customers left behind a few quarters. Once in a while, I would get a whole dollar. That was exciting.

The morning rush was over for today. So, I sat at a booth counting my tips. Rocky was waiting for Natalie. She was cleaning up the morning mess in the kitchen.

Rocky was right about Natalie. She was a great cook. The flaky biscuits covered in fresh sausage gravy were a customer favorite. The ham steak with hash browns was also a big seller. My favorite was the fluffy pancakes. They seemed to melt in my mouth.

The first plate I had surprised me. Natalie served a stack of two pancakes. They looked a little lumpy. I lifted the edge of the top pancake. Underneath were two sausage links.

Natalie saw the funny look on my face. "I call it Pigs in the Pancakes," she explained. "Sausage comes from pigs. I put the sausage in between two pancakes."

I wasn't too sure about eating it at first. Natalie poured on the syrup and waited. The first bite was a winner. The sweet syrup and spicy sausage was a great combination of flavors.

Now, I had it every morning. After most of the customers left, Natalie would give me a plate of Pigs in the Pancakes. I would sit down and count my tips, just like I was doing this morning. When I finished counting I would write down the amount on a piece of paper.

Next, I poured the money into my very own tips jar. I kept the paper with the total in the jar, too. Mom said it was good math practice. I counted money. I added totals. It was fun to count my own money.

"What are you going to do with all that cash?" asked Rocky.

"I'm hoping to buy a pet," I answered.

"A pet? What kind of pet?"

"I haven't decided. Maybe a dog or a cat," I answered.

Mom overheard me, "Remember, whatever it is, it has to be an outdoor pet."

"When are you getting this pet?" asked Rocky.

It wasn't like Rocky to ask a lot of questions, unless he was planning something. It reminded me of the day when Mom mentioned to him that we were wanting to serve breakfast. Rocky was planning something. I could tell.

I hadn't known Rocky long, but I knew one thing. When Rocky starting planning something, I knew it was probably going to be fun. So, I was willing to answer any questions he wanted to ask.

"As soon as I have enough money," I answered.

"Do you have $10?" asked Rocky.

"Yes," I smiled.

Buddy walked up. "I have $10, too. What do you need ten dollars for?"

"You have ten dollars, too. That's perfect," Rocky said to Buddy. "Follow me."

Buddy and I followed Rocky out to his truck. He unlatched the tailgate. In back on the truck was a large container. I had seen a container like this in pet stores. It was normally used for dogs. Rocky didn't have dogs in this container.

"I was just taking these little guys to an auction. If you'd like to buy them, they're yours for ten dollars each," offered Rocky. "I'd give them to you, but I think they would mean more to you if you actually had to pay for them."

I wasn't too sure. I don't think Mom was ready for this kind of pet. I was about to say we would need to talk to our parents about it. Then Buddy spoke first.

"We'll give you six dollars each for them," said Buddy.

Rocky laughed, "You've learned a few things about dickering from the farmers these last few weeks."

Rocky was right. Buddy had learned that you never pay the asking price for animals around here. You tried to get the best bargain. When someone said one price, you offered a lower price. That was called dickering.

You kept making offers until both people had an agreement. We had seen it in after lunch discussions with the farmers. Whether it was tractors, chickens, or even hay bales, the farmers always worked for the best deal.

"Nine dollars," Rocky was willing to play along.

Buddy shook his head. He stared at the ground and kicked some gravel. "I don't know. That's kind of steep. How about seven dollars?"

"I'll tell you what I'll do," said Rocky. "Eight dollars and I'll loan you this dog kennel until we get a better place for your pets."

"Deal," said Buddy as he held out his hand.

Rocky and Buddy shook on it. That made it a done deal. I looked at Buddy. He looked so proud. He felt he had made a great bargain.

I thought he had made a great disaster. What was he thinking? This wasn't the kind of pets I had in mind. I'm sure it wasn't the kind of pets Mom and Dad had in mind. And, I was beginning to think Buddy was out of his mind.

"Are you crazy?" I said to Buddy. "What are we going to do with them?"

"Play with them," said Buddy.

"I mean, where are we going to keep them? What are they going to eat?"

Rocky smiled. He had already begun working on a plan. "I'll take care of everything. Just keep them in this kennel until tomorrow."

Rocky lifted the container off the truck. He started carrying it around the back of Big Tom's. Just then, Natalie walked out the door. She looked horrified when she saw what Rocky was up to.

"Oh no," objected Natalie. "Are you trying to get me fired? You can't leave those here."

"I have to," explained Rocky. "They don't belong to me anymore. I sold them."

"Sold them?" asked Natalie.

"To Gracie and Buddy," added Rocky. "The perfect pets! Every child should have one."

"I don't think Oliver and Irene are going to like this," warned Natalie.

"Irene said Gracie could buy a pet. She said it was all right if it was an outdoor pet," said Rocky.

Natalie sighed, "Two little piglets are about as outdoor as you can get."

Chapter 3
Pig Tom's

"Tracy, did you find Buddy and Gracie?" my mom asked my sister.

Mom was scrubbing some pans. Her hands were covered with suds. It was Buddy's turn to dry the pans, and he was nowhere around. My dad had gone to the bank.

So, she had sent Tracy out to look for us.

"Uh...," stammered Tracy

Tracy looked shocked as she came in from the backyard. She didn't know what to say. Mom grabbed Tracy by the shoulders. The suds dripped on the floor. She stared into Tracy's eyes.

"Are they okay? Do they need help?" Mom was starting to get worried.

"No," said Tracy.

"No, they're not okay or no, they don't need help?"

Tracy was acting too strange. Mom wasn't waiting for an answer. She started to rush through the kitchen.

"Mom, they're okay," Tracy finally answered. "They're just playing with pigs!"

That's how Mom found out about our new pets. I wanted to talk to her first. I wanted to explain. It's just that the little piglets were so cute. Buddy and I were having lots of fun taking care of our pigs.

We poked grass and weeds through the cage door. The piglets snatched them right from our hands. Their little flat noses pressed against the cage, waiting for more. Buddy wanted to get a closer look at his pig. He decided to open the cage door, just a little.

"What are you two doing?" shouted my mom.

We hadn't seen her coming. Buddy jumped at the wrong time. He scared the two little pigs. The cage door swung open. The frightened pigs scampered out.

They grunted and squealed as they ran toward the street. Buddy chased them. I chased Buddy. Mom chased me. We were all shouting as we reached the front door of Big Tom's.

"What's going on?" asked Mark as he stepped outside.

At that exact moment, the two little pigs stepped on his toes. Mark danced around on one foot as the door closed behind him. Buddy ran right by him, hot on the trail of the pigs. He ran down the sidewalk. Mom came around the building.

"Mark, stop playing hopscotch and help us find some pigs," said my mom.

She ran after Buddy.

"But Mom!" Mark tried to run after them, but he was still hobbling. "Wait!"

I was about to start running again. Then I heard screaming in Big Tom's. It sounded like Tracy. Next, I heard pans crashing.

I quickly figured out what Mark had been trying to tell my mom. The pigs were Big Tom's next customers. I thought about chasing after Mom, but she was too far away. It also sounded like Tracy need a little help.

I saw Tracy as soon as I walked through the front door. She was in the kitchen. I saw her through the order taking window. She seemed taller than normal. Of course, this wasn't a normal situation.

Tracy had climbed on top of a counter to get away from the pigs. They wouldn't have hurt her, but Tracy didn't believe that. The pigs found something they were more interested in. Below Tracy was a garbage can full of leftover breakfast scraps. The pigs were happily munching on pancakes.

"Why didn't you tell me the pigs were in the café?" Mom talked excitedly to Mark as she came through the door.

"But Mom, I did," answered Mark.

Buddy, Mark, and Mom joined us in the kitchen.

"I know what to feed the pigs," I answered. "Leftovers!"

"We have a lot to talk about," said my mom. "But first we have to get these pigs out of the kitchen."

"I'm not getting down from here until those beasts are gone!" said Tracy.

"What do you think you are? A corncob? Those pigs aren't going to hurt you," said Mark. "Unless they step on your toes," he added.

"Mark, grab a pig," ordered my mom. "They can't eat in my kitchen!"

Mark reached for a pig. You must remember, Mark had never touched a pig in his life. He reached his arms around the pig's belly. The pig started squealing. It also started squiggling. Mark lost his balance and fell right into the garbage.

"This just isn't going to work," said my mom. "How will we get these pigs out of here?"

Buddy grabbed some pancakes off the floor. He ran into the dining room. We heard a familiar sound of a tiny motor running. A radio-controlled dump truck drove right under the cute little noses of the pigs. They took the bait.

The pigs followed the dump truck into the dining room. Dad opened the door just as Buddy reached it.

"Thanks, Dad," said Buddy as the dump truck full of pancakes and the two little pigs followed him.

My dad wasn't alone. A lady was standing behind him. They both looked very shocked at the sight. Mom came out of the kitchen with Mark. He was still covered with garbage.

"Irene," said my dad. "I met Mrs. Gray at the bank. She was just heading this way. She's the county health inspector."

Mom turned red. "What a surprise."

She didn't know what else to say. Mrs. Gray didn't say anything either. She was too busy writing on a clipboard.

"Shall we start the inspection?" sighed Dad.

We were in trouble. If a restaurant isn't clean, the health inspector could make it close. I had to think of something fast.

"Some of our customers are real pigs," I said.

That made Mrs. Gray smile. She held up her tablet and looked at me. "Is there something you'd like to explain to me?"

"Well," I said. "It all started when Rocky…"

Suddenly she really started laughing. "You don't have to explain a thing." She closed her tablet. "I'll be back tomorrow when you've had a chance to get things straightened out."

Dad and Mom looked very puzzled. "I think I missed something," said Dad.

"Like big fines?" said Mrs. Gray. "Or threats to close down Big Tom's?"

"Something like that," said Dad.

"If pigs and Uncle Rocky are involved, I'm sure there's a good explanation for all of this. I think your family has had enough stress for today."

"Uncle Rocky?" said Dad.

"He gave me my first pig when I was seven," answered Mrs. Gray. "He thinks every child should get to raise at least one pig."

Chapter 4
The Pig Palace

Dad poked some grass through the cage door. "Here, piggy wiggys."

"Did you just say, piggy wiggys?" I asked my dad.

"Oh," he stood up. "I didn't know you were there."

"You like the piglets, don't you?" I asked.

"Well," he hesitated. "They are cute little guys."

"Don't you mean cute little piggy wiggys?" I teased.

Dad smiled. He pulled a pancake from a bucket. The pigs seemed to enjoy them as much as our customers. The pigs grunted happily.

"So, we can keep them?" I finally had to ask.

"I'm not sure a restaurant is a good place to raise pigs," my dad tried to explain. "We can't exactly turn our yard into a pig pen. These little piglets are cute now, but they'll grow into big hogs. They could weigh a couple of hundred pounds. They're not like dogs."

"I've seen dogs that weighed over a hundred pounds," I tried to argue.

"I'm not sure what Rocky was thinking when he sold you these pigs," Dad shook his head.

"There you are," boomed a voice.

It was Rocky. He walked over to us. Buddy was right behind him. Buddy was carrying my tips jar.

"I just paid for my pig," explained Buddy as he handed me my jar. "You need to pay him for yours."

Dad frowned. "We were just talking about that. We can't keep the pigs."

"We've got to," said Buddy. "Rocky and I shook on it. I even had to dicker on the price."

Rocky smiled, "A deal's a deal. Now, I need to take my dog kennel back."

Dad waved his arms around the yard. "Where are we going to keep two pigs?"

Rocky pointed to some trees behind our yard. "Right over there."

"In the trees?" said Buddy. "I didn't know pigs could climb trees."

"No," chuckled Rocky, "Look past the trees. Follow me."

We walked to the patch of trees. A fence ran along the trees. Rocky pointed.

"I'm going to put in a little gate here."

He started climbing over the barbed wire fence. It was rusty and loose. He spread two strands apart and told Buddy and me to step through. Dad climbed through, too. It was just a tighter fit. His shirt caught on the wire.

"A gate would be a good idea," said my dad.

Past the trees was a little pen.

"Did somebody's house fall down?" asked Buddy.

In the middle of the pen was something that looked like the roof of a house. It was hard to see through the tall weeds. The roof of the short building was covered with tin. It wasn't very tall. Buddy and I couldn't even stand up in it.

"No, it didn't fall down," said Rocky. "That is a genuine pig palace."

"A palace?" I asked.

"Well, pigs don't live too high on the hog," answered Rocky.

Dad laughed. I guess Rocky had told a joke. Next, Rocky walked over to a funny looking box sticking out of a wooden deck.

It was gray colored with a little rust. On the side was a handle. Rocky told Buddy to turn the handle. Buddy cranked it once and stopped.

"Keep turning, fast," instructed Rocky.

Buddy cranked the handle four times. Suddenly the metal box made a strange sound. Water gushed out a spout. Buddy jumped back.

"I bet you never saw a real water pump," said Rocky. "It looks like you're a natural at using one though."

Buddy looked at his soaked tennis shoes. "How does washing my feet help the pigs?"

"We'll build a little trough to carry the water to the pig pen," explained Rocky.

"We?" I asked.

"I'll need you and Buddy to help me fix this place up," answered Rocky. "After all, it is for your pigs. We'll need to fix up the pen. You don't want your pigs running away. That could be big trouble."

"That *was* big trouble," said Buddy.

"Whoops. Did I forget to tell you not to open the cage?" asked Rocky. "You know that's not a good idea. I remembered when my niece did that once."

"Mrs. Gray?" I asked.

"Why, yes." Rocky was surprised. "Only she wasn't Mrs. anyone when she was only seven years old. I wonder if she remembers the first pig I gave her."

"She remembers," said Buddy, Dad, and I altogether.

"Well, pigs are great for creating memories," Rocky smiled. "You'll see."

"I think they've created a few memories already," said my dad.

"I have some tools in my truck. We're going to give those pigs a new home today!" declared Rocky.

That's just what we did the rest of the afternoon. The first thing we build was a water trough. We filled a large pan full of drinking water for the pigs. I liked cranking the handle on the pump.

After the pan was filled, Rocky moved the trough over. The water started running into a shallow hole. He had us keep pumping while he fixed the fence. The water created a little muddy pond.

I learned a lot about pigs that day. Pigs like the mud because it keeps them cool. They can also dig with their noses. That's why Rocky tacked a strand of barbed wire around the bottom of the pen.

I started to pull the weeds out. Rocky told me to leave them. Clearing the weeds would be a job the pigs would enjoy. Soon our piglets had their very own little palace, complete with an in-ground swimming pool. What more could a pig ask for?

We turned the piglets loose in their new home. It was a real piggy playground. The two little pigs ran around. Buddy and I joined them in a game of tag. The little piglets remembered all the pancakes we had fed them. They knew we were the best friends they had ever had.

Buddy and I named our pigs. My piglet had a big black spot on its back. Mark suggested I name him Spot. That didn't sound very creative to me. It just didn't have enough character.

Tracy said I should call it Stinky. My sister just didn't appreciate pigs like the rest of the family. It's a shame she hadn't met Rocky a few years earlier. He had a way of bringing kids and pigs together. Mom was beginning to think that was Rocky's mission in life.

I finally decided to call my pig, Abner. He just looked like an Abner to me. It sounded like a happy name. Abner was a happy pig. Why shouldn't he be happy? He dined on fresh scraps from Big Tom's every day. Plus, he lived in a pig palace.

The pig palace gave Buddy an idea for his pig's name. He called it Rex. Dad told him that Rex meant King. Since Rex lived in a pig palace, he must be a king, Buddy reasoned.

Chapter 5
The County Fair

First, I was a hostess. Then I became a waitress and a teacher. Now, I am also a pig farmer. I like being eight years old.

Buddy and I watched Abner and Rex munch happily on today's slop. That's what all the table scraps were called. We had to slop our pigs every day. Rocky taught us the right words that real pig farmers use.

"These pigs are going to make us rich," said Buddy as he watched them eat.

"You're not selling Abner," I said. He was too cute and sweet to sell.

"I don't want to sell them," said Buddy. "I want to enter them in a contest."

Buddy pulled a folded piece of paper from his pocket. I looked at it.

"Somebody brought a stack of these to Big Tom's today," explained Buddy. "The county fair is next week. I want to enter our pigs. We can win a prize. First prize is thirty dollars."

"Our pigs are too little," I said.

"Rex may be little, but he's a winner," defended Buddy. "Abner's a winner, too. All I need is four dollars from you to enter the contest."

I looked at the flier. "It says the contest only costs two dollars."

"Well," sighed Buddy. "I spent my money, and I owe Mark five dollars. I'll make you a deal, if Rex wins, I'll give you five dollars."

"Twenty-five dollars," I answered.

"Twenty-five dollars! Are you trying to rob me?" Buddy argued. "How about ten dollars?"

"Make it fifteen and you have a deal," I said.

"Shake," said Buddy as he held out his hand.

We shook hands. That made it a done deal.

"You sure know how to dicker," sighed Buddy.

"I learned a few things from the farmers, too," I answered.

The next few days we started getting our pigs ready. We weren't real sure what to do. We had never been to a county fair before.

Buddy and I had it all figured out. We knew we didn't have the biggest pigs. So, we were going to have the fanciest. Of course, we had to keep our strategy a secret.

Rocky told us our pigs were too small to win. Our parents said they agreed with Rocky. But they liked the fact that we were willing to try. They just told us to not be disappointed if we didn't win.

The morning of the fair, we woke up early. Abner and Rex had learned to walk with a leash. Well, it wasn't actually a leash. It was piece of rope. Buddy and I would let the pigs out of the pen and practice walking them around the pasture.

We roped our pigs. Then we gave them a bath with the cool water from the pump. Buddy used some of Mom's dishwashing soap. We would have the best smelling pigs at the fair.

Rocky had agreed to pick the pigs up in his truck. Our pigs had grown, but they still fit in the dog kennel. I grabbed my backpack. It had the rest of our surprise strategy in it. Buddy and I were riding to the fair with Rocky. We wanted to stay near our pigs.

Natalie was already there. She was flipping pancakes for the big pancake eating contest. The rest of my family left when Rocky arrived.

They wanted to get good seats in the grand stand. They didn't want to miss the pig judging contest. Okay, Tracy wanted to miss the pig judging contest. My parents wouldn't let her.

Rocky drove up to the livestock tent. He had some of his own pigs at the fair. He backed up to a little ramp. Buddy and I hopped in the back of the truck. We opened the door of the kennel. Abner and Rex poked out their heads. We slipped ropes around their necks and led them down the ramp.

Rocky walked around the livestock tent. He was looking for an empty pen. "You should have a pen somewhere in here," said Rocky as he started walking down the rows. After a few minutes, he gave up. "I need to find out where to put your pigs. I'll be back soon," said Rocky.

Rocky walked off. Buddy looked at his watch. "We're going to be late for the contest. We need to get Abner and Rex ready."

I agreed. I opened my backpack. Inside was everything we needed to make our pigs stand out. I looked around the other pens. They were filled with plain, ordinary pigs. I was sure Buddy's strategy was going to work.

Buddy and I had made special costumes for our pigs. He made a crown and a cape for Rex. The little pig really looked like a king. I made a bonnet and fake glasses for Abner. He looked adorable.

"We need to go now," said Buddy as he studied his watch.

Buddy was right. I had four dollars invested in this contest. We needed to win. We led our pigs through the crowds of people.

When they saw Rex and Abner, they smiled and backed out of the way. We made it to the contest just as the judge was calling for the contestants. The judge made us stand behind a table.

"Remember," said the judge. "The first one done wins the thirty-dollar prize. Ready…set… go."

Buddy and I each grabbed a plate and sat it on the ground. Buddy and I hadn't slopped the pigs last night. It was part of Rex and Abner's training for the contest. They were hungry little pigs. Natalie's pancakes were their favorite.

It took about fifteen seconds for Rex to finish his pancakes. Abner was finished a few seconds later.

"We won! We won!" shouted Buddy.

All the other contestants look up. That's when the judge noticed the pigs. "You can't feed your pancakes to pigs. You have to eat them yourself."

"But we're not entered in the pancake eating contest," Buddy explained.

He was right. Buddy and I didn't enter the contest. Abner and Rex were entered the contest. We explained that to the judge.

He didn't seem too happy. Just then, Rocky walked up.

"Why did you run off?" he asked.

"We didn't run off. We just needed to make it to the contest."

"I found out why you didn't have a pen for your pigs," Rocky explained. "You didn't enter them in the pig contest."

"Why would we do that?" asked Buddy. "Everyone told us Rex and Abner were too small."

"We entered them in a contest they could win. They're the best pancake eaters in the county. I know because we watched all the customers at Big Tom's. Rex and Abner can out eat anyone."

"But pigs can't enter a pancake eating contest," said the judge.

Rocky crossed his arms and smiled, "Where in the rules does it say that?"

The judge had a blank look on his face. "It doesn't," he sighed. "Everybody knows you can't enter pigs in the pancake contest."

"We didn't know that," I said.

"Abner and Rex didn't know that," said Buddy.

The judge grabbed a microphone. "The winner is Rex Pig. Second place goes to Abner Pig."

Buddy and I jumped up and down. The judge handed us a check and the crowd cheered. Some of the other contestants patted the pigs on the head and fed them their pancakes.

"You two are the cleverest pig farmers I ever met. I only have one question. Why are the pigs wearing costumes?"

Buddy looked at his watch, "We have just enough time."

"For what?" asked Rocky.

"For the costume contest," I answered as we lead our pigs away.

The Case of the Missing Trumpeter Part 1

Table of Contents

Chapter		Page
1	Rufus R. Goose	142
2	Missing Mr. Swan	144
3	The Egg-Sitters	147
4	A Stool Pigeon	150
5	Achoo!	152

by Brian Davis

Vocabulary Words

cautiously

daffodil

feline

ferocious

incubation

predator

Mr. Swan is missing from Blue Rocks Lake. Where there's trouble, they're there on the double. Rufus R. Goose, Private Eye and his assistant, Puffy Paws are on the case.

Chapter 1
Rufus R. Goose

The sign on the door read: Rufus R. Goose, Private Eye. Rufus admired his new door. One more thumbtack and the sign would be fully installed. The goose pecked at the last tack.

"Perfect," honked the goose as he backed up to take in the view.

His big web foot stepped on a crayon. The crayon rolled under the goose's weight. He stepped on another crayon, and another. The rolling goose lost his balance.

A big fluffy cat was bounding up the stairs. He reached the top just in time to meet the off-balance goose. The cat tried to duck the goose. It was too late.

A tumbling ball of feathers and furs rolled down the steps. Honking and hissing sounds filled the stairwell. Rufus and the cat came to a stop at the bottom of the stairs. The goose was dizzy from tumbling.

The cat hopped up and bounded back up the stairs. "My turn, my turn!" meowed the cat. "I'm king of the hill. Try to get past me."

"Puffy Paws, I'm not playing a game," honked Rufus. "All that fur is a built-in pillow for you."

"Plus, cats always land on their heads," added Puffy Paws.

"I think that's feet," corrected Rufus.

"Not me. A cat can damage their toes that way," meowed the cat. "Now come and get me! Are you a chicken or a goose?"

Just then the goose heard a ringing sound. It was coming from behind the door. The cat smiled. He spread out his big, fluffy paws to stop the goose.

Rufus flapped his wings and flew up the stairs. The cat was still determined. He leaped up at the goose. His waving paws came up empty. Instead, the cat landed on the steps and started tumbling down.

"Yee haw!" meowed the cat.

Rufus flew through a little window above the door. He swooped to a desk. His big webbed foot flipped up the phone.

"Rufus R. Goose, private eye speaking," he honked. "If you've got trouble, we'll be there on the double!"

"I see," Rufus honked into the phone. He clutched a crayon in his foot. The goose scribbled on a piece of paper. "Blue Rocks Lake, third rock on the right. I'll fly right over. Don't worry. Your case is in good hands."

Rufus frowned as he listened, "You're right, Ma'am. I don't actually have hands. Your case is in good webbed feet."

Rufus hung up the phone. He turned to leave his office. Suddenly, Puffy Paws filled the whole doorway. The cat smiled at the duck.

"I'm king of the doorway. You'll never get past me!" puffed Puffy Paws.

"No time to play now, Puffy. We have a case to solve." Rufus flew above the cat.

Puffy leaped up at the goose. Rufus was too quick. The cat landed on the crayons. He slipped and rolled across the hall. The cat slid and tumbled back down the stairs.

"Wahoo!" meowed Puffy Paws as he rolled. "We have a case!"

After coming to rest on his head, the cat popped up and followed the goose. Outside, the cat hopped in a bucket. Seconds later, a large red helium balloon rose from the bucket. It was soon joined by a blue balloon, then a green one. Finally, the cat in the bucket began to float. Rufus circled overhead.

A rope dangled from the bucket. Rufus swooped down and caught it in his beak. He strained as he flapped his wings.

"You need to go on a diet, Puffy Paws," complained Rufus.

"I can help," said Puffy Paws.

He pulled out a rocket on a stick. It was a leftover from the Fourth of July. He pulled out a roll of tape and fastened it to the bucket. The cat lit a match. Rufus looked back just as Puffy lit the rocket.

"No! Puff…"

The bucket took off. It flew past Rufus. The startled goose dropped the rope. The goose ducked the pail full of cat.

Rufus sniffed the air after the bucket sped away. There was a strange smell. Rufus thought it smelled like something cooking. He wondered what it could be.

"I know," said Rufus. "It smells like roasted goose."

"Roasted goose! That would be me!"

Sure enough, the sparks from the fire caught his feathers on fire. Rufus went into a dive. The flaming goose splashed into Blue Rocks Lake. Steam rose around him.

Rufus floated over to the third rock on the right. He emerged from the steam. A frightened white trumpeter swan peeked out from behind the rock. She was amazed at the sight.

"Rufus R. Goose, private eye, at your service," the goose introduced himself.

"You make quite an entrance, Mr. Goose," said the swan as she cautiously floated from behind the rock.

"No extra charge, Ma'am," the goose nodded at the swan.

"Yippee!" came a shout from behind him.

It was followed by a loud splash. The goose and the swan rose up and down on the wave. The swan once again looked frightened. Rufus saw the look on her beak.

"No need to worry, Ma'am. That's just my assistant, Puffy Paws," explained Rufus. "He's a few balloons short of a safe landing."

"Hello," yelled Puffy Paws from a distance. He pulled an oar out of the bucket and began to row to Rufus.

Chapter 2
Missing Mr. swan

The cat joined the two birds. He pulled out a notebook and began to take notes. Penny Swan had a sad story. Puffy had to wipe tears from his eyes.

"Stop, my eyes are getting puffy," meowed the cat.

"You're puffy all over, Puffy," Rufus pointed out.

"You're right," replied Puffy. "Where were we? Let me look at my notes." The cat looked over what he had written. "Here it is. You were telling us that you miss your cousins."

Rufus honked, "That's not what she was saying. Mrs. Swan said she saw her husband kissing a cow."

"No, no," squawked the swan. "My husband came up missing after I saw an owl."

"I like your story better," Puffy said to Rufus. "I think we should investigate. We can line up some cows and grill them."

"You're getting hungry, aren't you, Puffy?" asked Rufus.

"Just a little," whined Puffy.

"There's no time to eat right now. We need to hatch a plan to find Mr. Swan," said Rufus.

Oh no, you don't need to hatch a plan," Mrs. Swan explained.

"Then why did you call us?" asked Puffy.

"To hatch some eggs, of course," explained Mrs. Swan. "I can look for my husband. Someone's got to sit on the nest."

"I'm not sure we're qualified," explained Rufus.

"Were you an egg once?" asked Penny Swan.

"I wasn't," said Puffy. "So, I guess I'll be going. Good luck, Rufus."

"But Mr. Paws, I need a big, ferocious cat like you to help," pleaded Mrs. Swan. "You'll have Mr. Swan's job."

"I'm ferocious? Rufus, she called me ferocious. I'm ferocious!" Puffy puffed out his puffy chest. Suddenly, he looked confused. "What's ferocious? Is that a good thing?"

"It means that you're tough," explained Mrs. Swan. "You're scary. If you're around, nothing can happen to my beautiful, baby eggs."

A smile grew on Puffy's face. He looked down shyly. All of the sudden, Puffy gasped. Trembling, he pointed down at the water.

"Ah!" shouted the cat.

"What's wrong, Puffy?" asked Rufus.

"I just saw my reflection in the water. I am ferocious. I'd hate to meet me in a dark alley."

"You will help me, won't you?" asked Mrs. Swan sadly as she batted her eyes at Rufus.

How could Rufus say no? When he saw a need, he was ready for action. Right now, he really needed the work. He raised his wing and saluted Mrs. Swan.

"Rufus R. Goose, private eye and egg sitter at your service!"

"Ah!" shouted Puffy.

"What now?" asked Rufus.

"I just saw my own shadow. It scared me. That's how ferocious I am!" explained Puffy as he once more puffed out his puffy chest.

He saluted Mrs. Swan, too, "Puffy Paws, ferocious feline at your service, ma'am!"

Mrs. Swan started to swim away. Then she turned around and gave one final set of instructions, "Thanks, and keep your eyes open at all times for predators."

"I will," vowed Puffy Paws. "If I see any predators, I'll growl like this, grrrr."

"Ah!" shouted Puffy Paws.

"What?" asked Rufus.

"That sound scared me. I am so ferocious," explained Puffy.

Rufus looked around the lake. It was starting to get dark. Mrs. Swan flapped her wings and flew out of sight. Rufus looked over at the nest hidden in some brush. It suddenly seemed like a very lonely place. It even seemed a little spooky.

"Don't worry," smiled Puffy. "I'm here to protect you."

"That's what worries me," thought Rufus as he swam over to the nest.

Puffy scampered up a tree. He climbed out on a branch.

"See, I've already gone out on a limb for you," joked Puffy.

The cat waved at Rufus. He was right over the goose and the nest. From his perch, he could watch for predators. The cat was ready to pounce at the first sign of trouble.

Rufus settled into the nest. He sat atop three eggs. "Maybe this isn't such a bad job," thought the goose. He got to rest in a comfortable nest and watch the sunset. Rufus was just starting to relax.

Suddenly, he heard a rustling sound. His head flipped back and forth trying to hear where it was coming from. The goose was getting tense. The tall brush around him could be the hiding place for all kinds of predators.

Finally, he looked up. Rufus honked a sigh of relief.

"Sorry," apologized Puffy. "I had an itch." He scratched again and the whole tree limb shook.

Rufus began to relax once more. A buzzing sound grew louder and louder. The goose watched as the insect flew closer. Rufus started to snap at it.

Suddenly, his face was full of fur. The goose was under attack. Rufus heard growling and hissing. The next thing he knew, he was being swatted on the back. Then it stopped.

"The predator is gone!" announced Puffy.

"What was it?" asked Rufus. He was still a little shaken up.

"A dragonfly," answered Puffy Paws. "It landed on your beak, so I pounced on him."

"I think we need to narrow our definition of a predator," Rufus stood up and waved his wing at Puffy. "A predator is an animal that might actually hurt me or the eggs, besides you, I mean."

"And a dragonfly couldn't hurt you?" asked the cat.

"It's just a little insect," answered Rufus.

"But its name begins with dragon," explained Puffy. "A dragon could be a predator. It could breathe fire and cook the eggs."

Just then, a snapping turtle with and empty basket on its back swam up. "Pardon me," said the turtle. "I'm baking a cake. I need three eggs for the recipe. Could I buy these?" the turtle pointed to the nest.

Rufus did not like to be interrupted while he was explaining things to Puffy. "Sure, just bring them back when you're done," said the goose without giving it any thought.

"So, what would be a predator?" asked Puffy.

"Anything that takes the eggs," explained Rufus. "Can a dragonfly carry an egg?"

"Not as well as that turtle," said Puffy.

"Right," said Rufus. "So, a dragonfly is not a predator. A snapping turtle is a predator. Do you see the difference?"

"I think so," said Puffy. "But I don't see the eggs."

"Exactly," said Rufus. "The turtle took them."

Suddenly, Rufus realized what had happened. "Stop that snapping turtle!"

Puffy Paws grabbed the basket just before the turtle dove under the water.

Chapter 3
The Egg-Sitters

The eggs in the basket gave Rufus a great idea. Why spend the night at a dark, scary lake, not knowing when the cat above you is going to pounce? He had a nice cozy office. It had four walls to keep out predators. Puffy scribbled out a note for Penny Swan:

Dear Mrs. Swan,

We hope you found your husband. Please do not worry about the eggs. We have taken them to the safety of our office at 777 Quacker Lane.

Yours truly,

Puffy Paws, the ferocious feline.

P.S. Predators are not allowed to read this note.

The cat pinned the note to the nest. Then Puffy carried the basket to the bucket and climbed inside. The cat began to prepare for liftoff. He once again blew up some balloons. Rufus made sure there were no more fireworks in the bucket.

"Do you think our office is really safer?" asked Puffy.

"Yes, why do you ask?" questioned Rufus.

"Well, I did fall down the stairs three times today."

"True," said Rufus. "You go up first and pick up the crayons."

As soon as the cat, goose, and eggs arrived at the office building, Puffy bounded up the steps. The next thing he did was roll down the steps. The cat landed on his head. In each paw was a crayon.

"Here's two," smiled Puffy, although his smile looked like a frown since he was upside down. Rufus placed them in the basket.

Five more trips up the stairs and five more trips rolling down the stairs and the office was safe for the eggs. Once in the office, Rufus didn't need to sit on the eggs. He had a heat lamp that he used for tanning. The goose liked his big webbed feet to have that healthy orange glow.

Finally, the goose and cat could relax. Puffy Paws snuggled on his pillow in the corner. In his arms was his favorite stuffed puppy dog. Rufus propped his feet up on his desk, leaned back in his chair, and opened his newspaper.

He wanted something to keep his mind alert while he stood guard over the eggs. The sports section talked about the Duck, Duck, Goose playoffs. Next, he read his favorite comic strip. It was about a lovable cat called Fluffy Tail.

Rufus read an article about a bomb missing from the nearby Hare Force base. Rufus thought it was a mistake to teach rabbits to fly. He wondered whose hare-brained idea that was. As the night wore on, the goose finally drifted into dreamland.

Sunlight was streaming in the windows when the knocking started. The startled goose jumped. His office chair flipped over backwards. The goose tumbled onto the floor.

The noise woke Puffy Paws. He saw the chair. He glanced at the goose on the floor. The cat hopped up. He put the chair back on its feet.

"My turn," said the cat. He propped his feet on the desk and pushed off. "Ow!" cried the cat.

"Did you hit your head?" asked Rufus.

"No," cried Puffy Paws. "I hit my toes. I'm going to wear a helmet on my feet next time."

The knocking sound came from the door again. Rufus opened the door, expecting to see Mrs. Swan. Instead, there stood a raccoon. He was a tough looking raccoon. The raccoon was kind of short and fat with a scar over his right eye.

The raccoon pushed the door open and walked right in. The furry animal walked over to the eggs.

"Just as I thought," said the raccoon. "I'm going to have to remove these from the premises."

"That's not a premise," correct Puffy. "That's a basket."

"No, the premise is another name for a building," explained the raccoon. "This building is not zoned for incubation. I'm afraid you're in very big trouble."

"Wait a minute," said Rufus. "Just who do you think you are?"

The raccoon flashed a badge and quickly stuffed it back in his pocket, "Officer Lenny, Egg Patrol. I'm going to have to put you under arrest and take these eggs."

"But we were just egg sitting," explained Puffy.

"Oh," said the raccoon. "That's different. If you'll just show me your egg sitting license we can clear this up. Then you can go on your way and help Mrs. Swan find her husband."

"License?" frowned Rufus.

"I see," said the raccoon, grabbing the handle of the basket, "no license." He stepped to the door. "When you get the proper license, you can have your eggs back."

"Aren't you going to arrest us?" asked Puffy.

"Oh, yeah," said the raccoon. "My car is full right now. Why don't you boys just march down to the police station and turn yourselves in?"

"Yes, Sir," said Puffy.

"Yes, Sir," said Rufus.

The raccoon closed the door behind him. Puffy brushed his teeth. Rufus combed the ruffles out of his feathers. The cat and goose sadly went to the police station.

A duck in a blue uniform sat behind a desk at the station. The duck looked confused. "Explain it to me one more time. Why are you here?"

"We were incubating in a no incubation zone," said Puffy.

"And, we don't have an egg sitting license," added Rufus.

The duck was still puzzled, "There's no such thing as a no incubation zone, and you don't need a license to egg sit."

"But Officer Lenny Raccoon said…" Rufus started to explain.

"What did this raccoon look like?" asked the duck.

"I'm not sure," said Rufus. "I think he was wearing a mask."

The officer pulled a big book off the shelf. He flipped through the pages. It was filled with pictures of all kinds of egg predators, owls, turtles, snakes, lizards, and even raccoons. The duck pointed to a picture.

"Was this the raccoon, kind of short, kind of fat, with a scar over his right eye?" he quacked.

"Yes," answered Rufus.

"That's Lightfingers Lenny. He's a known bank robber."

"Why would a bank robber take eggs?" asked Rufus.

"He goes along the banks of rivers and lakes. He steals eggs from the nests. There's one thing I don't understand. How did he know you had eggs in your office?"

Puffy started getting angry, "I'd like to file a complaint. That raccoon read my note. Well, he read part of it. He must not have read the part that said predators were not to read the note."

"Oh no," sighed Rufus. "How are we going to get those eggs back?"

"I have an idea!" said Puffy after he thought for a moment. "We'll get an egg sitting license. Then that raccoon must give us the eggs back."

Chapter 4
A Stool Pigeon

The police officers scrambled to find the eggs. The problem was, only two police ducks were free to help. The others were guarding the prison. There was a big quackdown on crime in the city. The prison was filled with jailbirds. Left unguarded, they might fly the coop.

The two ducks flew off to all the doughnut shops to check for leads. Puffy and Rufus thought they were alone in the police station. Puffy started looking through some files. He wanted to find an application for an egg sitting license.

Rufus heard a soft cooing. It was coming from a cage at the back of the station. Inside was a pigeon perched up on a stool.

"Hey, goofy looking goose," cooed the pigeon.

"Who me?" honked Rufus.

"I'm not talking to the big furry creature that meows," said the pigeon.

"I'm not goofy looking," honked Rufus.

"Sure you are. All geese are goofy looking," answered the pigeon. "Now, why don't you grab those keys with your goofy looking bill and bring them right over here to Uncle Eddie."

"Why would I do that?" asked Rufus. "Certainly not because you're so polite."

"Oh," said the pigeon, "Did I forget to say, please? Maybe you ought to be saying please to me."

"Why would I do that?" asked Rufus.

"If you're looking for Lightfingers Lenny, I know where to find him," cooed the pigeon.

"If I let you out, how do I know you'll help us?" asked Rufus.

"Look at me," said Uncle Eddie, "I'm a pigeon sitting on a stool – a stool pigeon. Telling on my friends is what I'm born to do."

"Tell me where to find Lenny Raccoon, and I'll put a good word in for you with the police ducks," said Rufus. Rufus pointed to Puffy across the room. "Otherwise, my ferocious feline friend will come into that cage and ruffle your feathers."

The pigeon didn't look too impressed. "That cream puff?"

Puffy zipped over to the cage. He snarled and hissed. The cat started boxing at the air. The pigeon shrunk back.

"I'll tell! I'll tell you everything!" shivered the pigeon. "If you promise one thing."

"What is it?" asked the goose.

"Don't let me out of this cage," cried the pigeon. "I don't want to be Puffy food."

"Okay, but tell me everything you know about Lenny Raccoon."

"Lenny works for Big Owl," said Uncle Eddie. "You can find him on the boat dock and restaurant at Blue Lake. You've better hurry. The lunch special today is fried egg sandwiches."

The goose and cat left the police station. Puffy held the door open for a mink that was coming up the steps.

"Nice coat," said Puffy as the mink passed by.

"Thanks," mumbled the mink.

Inside the station, the mink was surprised to find it empty. He rang a bell that was on top of a desk. The pigeon started cooing. The mink walked back to the cage.

"Uncle Eddie, I'm here to bail you out," said the mink. "Where are the police ducks?"

"Out on an egg snatching case," said the pigeon. "They're looking for Lenny Raccoon. He took some swan eggs from a goose and a cat."

"Those two I saw outside?" asked the mink. "You didn't rat on Lenny, did you?"

"I'm not a fink, Mink," said Uncle Eddie.

"I know, but you are a stoolpigeon," the mink pointed out.

"Alright, I told them everything I know. I can't help it. I even told on myself."

"Big Owl isn't going to like this," said the mink as he unlocked the cage. "There's only one thing for us to do. We've got to stop the goose and the cat."

"That cat's pretty ferocious. How are we going to do that?" asked Eddie.

"What's this?" asked the mink as he picked something off the floor. "It's a bottle of allergy pills." The mink read the label, "Puffy Paws, 777 Quaker Lane. Take as needed."

A grin came on the face of the mink, "I know just how to take care of him."

"A warm bowl of milk and scratch his tummy?" asked the pigeon.

"No, what we need is a dog," said the mink as he picked up a telephone. "And I know just the one to call."

The bulldog answered the phone, "Bruiser speaking, what do you want?" The dog growled into the phone. "A cat, huh. Puffy Paws, 777 Quacker Lane. Got it." He scribbled something on a piece of paper. "I'll take care of him personally," laughed the dog.

Rufus and Puffy left the doughnut shop. It was the fifth one they had visited since leaving the police station. Puffy waved a jelly roll under the goose's beak.

"Sure you don't want a bite? It's really good. I just love the catfish jellyrolls. Yum, yum!" said Puffy.

Rufus turned his beak away, "How can you eat at a time like this?"

"Don't worry, it won't spoil my lunch," said Puffy.

"I mean, we have to rescue the eggs. We can't find the police ducks anywhere. I'm afraid we're going to have to go to Big Owl's by ourselves," explained Rufus.

"Why are you so worried?" asked Puffy. "Are you forgetting how ferocious I am?"

"Well, uh..." Rufus stammered. "Let me have a bite of that jelly roll. That looks really good."

"You do think I'm ferocious, don't you?" asked Puffy. Rufus was silent. "You don't believe I'm ferocious, do you?"

"You're cuddly," offered Rufus, "and lovable."

"I'm ferocious," pouted Puffy Paws. "And if you don't know that, you can rescue the eggs all by yourself!"

The cat slumped as he walked sadly down the street. Rufus watched the cat turn the corner. He felt sad. But he also thought of all the problems the cat seemed to cause.

"He would just get in the way," Rufus tried to convince himself it was for the best. "That cat was just slowing me down."

Chapter 5
Achoo!

Puffy didn't notice the van following him down the street. The words "Bruiser's Flower Shop" were painted on the side. It came up slowly behind him. The cat stopped at a lamppost. He leaned his head up against it and cried.

Bruiser saw his chance. The dog leaped from the van. He tossed a net over the cat. Puffy was tied, gagged, and tossed into the back of the van before he knew what hit him.

"Enjoy the flowers, Puffy Paws," laughed the bulldog. "You're going to be a big stuffed up fluff ball."

Daffodils, dozens of them filled the back of the van. Puffy Paws was allergic to daffodils. He tried to wiggle his paws free. The cat rolled around as the van took off. The daffodils were right under his nose.

Puffy knew he needed his allergy pills. His paws squirmed around until he could reach his pocket. He felt inside. The pocket was empty. The pills had fallen out at the police station when he was scaring Uncle Eddie the pigeon.

"Oh no," whined the cat. "My pills are gone. There's only one thing left to do…sneeze!"

One daffodil could make the cat sneeze a little. A few could make him sneeze a lot. Puffy had never been around dozens of daffodils. He felt a mega-sneeze coming on.

"Ah-choo!" Puffy sneezed the biggest sneeze he had ever sneezed. He sneezed so hard that he flew back and made a dent in the side of the van. Bruiser swerved as he was driving. He thought he ran over something in the road.

Puffy thought it was rather fun. He sneezed again. This sneeze was even bigger. Again, Puffy flew around the van. The cat sneezed again and again putting all kinds of dents in the van. He was like popcorn in a hot pan.

Bruiser tried to steer the van. It was impossible with Puffy flying all around the back. The van ran off the road and hit a fire hydrant. The back door flew open. Water sprayed up under the van.

Puffy bounced out the back of the van. His back paws were still tied. He hopped in the water. Some children saw him splashing. They thought it looked like lots of fun.
They all joined him.

Puffy hopped through the splashing children. He landed on a park bench and wiggled free of his ropes. The cat looked in the front of the van. The crash had knocked Bruiser out. Puffy noticed the pink order form.

The cat read it out loud, "Twelve dozen daffodils for Puffy Paws. Ordered by Mr. Mink. Bill to Big Owl. Beware of ferocious cat."

The cat put the paper down. "I am ferocious. Even dogs have to be warned!"

Suddenly, Puffy thought of the eggs, "Puffy Paws, ferocious feline to the rescue!"

He asked a child if he could get a ride on his scooter. The child looked at the big cat.

"I don't think I can push you," said the child.

"I just need you to steer. I've never ridden a scooter. I can supply the power."

"Okay," said the child.

Puffy grabbed a dozen daffodils. He faced the back of the scooter.

"Ready, set," Rufus put the daffodils under his nose. "Achoo!"

The sneeze made the scooter fly forward. The cat sneezed again. The scooter went faster. The child smiled.

"Wee, this is fun," said the child.

The scooter ran right through a red light. The two ducks were just coming out of the doughnut shop on the corner. The police ducks couldn't believe how fast the scooter was moving. They hopped on bicycles and began to chase the scooter.

"Oh, good," said Puffy Paws in between sneezes. "What luck, the ducks are coming to help us."

The scooter took a sharp corner. Puffy and the child passed through a yard full of blooming daffodils. Puffy sneezed harder than ever. The cat flew up into a tree.

The scooter came to a stop. The child

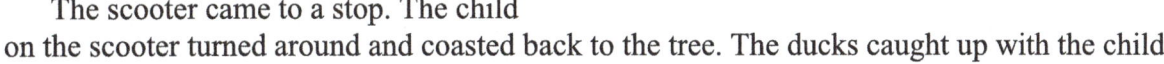

on the scooter turned around and coasted back to the tree. The ducks caught up with the child.

"We need to see your license," said a duck.

The child pulled out a card. The police duck look at it.

"This is an egg sitting license," said the duck.

"Wow, they do make those," said the other police duck. "I didn't know that."

"Hello," said Puffy

The ducks looked up in the tree. Puffy was caught in the branches. The cat waved.

"I think I'm stuck," said Puffy.

The police duck spoke into his radio. "We have an 11-19 on the corner of Fourth and Sparrow."

"What's an 11-19?" asked the child.

"A big, fluffy cat stuck in a tree," explained the police duck. "This is going to take heavy duty equipment."

Suddenly there was a loud cracking sound. The child jumped back. The tree limb crashed to the street. Puffy landed on the police ducks.

"Officers down," groaned a flattened police duck into his radio.

The Case of the Missing Trumpeter Part 2

Table of Contents

Chapter		Page
6	Lunch at Big Owl's	155
7	The Laughing Lizard	157
8	The Star Trumpeter	159
9	The Mystery Creature	161
10	The New Big Owl	163
11	Puffy and the Eagles	165

by Brian Davis

Vocabulary Words

cygnets

delightful

distracting

undercover

Something is going on at Big Owl's Restaurant and Boat Dock. Rufus R. Goose goes undercover to discover Big Owl's terrible plan.

Chapter 6
Lunch at Big Owl's

Meanwhile, Rufus R. Goose had flown to Big Owl's Restaurant and Boat Dock. He floated under the dock and listened. Two hawks stood guard.

"The boss says to be on the look-out for a cat and a goose," said one hawk. "Some stoolpigeon said they were heading this way."

"They won't get past me," said the other. "They don't call me Eagle Eyes for nothing."

Rufus quietly floated back to shore. He scampered into the woods. It was a good thing Rufus had stopped by his office before coming. He found his duffle bag. It was filled with his disguises.

The goose found just what he was looking for. First, he put on the see-through eye patch. Next, he would need to do something with the beak.

"This should do," he said to himself as he pulled out just the right beak, "and the red bandana. Now, I'll just slip this over my foot."

When he finished, the goose looked in a little mirror he had brought along. "I think this would fool my own mother," said the goose, quite pleased with his disguise.

Rufus hobbled past the two hawks. The two hawks were still talking.

"Did you just see someone walk past us?" said the first hawk.

"I didn't notice anyone," said Eagle Eyes.

The first hawk turned around and saw Rufus waddling to the restaurant. From the back, he looked just like a goose with a wooden leg.

"Hey you! Stop!" said the hawk.

Rufus froze. He was afraid he had been caught. He turned around slowly. The two hawks stared at him.

Eagle Eyes looked him in the eyes, "What's your name?"

"Captain Jack Pelican, master of the sea," answered Rufus.

"You're pretty sneaky for a pelican," said Eagle Eyes. "You thought you could slip right by us. Well, you're not going in there without talking to us first." The hawk tapped Rufus on the beak.

The beak slid down slightly. Rufus quickly readjusted it. Eagle Eyes didn't seem to notice. He just kept on talking.

"No one goes in there without hearing our list of daily specials!" said Eagle Eyes. "Now, our appetizer of the day is cattail roots with a delightful sauce made from bulrushes. After that, you may want our fresh roast swan."

"That's tomorrow's special," interrupted the other hawk. "Today's special is fresh swan eggs. But you better hurry. We only have three eggs today."

"That sounds like what I'm looking for," said Rufus.

"Great," said Eagle Eyes. "Have a delightful meal."

"And if you're still hungry," said the other hawk. "We may have some fresh goose coming in soon."

Inside the restaurant was filled with all kinds of predatory creatures and criminal type birds. Three black birds sat at the crow bar sipping root beer. Rufus found a table in a dark corner.

"What'll it be?" asked a parrot.

"I'll have the swan egg special," said Rufus.

"How would you like that cooked?" asked the parrot.

"I'd like them raw and in the shell," answered Rufus.

The waitress came back with the eggs. Rufus quickly put them in the pelican pouch on his disguise. That was easy enough, thought Rufus. Suddenly, there was loud talking on the stairway that led to the office.

"I told you to bring those eggs to me!" screeched Big Owl.

"I thought they were for the lunch special," explained Lightfingers Lenny.

"If anything happened to those eggs, you'll be the lunch special!" warned the owl.

Rufus knew he needed to leave right away. He kept his beak down and tried not to look suspicious. The goose had to pass by the raccoon and Big Owl. Rufus was relieved when Lenny didn't recognize him.

"Wait just one minute!" said a voice behind him.

Rufus hoped the voice wasn't speaking to him.

"Stop that pelican with the peg leg," ordered the voice.

The two hawks blocked the door. Rufus was trapped. He turned around. An angry parrot was glaring at him. All the commotion had gotten Big Owl's attention.

"What seems to be the problem?" asked Big Owl.

"This pelican orders the lunch special, then walks out without paying. I didn't even get a tip!" complained the parrot waitress.

"The swan egg special?" asked Big Owl.

"All three of them," said the parrot.

Big Owl turned and pecked the raccoon on the head, "We're too late, and it's all your fault."

Just then, something strange started to happen in the pelican beak. It bulged on the left. Then it wiggled on the right. The owl, raccoon, and parrot stood in amazement.

The beak fell open. Inside were three cygnets. That's what baby swans are called. The newly hatched cygnets had shaken free from their shells. Rufus was so surprised, that his beak fell off his face.

"It's Rufus R. Goose, private eye," Lenny pointed at Rufus.

Rufus scrambled for the cygnets. It was hard to bend over with the peg leg. He wasn't quick enough. Big Owl scooped the cygnets up in his wing.

Rufus dove for the owl. One of the hawks grabbed the goose's peg leg. It pulled loose and the hawk flew backwards. The goose hopped to his feet. This time Lenny blocked him.

The goose turned to go the other way. The angry parrot wouldn't let him by. He turned to his left and right. Hawks were on both sides of him. Rufus R. Goose was surrounded.

"Yahoo wee!" cried a voice from the top of the stairs.

Down came a rolling fluff ball. The goose ducked just in time. The hawks, raccoon, and parrot fell like bowling pins. They didn't know what hit them.

"Puffy Paws, ferocious feline to the rescue!" shouted Puffy.

Just then, the duck police came in blowing whistles. They quickly slapped wing-cuffs on the hawks and parrot. They put paw-cuffs on Lenny. Rufus gave Puffy a light peck on the whiskers.

"Am I ever glad to see you! I thought this goose was cooked." Rufus said as he pointed to himself.

"And..." said Puffy.

"And you are the most ferocious feline I've ever met," said Rufus.

Puffy smiled and hugged the neck of Rufus. "Now that you know I'm ferocious, I'll have to try harder not to scare you."

"I'm...choking..." the goose grunted. Puffy was hugging just a little too tightly.

"I'm kind of choked up, too," said Puffy. He let Rufus go to wipe a tear from his eyes.

Rufus slumped to the floor and panted. When he caught his breath, he looked around the restaurant. He didn't see Big Owl. There was no sign of the cygnets.

Chapter 7
The Laughing Lizard

Rufus and Puffy searched the restaurant. Big Owl and the cygnets were nowhere to be found. A lizard and a skink were in the kitchen. They were both wearing aprons. The lizard was flipping burgers on a grill. The skink was at the sink washing dishes.

"Did Big Owl come through here?" Rufus asked the cook.

"Are you one of those police ducks?" asked the cook. "I don't talk to the police."

"I'm a goose," said Rufus.

The lizard looked closely at the goose. "I think you're one of those undercover police ducks. You're just disguised as a goose, and a very poor disguise I might add."

Rufus had no time to waste on the lizard. The goose turned to the skink at the sink, "Have you seen Big Owl?"

Before the dishwashing skink could answer, the lizard started laughing. The cat whipped around.

"Who are you laughing at?" asked Rufus.

"No one," said the lizard. "Your tail feathers tickled my chin."

That gave the goose an idea. He stretched out his wing and tickled the lizard under the chin. The lizard started giggling. Rufus tickled the lizard more.

"Stop," gasped the lizard between laughs, "I can't breathe."

"Will you tell me what happened to Big Owl?"

"Yes, yes!" said the lizard. "He went out the back. He left on his old boat with three chicks."

"Let's go, Puffy," said Rufus. "Puffy?"

The goose turned around. Puffy was standing at the grill flipping burgers. He was flipping them right into his mouth. Rufus grabbed him and pulled him away.

"Great burgers," said Puffy to the lizard. "I'll be sure to tell all my friends."

"Thank you very much," said the lizard.

"No problem," said Puffy. He handed Rufus a burger. "These are really good."

Rufus handed it back. "You know I don't eat meat."

"I know," said Puffy. "But I promised to tell all my friends. You are all my friends."

"I'm a blessed goose," sighed Rufus.

The cat and the duck ran out the door in the kitchen. They saw Big Owl's boat in the distance. It was speeding away. They ran to an old fishing boat tied at the dock. Rufus told Puffy to climb into the boat.

"I don't want to," said Puffy. "I'm afraid of boats."

"Why?" asked Rufus.

"Because they're in water," said Puffy.

"You floated on the water in a bucket," Rufus pointed out.

"But my bucket is comfy and safe," explained Puffy.

"I thought you were ferocious," said Rufus.

"I'm ferocious, but not fearless," answered Puffy.

Rufus thought they were wasting too much time. He looked around the dock. A bucket sat next to some old wooden crates and a stack of fishing poles. The goose tipped over the bucket. He hopped on top and rolled it to Puffy.

"Put this in the boat," ordered Rufus.

The cat placed it toward the front of the small boat. Then he snuggled down inside it.

"I just love a boat with bucket seats," said Puffy.

The goose hopped in the back. Rufus started the motor. Then he remembered something. Rufus told Puffy to take over steering the boat.

The goose flew back toward Big Owl's Restaurant. He landed in the woods. Rufus found his disguise kit. He gathered it up and flew back to Puffy.

The cat was spinning around in circles on the lake. He had never driven a boat before. Plus, he was too afraid to get out of the bucket. The boat was driving by itself.

Rufus was getting dizzy trying to find a landing place. Finally, the boat started to zoom toward the lakeshore. The goose chased it. Rufus dropped his bag in the boat and landed right next to the motor.

The boat was speeding right toward a log. Rufus turned the boat sharply. Puffy and the bucket rolled to the back of the boat. The cat landed on top of the goose. Now, Puffy and Rufus were in the bucket.

"See, it is comfy. Isn't it?" said Puffy. "But you really should have brought your own bucket."

"I don't want a bucket," said Rufus angrily as the boats motor stopped. "I just want to rescue the cygnets. Now, Big Owl is completely out of sight. We'll never find him."

Rufus tried to restart the motor. The boat drifted behind the log. Puffy was busy moving to the front of the boat. It wasn't easy with a bucket on his back.

"I don't see how turtles can do this all day," said Puffy.

In the distance, they heard another motor sound. Rufus peeked over the log. The lizard cook was speeding by. He was riding his own jet ski. Rufus knew the lizard was going to warn Big Owl. So, all they needed to do was follow the lizard.

The goose gave one more pull on the boat motor's rope. The motor roared to life. Rufus and Puffy followed the lizard. The lizard didn't go to Big Owl. Instead, it landed on a tree-covered island. The lizard slithered into the woods.

Chapter 8
The Star Trumpeter

Rufus and Puffy followed. Soon the lizard came to a clearing. In the clearing was a small stage. The lizard slithered onto the stage. He popped up behind a set of bongo drums. The lizard started pounding out a beat.

"He's good," said Puffy as Rufus and he peeked through the bushes.

Soon, three horned owls flew in along with a large white bird. Rufus was very surprise.

"I think that's Mr. Swan," whispered Rufus.

"Let's go get him," said Puffy.

"Wait," said Rufus as he spread out his wing to stop Puffy. "Let's see what they're up to."

The birds opened cases. Inside were musical instruments. The largest owl had a tuba. Another had a trombone. The third owl had a saxophone. Mr. Swan pulled out a trumpet. He was, after all, a trumpeter swan.

The birds and the lizard started to play. It was a lively jazz tune. The owls and the lizard seemed to really be enjoying themselves. The swan didn't look so happy, yet he didn't try to get away.

Rufus and Fuzzy hid in the bushes and watched for an hour. Puffy really enjoyed the music. Rufus kept his eye on Mr. Swan. The more the goose watched, the more Rufus was sure Mr. Swan didn't want to play with the band.

"What we need is some kind of a distraction," said Rufus. "Then I could sneak in and try to rescue Mr. Swan."

"I can take care of that," said Puffy Paws. "I am good at being distracting."

"That's true," said Rufus. "You are even more distracting than you are ferocious."

"You're not the first one to tell me that," smiled Puffy.

Rufus sneaked around the back of the stage. Puffy was watching for just the right moment. The band had just finished a song. The owls couldn't believe their eyes.

Puffy popped out of the top of a tree. He swung from a vine and landed on the stage right in the middle of the three owls. The cat was ready for a fight. He spun in circles. His paws were flying. He was being as ferocious as he could be.

Still the owls weren't afraid. Nor were they upset. Instead, they seemed to be enjoying themselves. They picked up their horns.

"That cat can dance!" said the owl that was the band leader.

The lizard started playing a beat on the bongos. The owls joined in with their horns. Puffy's ferocious dance proved to be a very good distraction. In fact, it was so distracting Rufus almost forgot the plan.

He pecked at the swan's feet. The swan turned around. The goose motioned with his wing. The swan followed the goose into the woods.

"We're here to rescue you," said Rufus R. Goose.

"I can't be rescued," said Mr. Swan.

"Yes, you can," said Rufus.

He tugged the swan's wing. Mr. Swan pulled away. He headed back to the stage. Rufus followed him.

"Mrs. Swan is looking for you," said Rufus.

"No, she's not," answered Mr. Swan.

"Yes..." Rufus started to argue.

The swan interrupted, "She found me. That's why I can't leave."

"I don't understand," said Rufus.

"Big Owl kidnapped me. He's forcing me to play with The Horned Owls in a talent contest at the Condor Club tonight. I'm sure Big Owl is up to no good. That's why I tried to escape from his boat."

"When the guard hawk, Eagle Eye, came to bring me dinner one night, I hid behind the door. He didn't see me. I snuck out and locked the hawk in. I was ready to leave then I heard a commotion below deck. I peeked through a window. There was Penny. Big Owl had her tied up."

Big Owl was threatening to put her on the menu at his restaurant. I had to stay. I decided the best thing to do was play in the band. If we win the contest tonight, Big Owl said he would let us go."

"The only good thing is that Penny left our eggs with a private eye goose and his cat…" suddenly the swan stopped. "Is your name, Rufus R. Goose by any chance?"

"At your service," Rufus frowned.

"Are the eggs safe?" the swan was worried.

"I have good news, bad news, and good news," said the goose. "The good news is that you're a father."

"And the bad?" asked Mr. Swan.

"Big Owl kidnapped your three cygnets," sighed Rufus.

Mr. Swan frowned, "So what's the other good news?"

"We're willing to rescue the cygnets for no extra charge," Rufus smiled weakly.

The swan pointed a wing at Rufus, "I think you've done enough. Just leave us alone. I'll win that contest for Big Owl. I'll rescue my family."

He turned to go back to the band before he was missed. Rufus tried to stop him.

"You can't trust Big Owl. Tomorrow's special is roast swan," said Rufus.

"Go away," said Mr. Swan. "I don't need Gufus Goose and Poofy Paws getting me in deeper trouble."

"That's Puffy Paws and Rufus Goose. Don't you understand? We're here to help," Rufus tried to explain.

"Like you did with my eggs?" said the angry swan.

The swan waddled back to the stage. The owls were still playing. Puffy Paws was still putting on a show. The swan picked up his horn and blew it loudly to get everyone's attention. The band stopped playing.

"We've got work to do," commanded the swan. "Stop playing around."

"Sure thing, Cobb," said the lizard.

Then he looked at Puffy. "Your goose friend is waiting for you in the woods. You're just a big distraction."

"Thanks," said Puffy happily. "I try to be."

Puffy joined Rufus in the woods. The cat followed the goose back to the lake. Puffy climbed in his bucket. Rufus climbed back to the motor.

"Where are we going now?" asked Puffy happily. He had a good time dancing.

"Home," said Rufus. "We're done here."

"But we're private eyes," argued Puffy. "When there's trouble, we're there on the double. Remember?"

"We're terrible private eyes," sighed Rufus. "We're not even good egg sitters."

Chapter 9
The Mystery Creature

Rufus stopped the boat in the middle of the lake. The goose hopped out of the boat and floated on the water. Puffy didn't know what to think. The goose honked softly.

"Puffy, get out of the boat," whispered Rufus.

"No," said Puffy. "It's wet out there."

Rufus pointed to his bag of disguises. Puffy soon saw what the goose was whispering about. The bag moved. Puffy knew he was ferocious, but he decided it was better to be ferocious outside the boat.

The cat quietly lowered his bucket over the side of the boat. Next, he climbed in it carefully. He jumped once when his tail almost got wet. The goose and the cat floated alongside the boat.

"Now what?" asked the cat. It was too far to float to shore.

"One of us is going to have to see what's in that bag," said Rufus.

"Good idea," said Puffy. "You open the bag. If it's something bad, I'll scare it."

Rufus sighed. He could just fly away. Then again, he didn't want to leave Puffy behind. He also wanted his disguises back.

The goose cautiously approached the boat, "Hello in the bag. Can we help you?"

A face with black glasses, a big nose, and a black moustache peeked out at Rufus. The goose recognized the face. Then he realized the face was wearing one of his disguises.

"Hello," the face spoke slowly. "I… need… a… ride… to… town."

The voice spoke very slowly. Rufus was a little less afraid. The goose swam closer to the boat. Puffy did face exercises to get ready to look ferocious, just in case he was needed.

"I…need…to…find…Rufus…R…Goose," spoke the voice.

"Why?" asked Rufus. He wasn't ready to tell the voice who he was until he knew more about the creature in the bag.

"Where's…there's…trouble…he's…there…on…the…double," said the voice.

"And don't forget the ferocious Puffy Paws," said Puffy from the bucket.

"I…won't," answered the voice.

"Climb out of the bag," ordered Rufus.

Slowly the head poked out. Then a claw scratched against the bottom of the boat. By now Rufus could see the shell forcing open the zipper. After seeing the animal, Rufus flapped his wings and fluttered back into the boat. Puffy soon joined him, but he wasn't nearly as graceful as he stumbled over the side, rocking the boat.

The turtle slowly explained that her husband was missing.

"And you want us to egg sit?" asked Puffy.

The turtle looked confused, "Of…course…not…please… find…him."

It took a while, but Rufus finally got the whole story out of the turtle. Her husband had gone out to buy some eggs. After a goose refused to sell him some swan eggs, he went to Big Owl's Grocery Store. Mr. Turtle never returned.

Mrs. Turtle said she could pay Rufus to find her husband. She reached back into the duffle bag. The turtle slowly pulled out a little purse. She turned it upside down and shook it.

Five coins fell on the bottom of the boat. Rufus was surprised to see that much money. He had never met a rich turtle before. Suddenly, Rufus was very interested, but not because he wanted the money.

There was something strange about the coins. They had a nice yellow color. They also looked very old. The goose scooped one up in his wings. He looked at it very closely.

"Where did you get this money?" he asked the turtle.

"From…the…Golden…Salamander," answered the turtle.

"There's a salamander made of gold that gives you coins?" asked Puffy.

"No, no," The turtle went on to explain that the Golden Salamander was a steamboat. Before Blue Rock Lake became a lake, it was Blue Rock River. A boat load of gold sank in the river over 150 years ago. That boat was called the Golden Salamander.

Then a dam was built on the river. The river became a lake. Mr. Turtle was diving one day and found the sunken boat. He took a few of the coins, just because they were shiny. Then the turtle discovered he could buy things with the coins. That's when he went to Mr. Owl's store.

"I wonder what Mr. Owl is up to," said Rufus.

"He's probably resting," said Puffy. "Kidnapping all those animals has got to be tiring."

Rufus scooped up the rest of the coins. He slipped them back into the purse. He handed it back to Mrs. Turtle. The turtle frowned.

"Don't worry, Mrs. Turtle. We'll help you for free. Big Owl is up to something and if we don't figure it out, I have a feeling we'll all be in trouble."

Rufus looked at Puffy. "I need you to find the most talented animals you can. We have a contest to win tonight."

"I can help," said Mrs. Turtle.

"You didn't talk slowly," Puffy pointed out.

The turtle blushed, "I'm just so excited." She chattered.

"What are you going to do?" Puffy asked Rufus.

The goose reached into his disguise bag. He pulled out an inflatable costume. He pulled a cord. The costume made a hissing sound as it filled with air. The huge wings stuck out over the edge of the boat.

"I'm going undercover at the condor club."

The goose climbed into the costume. He pushed a button. Little propellers on the wings began to spin. The condor lifted off from the boat.

Chapter 10
The New Big Owl

Rufus flew toward the Condor Club. As he passed over the dam, the goose noticed something strange. Lightfingers Lenny was painting red circles on the top of the dam. Rufus would have stopped to investigate, but he didn't have any time to waste.

Rufus blended right in as he landed his costume. Dozens of condors were busy getting ready for the big contest. Condors were sweeping the aisles. A few were on stage painting scenery. It was the biggest event of the year. This was the major fundraiser for the Save the Condor Foundation. It was all for a good cause.

The Condor Club was a huge outdoor theater. It had to be huge. Condors are big birds. Rufus knew what it felt like to be huge.

The condor costume worked great in the air. It was hard for a goose to move around in on the ground. The goose decided it was time for a disguise change. It was a good thing he has stuffed his disguise kit in the storage bay of the condor costume.

The goose stepped behind some bushes. He slipped out of the condor costume. He was trying to decide what to put on next. Suddenly, he heard two birds talking on the other side of the bushes.

"When my Horned Owls band wins, I want you to deliver the trophy to Lightfingers Lenny. He'll be standing in a big red circle so you can't miss him."

"That's if you win the contest," corrected a condor. "As head judge, I'm going to make sure this contest is fair and square."

Rufus peaked through the bushes. Big Owl didn't look so big next to a condor. The huge bird towered over Big Owl. Rufus began to understand something.

Big Owl wanted that trophy very badly. He also couldn't bully the condors into it, like he could with the smaller animals. There was only one thing he could do. Big Owl's band had to win fair and square. Well, sort of. He had to force Mr. Swan, the best trumpeter on the whole lake, to play with the group.

As he watched Big Owl and the condor walk off in two different directions, Rufus suddenly got inspired. He knew exactly what costume he should wear. He was surprised he hadn't thought of it sooner.

As Rufus stepped from the bushed he was knocked over by a cart. The condor who had been pushing the cart stopped.

"Are you okay little fella?" asked the condor.

Rufus was a little woozy. As his head cleared up, he pointed to the cart.

"Where did you get that?"

"Isn't it a beauty? We bought this from a weasel. We just painted it gold."

Rufus recognized it as the bomb that was stolen from the hare force base.

"What are you going to do with it?" stammered Rufus.

"It's the first prize trophy for the contest tonight," said the condor. "Are you in it? If so, this could be yours."

Rufus suddenly had all the information he needed. He wondered if he had enough time to use all he knew, before it was too late. He quickly ducked into the bushes again. He pulled out a notepad and scribbled some directions. The next thing he needed was on the stage. He found just what he was looking for, a half-full bucket of gray paint.

A half-hour later, Lightfingers Lenny was surprised to see his boss. He wasn't surprised when he found out his boss was angry with him again. He was always doing something wrong. Like the time Big Owl asked for a chocolate shake. Lenny brought him a chocolate covered rattle snake. Big Owl wasn't happy. The snake was one of his best customers. The snake wasn't very happy, either. Chocolate made its skin break out.

"You put the red circle in the wrong place!" said Big Owl.

"You gave me directions, see?" Lightfingers held out a piece of paper.

"Those are the wrong directions," said Big Owl. "You've made a mess here."

He handed the raccoon another piece of paper and a small bucket of gray paint.

"Paint over these red circles with the gray paint. Then paint ☐ the red circles in the right place."

"Do you still want me to catch the trophy?" asked Lightfingers.

Big Owl thought for a moment, "No. Take the night off."

Lightfingers smiled, "Yes sir, Boss."

"And tell everyone at the restaurant to take the night off, too," added Big Owl as he flew off.

Rufus was rather pleased with himself as he flew off. Lenny completely fell for the costume.

By the time Rufus arrived at the Condor Club, the talent contest was well underway. He hoped he wasn't too late. He also hoped Puffy had made it.

Rufus decided to try out the owl costume one more time. He circled over the theater until he spotted Big Owl. Rufus was glad to see that he wasn't on the boat. The goose flew to the boat.

Two vultures were guarding the walkway to the boat. They were half asleep. Rufus landed right in front of them. The startled birds jumped to attention and saluted.

"It's good to see you two working so hard," said Rufus, speaking in his deepest voice to sound like Big Owl.

Just then, the crowds began to cheer. Cobb and the Horned Owls were taking the stage. The vultures strained to see the show. They expected the boss's band to win easily.

"Why don't you two go enjoy the show?" asked Rufus.

"Thanks, Big Owl," said the vulture.

"You can call me, Big," said Rufus.

The two vultures strolled off. One of them turned back to say thanks. Instead, he got a puzzled look on his face. He watched Rufus walk on up to the boat.

"Did you notice something different about the boss?" said the vulture who had been watching Rufus.

"Not at all," said the other vulture. "If there was something different I would have picked up on it. They don't call me hawk eye for nothing."

Rufus began peaking in windows. Most of the rooms were empty. Finally, he came to a window covered with bars. He looked inside. First, he saw Penny Swan. Then he saw the three cygnets and Mr. Turtle. He was keeping the cygnets entertained.

They were playing hide-n-seek. Mr. Turtle would duck into his shell. The cygnets were running all around the room looking for him. Then he would pop his head out of his shell and surprise them.

Rufus found a set of keys next to the padlocked door. He quickly opened the door. Mrs. Swan spread her wings. She covered her cygnets.

"Stay away from us Big Owl," warned the swan.

The goose pulled off his mask.

"Rufus? Rufus R. Goose?" replied Penny Swan in great surprise.

"Where there's trouble, I'm there on the double," smiled Rufus.

Chapter 11
Puffy and the Eagles

Rufus led Penny, Mr. Turtle, and the cygnets to the bushes. He found each of them costumes. The cygnets were disguised as cute ducklings. Mr. Turtle was disguised as a crab. Penny was disguised as a peacock.

Penny got to see her husband play one song with the Horned Owls. Mr. Swan was a magnificent trumpeter. She was as proud as a peacock. She was certainly dressed right.

Everyone was sure that Cobb and the Horned Owls were going to win. The three owls and the lizard took a bow. Cobb looked so worried. The cheering crowds didn't make him happy.

One last group had to perform. A condor in a tuxedo came on stage. He read off a note card.

"Our last group is called Puffy and the Eagles singing their newest song called: I'm Not Bald, I'm Just Feather Challenged."

The curtain pulled back. Four turtles began to snap in unison. Three eagles played instruments. One played guitar, another played bass. The third played keyboards. Five hummingbirds and two canaries gathered around microphones. On a stool behind the drum set was a bucket. Out of it flopped a fish. It bounced between the drums. It was Jo Jo Finn, the most famous drum fish in the whole lake.

The eagles started playing. The birds began to hum and sing. The lights grew brighter on stage. Suddenly, stick rockets flew above the stage. It created smoke that floated around the musicians.

Out of the smoke came an animal. Rufus couldn't believe his eyes. It was Puffy Paws. The cat began to do his ferocious feline dance. The crowd cheered.

The more they cheered, the more ferocious Puffy felt. The animals were going wild. There were wings flapping, paws clapping, and talons tapping. Puffy and the Eagles was a hit with everyone, except Big Owl.

All the animals were paying attention to the band. They didn't notice what the old owl was up to. He had gotten the attention of the two vultures. He led them to the trophy.

The owl realized he wasn't going to win the trophy. Still the condors were so distracted by Puffy Paws, they didn't notice as the owl stole the bomb trophy. He gave the vultures the same instructions that he had told the condor earlier that day. They were to drop it on the red circle target. Next, he found a couple of falcons that worked for him.

"It's time to prepare my boat guests for tomorrow's special," he told them. "Turtle soup and roast swan with cygnet appetizers."

"I just love this kind of work," said one of the falcons as they swooped toward the boat.

"They don't call you the Vulture for nothing," smiled the other falcon.

Puffy and the Eagles were near the end of their second song when there was a loud explosion by the lake. Big Owl had a wide smile on his face as all the animals ran and flew by to see what had happened.

"I believe the trophy went boom, boom," he laughed to himself. "Bye, bye Blue Rocks Lake. Hello Golden Salamander sunken treasure. I'm rich! I'm rich!"

Big Owl joyfully followed the crowd, expecting to see Blue Rocks Lake draining into the town. He thought it was such a perfect plan. The turtle told him where to find the ship. With the water gone, he could get all the gold. He would be the richest owl, ever.

When Big Owl reached the lake shore, the animals weren't staring at the dam. They were looking the other way. There was a bright fire in the sky. It was coming from a pile of rubble that used to be Big Owl's Restaurant and Boat Dock.

Lightfingers Lenny came up to Big Owl, "I followed your directions. I painted the circles on the roof of the restaurant. Thanks for not having me catch the trophy. It would have taken some pretty heavy fingers to catch that."

"What!" cried Big Owl as his beak turned red.

Just then, a whole flock of police ducks landed around Big Owl. It just so happened that most of the jailbirds had been taken off to another prison that day. The ducks needed the extra space for Big Owl and his gang.

Penny found her husband, Cobb, in the crowd. She introduced the cygnets to their father. He didn't know what to say. He was happy to see his family, but the cygnets looked like ugly ducklings. Then Penny had them take off their disguises. Cobb was relieved to see his children were beautiful swans.

Mrs. Turtle was happy to see her husband. The two said goodbye to Rufus. Mrs. Turtle gave the goose a quick hug. Then the two turtles slipped into the lake and swam home. Rufus felt something in his pocket. Inside was the little coin purse filled with five gold coins. Four police ducks surrounded Rufus.

"You're under arrest Big Owl," said the duck from the police station.

Rufus pulled off his Big Owl disguise. Just then, Puffy Paws walked up. The police duck smiled. He handed a card to Puffy and another card to Rufus. The two looked at the cards.

"We're licensed egg sitters!" cheered Puffy.

"Are you sure you don't want to be a big star? You were a real hit tonight," honked Rufus.

"No," said Puffy Paws. "I need something that takes advantage of my ferociousness, like private eye work and egg sitting. Hopefully the eagles can make it without me."

"I know I couldn't Puffy," smiled Rufus. "I wouldn't even want to try."

The Bobcat Cowboys Take the Cake Part 1

Table of Contents

Chapter		Page
1	Here Comes the Bridle	168
2	The White Horse	171
3	Time in the Pen	174
4	Frazzle and Starlet	177
5	Ewe-haw!	179

Vocabulary Words

appetizer

bridle

corral

mutton

notorious

by Brian Davis

Starlet Fussybunny and Frazzle O'Hare are about to be married. They are planning a wedding without bobcats. Is that possible in Rowdent Gulch?

Chapter 1
Here Comes the Bridle

Bobbybill and Bubba lifted the gate onto the hinges. The new corral was now finished. Billybob would be back at anytime with their new livestock. He had the animals hidden on the mountain. The bobcats didn't want the rightful owners to steal them back.

"It's good to learn something new," said Bubba.

"You mean corral building or sheep rustling?" asked Bobbybill.

"Sheepback riding," said Bubba. "It will be nice to not have to walk everywhere."

"Oh, that," said Bobbybill. "It will also make our getaways much quicker. Think of all the time we'll save. We were really getting behind on our bank robbing."

"If we don't have the time, we can't do the crime," grunted Billybob as he joined the conversation.

He'd just arrived with the sheep. The bobcat had ropes around the sheep's necks. Billybob led them into the corral. The sheep trotted around the pen looking for a way to escape.

"I know how we can save time," said Bobbybill. "We can just eat the sheep. That way we don't have to steal to get money to buy things from Otto Muskrat's store."

Billybob sighed, "It was a lot easier when we could just steal things from Otto's store."

"Then he went and put up that NO STEALING sign," nodded Bobbybill.

"Oh well. After we paid Otto to have Davy Beaver deliver all the stuff we stole, it was cheaper to buy it anyway," said Billybob. "Now that Davy's working for him again, he has free delivery when you actually pay for your stuff."

"Maybe we should have stolen Davy Beaver, too," suggested Bobbybill.

"Oh no! He would eat us out of house and home," said Billybob. "Think of all the things we have that are made from wood."

"We could steal the NO STEALING sign," suggested Bobbybill.

Billybob smiled, "That's a good idea. I'm glad to see my smartness rubbing off on you."

"Some rubbed off on me, too," said Bubba. "Then I took a bath."

"You're right there," said Bobbybill. "You're clean out of smartness."

"I like the sheep," said Bubba as he reached through the corral and patted them on the head. "They're so wooly. They'll be comfortable to ride."

"When can we start?" asked Bobbybill.

"As soon as those bridles arrive," answered Billybob. "We can't go sheepback riding if we can't steer. You did order those bridles, didn't you Bubba?"

"I put the order in the mail today. I still have an extra order form if we ever need to replace one. Here it is," Bubba handed the paper to Billybob.

"Why would we need to replace one?" asked Billybob.

"I've heard a lot of sheep have been stolen lately. Three were taken outside of Rowdent Gulch two days ago," explained Bubba.

"Two days ago?" asked Bobbybill. "Isn't that when we were stealing these three sheep outside of Rowdent Gulch?"

"Yep," said Bubba. "It's a good thing we didn't run into those sheep wrestlers."

"That's sheep rustlers, Bubba," corrected Billybob. "Not sheep wrestlers."

"So, don't wrestle with them again, Bubba. You got them all dizzy," added Bobbybill.

"But I was winning," smiled Bubba. "I'm pretty good at sheep wrestling."

"Bubba," Billybob was looking at the order form. "What is this?"

"That's the order form for the bridles. See?" Bubba pointed to the lines on the paper. "I put our names on this line. Then I put our ages here, and our height and weight on the next line. Then you check a box that asks if you're ugly or good looking."

"Why would they ask us all those questions?" asked Bobbybill.

"To make sure we get the right kind of bridle," explained Bubba. "And, if you're ugly, they'll send you a handsome bridle so everyone has something nice to look at."

"Did you check ugly or good looking for me?" asked Bobbybill.

"Ugly, of course. I knew you'd want a handsome bridle," said Bubba.

"Thanks," smiled Bobbybill.

"Wait," said Billybob. He shook the order form. "This isn't for mail order bridles. It says mail order brides. Bubba, you went and ordered us some wives!"

"Oh no!" cried Bubba. "We're going to need three more sheep. Give me that order form and I'll send for more bridles."

Billybob tore the order form into tiny pieces. He ground it into the dirt with the heel of his boot. Bubba looked upset. He picked up the pieces of paper.

"Our wives aren't going to like riding sheep they can't steer," said Bubba.

"Hush-up, Bubba," said Billybob. "We're not getting married to some mail order brides."

"Because it would break the hearts of all the girl bobcats around here?" asked Bobbybill.

"No," explained Billybob. "Mrs. Bobcats think they have to run everything. First, they'll want us to wash our paws before eating. Then they'll want us to say please and thank you when we're holding up stagecoaches. The next thing you know, they'll only want us to rob slow trains, because fast ones are too dangerous."

"But isn't that like mom?" asked Bobbybill.

"Before Daddybob married Momma, he was the most notorious bobcat in the whole territory. Afterwards, he was only the most notorious bobcat in Rowdent Gulch," Billybob reminded them.

"Momma didn't want Daddybob to travel," Bobbybill remembered.

"She wanted Daddybob to teach us everything he knew," said Bubba. "Remember when he used to take us ambushing?"

"And chicken thievin'," Billybob remembered with a smile. "Those were great father-cub times. I don't think we would have turned out as well as we did if it weren't for those times with Daddybob."

"We might have ended up honest," Bobbybill shuddered.

"Then poor old Sheriff Prairie Dog would have nothing to do," said Bubba.

"What would the whole town do without us?" added Bobbybill. "If we didn't break things and steal things, half the stores would close down. Critters would lose their jobs. Cubs and pups would go hungry. Rowdent Gulch might become a ghost town."

"And ghosts are scary," added Bubba.

"There's only one thing to do," said Billybob. "We'll have to stop the pony express and get the order back. We don't want to end up with three brides."

"We were supposed to rob the toy store today," said Bobbybill.

"We'll just have to reschedule," said Billybob.

"But I'm out of bubbles," sighed Bubba.

Chapter 2
The White Horse

A white horse rested by a little stream. It pulled a little snack from a leather pouch. The horse bit off the end and spit it on the ground. The horse whinnied happily.

"My favorite, a Horsy Way Bar. Chocolate coating, creamy filling, and crispy clover hay. Yum, yum."

The horse was enjoying the candy so much; he didn't notice what was happening on the rocks above him. Billybob lowered the fishing line. The mailbag was almost hooked. Just then, a large fish splashed out of the water and snatched the hook.

The fish dove under the water. The line pulled tight. Billybob was pulled right off the rocks. The bobcat landed squarely on the back of the horse. The horse choked on the Horsy Way Bar. The coughing horse tossed Billybob right in the stream.

Bobbybill didn't want to waste the opportunity. While the horse was trying to breathe and Billybob was trying to swim, Bobbybill climbed down the rocks to take the mail bag. Bubba noticed the white horse was turning red.

The horse's face was turning red. Bubba grabbed the horse around the middle and squeezed. The Horsy Way Bar flew out of the horse's throat. The white horse gasped to catch his breath. Bubba set him back down.

"That was a pretty powerful squeeze," said the horse. "I think you'd be a good sheep wrestler."

"I try to practice whenever I can," said Bubba.

Bobbybill interrupted, "I can't find the order form."

The horse turned around and saw the bobcat, "Stop that. It's against the law to steal mail."

"It's okay," explained Bobbybill. "I have lots of experience breaking laws."

"We're not stealing the mail," Bubba explained. "We're just taking it."

"Oh, that's different," said the horse. Then he thought for a second. "How is that different?"

"We're taking our own mail," said Bubba. "I accidentally ordered three wives. I'm sure that happens all the time."

"Not often," said the horse. "I did have someone accidentally order three bridles last week, but never three wives. Three of their children were getting married. It was a pig family if I remember right."

"What were they if you didn't remember right?" asked Bubba.

The horse started laughing as he thought of the story. "It had to have been pigs. I remember putting the letter in the pig pocket now. I don't like to get the rest of the mail muddy. Let me remember. They were trying to get their sons mail order brides. Instead, they ordered mail order bridles. Have you ever heard of anything so silly?"

Bobbybill and Bubba were laughing, too. They couldn't believe someone could make such a silly mistake. That suddenly reminded them of their own problem. They still hadn't found their order form.

"But where's our letter?" asked Bobbybill. "You didn't steal it, did you? That would be a low-down, good-for-nothing thing to do."

"Did you mail your letter at a farm or in Rowdent Gulch?" asked the horse.

"In Rowdent Gulch, just after we robbed Peppy Possum's Pizza Parlor," explained Bobbybill.

"You stole pizza?" asked the horse.

"No," explained Bobbybill. "I stole some soap bubbles. I had some dirty pans to wash."

"That will take the grime out of crime," said the horse. "But you know stealing soap bubbles is a hangin' crime."

"I know," said Bobbybill. "Judge Polecat made me wash Peppy's pans after I got caught. That's hard to do when I'm hanging upside down from a tree limb like a possum."

"I guess you learned your lesson," said the horse.

"Yes," answered Bobbybill, "Always wear rubber gloves when scrubbing pans. My paws were getting red. I'll have to steal some when I get a chance."

The horse took the mail bag away from Bobbybill. He fastened the buckle. The horse tossed his baggage on his back. He checked his watch.

"My break time is over. I need to get going," said the horse. "I never had your letter."

"How do you know?" asked Bubba.

"I'm the white horse. I carry letters for the Livestock Postal Service. You need to find the brown horse. She carries the letters for the Critter Postal Service," explained the horse.

The two bobcats thanked the horse. They walked off to find the brown horse. As they left the stream, something didn't feel quite the same. Bubba and Bobbybill seemed to be missing something. They sat down on a rock and tried to figure out what it was. They thought and thought.

"Is it bigger than a breadbox?" asked Bubba.

"I think so," answered Bobbybill.

"Is it animal, vegetable, or mineral?" asked Bubba.

"I'm thinking it was some low-down critter, so let's go with animal," answered Bobbybill.

"Was it a pig?" asked Bubba.

"It did have a funny smell, but I don't think it was a pig," answered Bobbybill.

"Was it something you try to avoid, like a skunk?" asked Bubba.

"Yes, I think we do try to avoid it. But what is it?" asked Bobbybill.

"I give up," said Bubba. "Maybe we should ask Billybob."

"Right, let's ask…Billybob!" exclaimed Bobbybill. "That's it. We're missing Billybob."

The two bobcats retraced their steps. They went back to the stream. Bubba pretended to save the horse. The two bobcats climbed back up the rocks. Finally, they remembered. The last time they saw Billybob, he was flying off the rocks toward the stream.

"Billybob!" yelled Bobbybill.

"Billybob Bobcat, where are you?" yelled Bubba.

There was no answer. The bobcats waded out into the stream. The water was up over their paws. They didn't like getting wet.

"Maybe he's looking for the brown horse," said Bubba.

Bobbybill shook his head no. "He doesn't know about the brown horse."

"You don't think he…," Bubba started to say.

Bobbybill interrupted, "Don't even say it. It's unthinkable."

"Took a bath?" Bubba finished anyway.

"I told you not to say it," groaned Bobbybill.

Bobbybill and Bubba took another step to see if they could see further downstream. Instead, Bubba slipped on a rock. He reached out for Bobbybill. The two bobcats splashed in the stream. The current swept them away.

Chapter 3
Time in the Pen

Harley Hawg was sitting on a log at the edge of a steam. His bamboo fishing pole suddenly began to bend. The hog pulled and pulled. He was afraid his pole was going to break. Finally, the hog landed his catch.

"What did you catch?" grunted Ima Hawg.

She was just walking back from the garden. The hog carried a basket of corn. Mrs. Hawg bent over the catch.

"Is it alive?" squealed Ima.

Harley poked it with his fishing pole. Water squirted from its mouth. The big hog picked it up with by the tail. Water dripped off the catch.

"It's alive," snorted Harley. "These things have nine lives. I think it just needs a little first aid. Just put your snout over that mouth and breathe."

"I'm not letting my snout touch that thing," said Ima Hawg. "It better start breathing on its own."

Suddenly, the soaked body let out a gasp. It started to sputter. The animal shook all over. It splattered all over the two hogs.

Ima was upset, "I just took a mud bath. Now look at me. I'm all wet."

"You don't need mud on your face to look beautiful," smiled Harley.

"Harley! I think I recognize that thing," said Ima as she pointed at his catch. "It's another one of those bobcat cowboys. I wonder which one it is."

Harley sniffed at the bobcat, "I think it smells like Bubba. He has that pineapple, marshmallow burger smell."

Just then a piglet came squealing, "Look, look, I caught something. Can we eat it for lunch?"

He pointed to his fishing pole. At the end of it was Bobbybill. The cat was clawing at the ground, trying to get away. The piglet pulled the rod.

"You're not getting away. I caught you fair and square," said the piglet.

"Honey," said Ima, "We don't eat bobcats. They're bad for you. They'll give you a tummy ache. Besides, we know these bobcats. We don't eat our friends."

"Can't we just this one time?" asked the piglet.

"Do what your mommy says," groaned Bobbybill.

The piglet put down the pole. "Will you at least spit out my rubber frog?"

"I wondered why it was so chewy," said Bobbybill.

He gave the frog back to the piglet. Bubba and Bobbybill were shivering. They weren't used to getting wet. Ima began to feel motherly toward the bobcats.

"I'll take these two bobcats to the other one," said Ima. "Then I guess I better pick some more corn. We're having a lot of guests tonight."

"The other one?" asked Bobbybill. "Is Billybob here?"

"We caught him trying to steal our bridles," explained Ima. "If he had asked for the bridles we would have given them to him. We don't need them. We ordered them by mistake. But he was trying to rob us so he's doing time in the pen"

"Oh no," said Bobbybill. "He's not very good at multiplication problems."

"Not times," said Ima as she walked the bobcats up to the barn. "Today, my piglets are learning how to read clocks. My oldest daughter, Ada is teaching them."

"I want to do time, too," said Bubba excitedly. "I don't think a bobcat can ever be too smart."

"I have to agree with you, Bubba," said Ima.

"Do I have to steal something first?" asked Bubba.

Ima nudged the latch on the gate. She trotted through the mud. The piglets were in the corner learning all about clock reading. The mother hog dumped the corn in a trough.

"Now that I have dinner ready, we can eat right after school. You two go on over and learn all you can. We'll be eating in a few minutes. And don't get any dust on my muddy floor. I just watered it."

Bobbybill and Bubba shook the dust off their feet. They walked over to the little desk and took a seat. Ada Hawg was pointing to a large teaching clock. She explained that their clock had two hooves. The large hoof pointed to the minutes. The small hoof pointed to the hours.

Billybob looked like he was in pain. Having to think hard gave him headaches. He was glad to see his brothers. He hoped they could do some of the thinking for him. He asked Bobbybill to study the long hoof. Billybob would study the short hoof. Bubba would try to remember the order of the numbers on the clock. Together, they could almost tell time.

The class time was soon over. The piglets were dismissed. They all rushed to the trough. Ima pulled out a few ears of corn for the bobcats. She had them sit at the guest trough. Ima soon returned to the piglets' trough. Two of her children were fighting over a worm they found in an ear of corn. She took it away from them.

"No dessert until you've finished eating your dinner," she scolded them.

The bobcats looked at the muddy corn. It wasn't their favorite meal. Harley joined them at the trough. Bobbybill didn't want to eat corn, but he knew Ima would never let him just walk away.
He would need to make her angry. It was the only polite thing a bobcat could do. He decided to tell a joke instead.

"What's the difference between an ear of corn with a beard and a bunny rabbit?" said Bobbybill loudly.

All the pigs stopped to listen. Bobbybill went on.

"One is a long ear with hairs. The other is a hare with long ears!"

The piglets started squealing with laughter. Ima wasn't smiling. Bobbybill had broken her number one rule; no corny jokes at the table. You could joke about tomatoes, carrots, or even watermelon, but not corn.

Ima was very fond of the sweet, golden kernels. And no one could dump it in a trough quite like her. Harley said she always added in just the right amount of mud.

Ima kicked Bobbybill out of the pen. "If you're going to joke about corn, you'll just have to sit out here and eat some of the fish Harley caught."

"This is what I deserve," said Bobbybill as he licked his lips.

Ima Hawg sighed, "I just can't do this to you. Come back in and get your snout into the guest trough. You've been through enough today."

"Why did the ear of corn jump in the milk pail?" Bobbybill quickly replied.

Ima got a scowl on her face. "Why," she snorted.

"Because it wanted to get creamed!" he answered.

All the piglets squealed with delight. "Tell some more," they begged.

Bobbybill was sure he was going to get the fish now. Instead, Ima led him to the head of the trough. She piled up several ears of corn. Then she added a fresh topping of mud.

"Anyone who brings my children so much joy, deserve all the corn they can eat."

So, Ima watched while Bobbybill ate every miserable bite. Then Harley gave each of the bobcats a catfish. Bobbybill was too stuffed with muddy corn to eat his. So, Bubba and Billybob helped him out.

The hogs gave the bobcats three bridles. The bobcats said thank you. The little hoof was pointing on the eight. The big hoof was pointing to the twelve. It was time for the piglets to go to bed. So, the bobcats took the bridles and left.

"I wonder why the piglets had to go to bed at 4:30?" asked Bobbybill.

"They're just not good at telling time like us," said Billybob.

"It was good to see the Hawgs again," sighed Bubba. "And that corn was delicious. We even got free bridles. It was a perfect day!"

"You forgot about almost drowning, eating mud, doing time in the pen, and most of all, ordering us some wives," corrected Billybob.

"You're right," admitted Bubba. "It was almost a perfect day."

"Hush-up, Bubba," said Billybob.

Chapter 4
Frazzle and Starlet

It had been a perfect day. The food was delicious. The smell in the air was sweet. The water in the stream was cool and relaxing.

It's hard to believe how different Frazzle O'Hare's day was from the bobcat cowboys. He had spent the afternoon on a picnic with his beloved and beautiful Miss Starlet Fussybunny. They had hopped among the sweet-smelling wildflowers, dipped their big bunny feet into the stream. Then the couple dined on fresh carrot cake and strawberries.

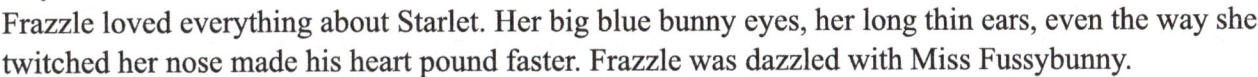

Now, they soaked in the last sun rays as they sat on a rock and watched the sunset. Frazzle loved everything about Starlet. Her big blue bunny eyes, her long thin ears, even the way she twitched her nose made his heart pound faster. Frazzle was dazzled with Miss Fussybunny.

"I'm thinking of a June wedding," Starlet said softly.

"That's several months away," Frazzle pointed out. "Are you sure you want to wait that long?"

"It's not several months away," Starlet pointed out. "June is several miles away."

"How can a month be miles away?" Frazzle was confused.

"Not the month, Silly," said Miss Fussybunny. "June LaPurr."

Miss Fussybunny pulled out the latest issue of Gettin' Hitched Magazine. It was the favorite source for wedding ideas in Rowdent Gulch. The March issue had an article about a famous wedding planner named, June LaPurr.

Her sisters, April and May also helped with the weddings. May was a famous florist. May Flowers were shipped all around the territory. April loved to plan the bridal showers. April always brought May Flowers to the showers.

"I want our wedding to be perfect," said Starlet. "Just like my future husband."

"I'll tell the bobcats to be on their best behavior," said Frazzle.

"Bobcats! Do you mean those bobcat cowboys?" The hair raised on the back of her neck at the mention of the notorious bobcat cowboys.

"I've got to invite them," explained Frazzle. "I'm their attorney. They're my best customers."

"Well," sighed Miss Fussybunny. "You did defend them brilliantly. You did get them off with only some time in the pen."

"And hangin'," added Frazzle proudly. "Don't forget all three bobcats had to hang."

"Bubba did do a nice job hanging my curtains," admitted Miss Fussybunny. "Still I'm not sure how our other guests will feel about bobcats at the wedding."

"Maybe if we had lots of appetizers on hand," thought Frazzle.

"What would be good appetizers for bobcats?" asked Starlet.

"You mean, besides the other guests?" replied Frazzle. "Maybe I should ask Alice McHoot in court next week. Wait, I don't want to ask an owl about food. She may decide to show me rather than tell me."

"I don't want you hanging around that owl anyway. You'll be a married rabbit soon. I don't want you to fall for her owly ways. I've seen the way she looks at you," warned Miss Starlet.

"I'll keep my distance," shuddered Frazzle at the thought.

"Now, if you could just keep your distance from those bobcats, we'll have the perfect wedding," added Starlet.

"They're sure to find out," said Frazzle. "The whole town will know about the wedding. If we don't invite the bobcats, it will hurt their feelings."

"The bobcats have feelings?" Miss Fussybunny was genuinely surprised.

"Underneath all those teeth and claws, they're just like little kittens," explained Frazzle, "Especially Bubba. They wouldn't want to be left out. It's not like we're eloping or anything."

"Eloping?" asked Miss Fussybunny.

"You know. Getting married without a big wedding, just a few critters," Frazzle explained. "If no one came to the wedding, how could the bobcats feel left out?"

"Hmmm…" thought Miss Fussybunny. "We could have a secret wedding. We would invite all the best critters in town, no predators. Then when the bobcats find out you got married, you could say you eloped."

"It sounds awfully tough to do," sighed Frazzle. "All the critters in town will have to keep it a secret."

"Now, we'll have the wedding at the church and the reception at the Checker Hall."

Frazzle nodded in agreement, "Then we'll get married the last Saturday of the month."

"Why then?" asked Starlet.

"That's when they play for all the new wedding gifts at the Saturday checker tournament," answered Frazzle.

"Perfect!" smiled Miss Fussybunny. "I'm pretty good at checkers."

Frazzle would do anything to make his beloved Miss Fussybunny happy. He agreed not to invite the Bobcats. They would have their secret wedding. It would still be a big wedding planned by June LaPurr and her sisters, April and May.

Frazzle hitched the sheep back to the buggy. The couple rode back into town. Miss Fussybunny wanted to start making plans right away.

They stopped at the telegraph office. The couple sent for the LaPurr sisters. Frazzle was going to make sure his bride had the most beautiful, secret wedding ever in Rowdent Gulch.

"Imagine," smiled Starlet Fussybunny, "A wedding without any bobcats. It will be wonderful."

Chapter 5
Ewe-haw!

The bobcats hid out in their cave for two weeks. They didn't go into town to pick up their mail. The bobcats were afraid they would get a box full of brides. They knew the mail carrier wouldn't leave them in the mailbox. Bobcat brides are too big for that.

"If we see a female bobcat, how will we know it's our mail order brides?" asked Bubba. "We can't run and hide from every female bobcat we meet."

"We can try," answered Billybob.

"Won't that break all their hearts?" asked Bobbybill.

"You've got a point there, Bobbybill," said Billybob. "Well, it's got to cost some money to mail three bobcats. I guess we look for the bobcats that are covered with stamps."

"That should be easy enough," said Bobbybill. "Can we leave the cave, now? I'm getting hungry."

"I've been cooking every day," said Bubba. "Don't you like that new recipe I got?"

"The one from Ima Hawg?" asked Bobbybill. "I can't eat another bite of that low-down, good for nothing muddy corn. In fact, I haven't eaten it for the last week."

"And look how fit and trim you are," said Bubba. "I think my cooking is good for you."

Bobbybill rubbed the spot in the air where his chubby tummy used to be. "That's what I said. It's good for nothing. There's nothing here anymore. Maybe one of those mail order brides would be a good thing. Maybe she could cook some real bobcat food: blueberry possum pie, roasted blackbirds with homemade gravy…"

All that talk was making Billybob hungry, too. The bobcats decided it was worth the risk to go out. They would just be careful to avoid any stamp covered female bobcats. They had just enough time to catch the noon stagecoach.

The bobcats went out to their new corral. Each of them held a bridle. The bobcats called for the sheep. To the sheep, the bobcats seemed to be growling. That scared them. Then Bobbybill's stomach started growling, too. That scared them even more.

Billybob climbed up on a rail. He jumped onto the back of a sheep. It started twisting, turning, and bucking wildly.

"Ewe-haw!" yelled Billybob as he bounced around the corral. The sheep finally managed to throw him off into the water trough.

Bobbybill laughed, "Two baths in two weeks. That's a record for you Billybob."

Bubba gripped his bridle and picked out a sheep. He wrestled with the wooly creature. They tumbled in the dust. Soon, the bridle was in place. Only, it wasn't on the sheep.

"Baa-haw!" yelled the sheep as it rode on Bubba's back around the corral.

Bubba finally managed to buck the sheep off into the water trough. The sheep landed right next to Billybob. Bobbybill decided sheep weren't for riding. He simply built a roasting pit, instead. Then he brought out a jug of barbecue sauce. Finally, he opened the mutton cookbook.

The sheep watched all this from their corral. They each ran over to their bridles and slipped them on. They decided it was a good idea to be a little less stubborn. They thought it would be best to take the bobcats out for lunch.

The bobcats climbed aboard the sheep. Billybob and Bobbybill rode up to the gate. They looked around. Bubba's sheep hadn't moved.

"My sheep is missing its head," complained Bubba.

"You're sitting on it backwards," said Billybob.

"I thought it had an awfully big tail when I hopped on," said Bubba.

They were about to leave. Then they heard someone coming up the trail. It was Bessybob Bobcat, their dear old mother. She brought them a fresh mousemeat pie. The three bobcats ate the whole thing in just a few seconds.

Bessybob looked at Billybob. "There's something different about you."

"He took a bath," laughed Bobbybill.

"That's it," said Bessybob. "You clean up pretty well, Son."

"Thanks for the pie, Momma," said Billybob, "But we have to be going now. We have some important work to catch up on."

"You're not going like that, Young Bobcat," she said.

"What do you mean?" asked Billybob.

"You were raised better than this. What have I always told you about sheep riding?" Bessybob asked as she scolded her sons.

"Always wear a helmet," they said in unison.

"You know what's in your head?" she asked.

"Fluff?" answered Bubba.

"Noodles?" was Bobbybill's answer.

"Hush-up, you two," said Billybob. "I know the answer. Hair roots, otherwise all our fur would fall out."

Bessybob sighed, "No, it's brains. That's why you're so smart, just like your papa, Daddybob. You got your good looks from me and your brains from him."

"If we got our brains from Daddybob, what does he use for thinking?" asked Bubba.

"That's a silly question," said Billybob. "First it was Momma. Now, the prison warden does all the thinking for Daddybob."

"What I want to know," said Bobbybill, "is if we got our good looks from Momma, why is she still so purdy?"

"Well, you didn't take too much of your share," answered Billybob.

"You boys are so sweet," sighed Bessybob. "You're going to make some young female bobcats happy someday. That's why you need to protect those brains. You'll be passing them along to your youngins' someday."

"Not if we can help it," said Billybob. "I'm going to use my brains to figure out how not to get married."

The bobcat cowboys put helmets on over their cowboy hats and road off on the sheep.

"Don't trot too fast. Don't do any crazy stunts on those sheep," Bessybob warned them as they rode by her.

The Bobcat Cowboys Take the Cake Part 2

Table of Contents

Chapter		Page
6	April, May, and June	182
7	The Bobcat Surprise	184
8	Sheep Kissing	186
9	The Plan	188
10	Two Hundred Children	189
11	The Bobcat Trap	191
12	The Wedding Day	193

by Brian Davis

Vocabulary Words

concentrate

evidence

reception

April, May, and June LaPurr arrive in Rowdent Gulch to plan Starlet and Frazzle's wedding. Meanwhile, the bobcat cowboys are making their own plans.

Chapter 6
April, May, and June

The road to Rowdent Gulch was a bumpy one. There were potholes and rocks all along the way. The passengers were not used to the rough riding stagecoach.

June LaPurr and her sisters, April and May, hoped the ride would be over soon. The only other passenger was a kind looking old woodchuck named Walt. He did manage to keep the ladies entertained. He had a very interesting hobby.

The woodchuck collected stamps. He had several books of them with him. The woodchuck passed one out to each of the ladies. The passengers were glad to have something to look at. The DVD wasn't working.

That was a shame. It was one of the most popular features on the stagecoach. The DVD was a small stage mounted to the ceiling of the stagecoach. It featured the Dancing Varmint Duo, two very talented mice named Blue and Ray.

It hadn't worked since they had to stop for repairs. The stagecoach wheel broke right in front of the cheese factory. After that, the mice never came out of their dressing rooms. They couldn't fit through the dressing room door. The stagecoach driver worked for an hour trying to pull them out.

At least the passengers could get a tall glass of lemonade at the roadside stand. Sipping lemonade and looking at stamps did make the time go faster. Walt pulled out a whole box of stamps that needed to be put into the books. He thought the LaPurr sisters would enjoy arranging the stamps.

Suddenly, the stagecoach sped up. Walt Woodchuck leaned out the window. He saw what the problem was. Three helmet wearing, sheepback riding bobcat cowboys were gaining on them. Walt knew this could mean nothing but trouble. He tried to gather in his stamp collection. He didn't want those bobcats to steal it.

The stagecoach was bouncing too much. The lids popped off the lemonade glasses. The sticky liquid splattered all over the passengers. Then the loose stamps flew into the air. They fell right on the LaPurr sisters.

Larry the rat couldn't outrun the speedy sheepback riding bobcats. The stagecoach driver pulled back on the reins. The stagecoach came to a stop. Larry pulled out a triple-barrel rubber band slinging shotgun. He used it for going on posses with Deputy Guinea Pig.

Unfortunately, he wasn't allowed to use rubber bands, yet. He hadn't passed the rubber band slinging gun safety course. Papa Prairie Dog taught the class. So far, none of the students had passed. Most had recovered from Papa Prairie Dogs demonstrations, though.

There was little Larry could do except yell bang, bang, as he pointed the gun. He did have one idea as the bobcats surrounded the stagecoach.

"Throw down that food supply," said Billybob.

Larry raised the gun and pointed it at Billybob. The bobcats laughed. Billybob pointed back at Larry

"You don't have any rubber bands on that there rubber band blasting shotgun. How are you going to shoot us?" asked Billybob.

"These are invisible rubber bands," said Larry. "It's the latest development in rubber band firearms."

June LaPurr leaned out the window, "Could you gentlemen speed this up? We have a very important meeting about a wedding."

The bobcat cowboys turned around. What they saw shocked them. Three bobcat sisters leaned out the window. They were covered with stamps.

The bobcat cowboys rode away as fast as they could. Larry the rat put away the triple barrel rubber band blasting shotgun. He was sure the bobcats wouldn't try to mess with him again.

"I was worried they might be wearing invisible rubber band deflecting vests," said Larry.

"Those were some smart bobcats," said May LaPurr. "They wore helmets."

"I liked the big one," said April. "Notice how he was riding his sheep backward. I've never seen someone so skilled at sheepback riding. He was also kind of cute."

Walt Woodchuck nearly jumped out of his seat, "A low down, good for nothing bobcat?"

The three bobcats looked at him angrily, "Not all bobcats are low down. I'm sure you lovely ladies are rather high-up bobcats. Those three that stopped the stage are nothing but trouble. They're always stealin' goldfish, cheatin' at checkers, and even wrestlin' with sheep."

"So, you're saying they're very hard working," said May.

"No, no, no!" said Walt. "The only thing they work hard at is causing trouble."

"Maybe they just need some settling down," smiled June.

Walt got a chill down his spine. The thought of the bobcat cowboys getting married was a scary thought. First, there would be three more bobcats around. Next thing you know, they'd be having bobcat cubs.

The woodchuck knew he had to keep the lady bobcats away from the bobcat cowboys. Otherwise, the three bobcats across from him may start to plan their own weddings. Walt couldn't figure out why Miss Fussybunny wanted bobcats to plan a rabbit wedding. He just knew this was the start of some big trouble in Rowdent Gulch.

Chapter 7
The Bobcat Surprise

Miss Fussybunny and Mr. O'Hare waited eagerly at the stagecoach station. Starlet wanted to start planning her wedding. She was getting impatient. The bunny hopped over to the ticket window.

"When will June be here?" asked Starlet.

"A few more months," said the station master.

"But she left yesterday. Her stage was supposed to be here an hour ago," said Starlet.

"The stage is late. The DVD player broke down. It has the new wireless mouse system. The wire used to keep them in the little box. Now, they run off to the cheese factory any chance they get. Give the mice a little freedom, next thing you know they're too chubby to bend over to slip on their dancing shoes."

"That makes the stagecoach a few months late?" asked Starlet.

"No," said the station master. "The stagecoach is just around the corner."

Starlet hopped with joy back to Frazzle. "June is just around the corner."

"I thought it was a few months away," said Frazzle.

Miss Fussybunny hopped to the platform and waited. Three bobcats climbed out of the stage. Next, came Walt Woodchuck. He didn't look too happy to see Starlet.

He pulled her and Frazzle away from the bobcats. He didn't want the bobcats to hear what he had to say.

"Do you think we don't have enough bobcats around here?" he scolded. "What were you thinking?"

"What ever do you mean, Mr. Woodchuck?" gasped Miss Fussybunny.

"Those LaPurr sisters over there. You're the one that invited them," said Walt as he pointed to the bobcats.

"Those are the LaPurr sisters?" asked Fussybunny as she turned pale.

"April, May, and June," said Walt.

Miss Fussybunny whipped out her fan. She tried to stay cool. It was just too much for the rabbit to take. Miss Fussybunny fainted right on the stagecoach platform.

The next thing she remembered was waking up inside the stagecoach station. Frazzle cradled her head in his lap. Everything was a little fuzzy. That wasn't an unusual experience for a rabbit. They were fuzzy all the time.

Miss Fussybunny started to speak, "I must have taken a nap waiting for the stagecoach. I just had this terrible dream. I think you'll find it funny. I dreamed the LaPurr sisters were…"

Just then, April, May and June walked up.

"Bobcats!" shouted Starlet.

"We're excited to meet you, too," said June. "I can tell by how finely you're dressed that you have great taste."

"We do like well-dressed rabbits," added May. "Would you like to hear about our plans over dinner?"

Frazzle gulped, "Maybe you'd better change into your gardening clothes first, dear."

Starlet gasped. This was not a part of her plan. Still the wedding was only a few weeks away. It took quite a few carrots to hire the LaPurr sisters. Miss Fussybunny had no choice but to get used to working with bobcats.

She took them to the church so the bobcats could start making decorating plans. The sisters were very professional. They knew just what to do. Starlet was impressed. She was starting to feel better about the bobcat sisters.

They wanted the church to look beautiful for Starlet. The sisters took turns walking down the aisle. They explained they wanted to get a bride's eye view. It helped May plan for the flowers. It helped June know where everyone should stand. And of course, April didn't want to be left out, so she took a turn.

The five critters in the church didn't notice the three critters peeking in the back door. They were too far away to hear anything. They were close enough to see plenty. The bobcat cowboys were shaking in their boots.

"Those female bobcats are already practicing to marry us," said Billybob.

"They look kind of purdy without the stamps on their faces," said Bubba. "Do you think we should go in and practice with them?"

"Bubba, we don't want to get married," explained Bobbybill.

"How do we know unless we try?" asked Bubba. "It doesn't look too tough. All you have to do is walk down the aisle."

"There's a lot more to it than that," said Billybob. "There's the I do's and then there's kissin' and huggin',"

"Kissin' and huggin'? At the same time?" asked Bubba.

"Right smack on the lips," added Bobbybill.

"We have to hug their lips?" asked Bubba.

"Hush-up, Bubba," said Billybob. "You're not ready for the complexities of getting hitched."

"Okay," said Bubba. "But why is our attorney in there with them."

"That is Frazzle O'Hare," said Billybob. "I didn't recognize him. This is worse than I thought. He's there to make sure everything is done legal."

Just then, they were joined by another visitor at the backdoor. This one had a triple barrel rubber band blasting shotgun. The gun was loaded with real rubber bands. Deputy Guinea Pig was always on the lookout for bobcats.

"Don't you know spying on a secret wedding practice is against the law?" asked the deputy.

"Nobody told us it was a secret," said Bubba.

"That's because it's a secret," said the deputy. "I can't tell you whose wedding it is. Miss Fussybunny and Mr. O'Hare made me promise not to tell. Now, get on out of here before I try to shoot you with this here rubber band blasting shotgun."

"*Try* to shoot us?" questioned Billybob.

"I'm not sure this thing will fire. The safety button's been sticking lately. You push this button here. Then you turn this knob. This isn't going to work."

"Ow!" cried Bobbybill. "That stings!" He was holding his shoulder. A rubber band lay at his feet.

"Oops, I guess it does work," said the deputy. "I'm sure I'll shoot you now. There's no guarantee I'll hit you though. I'm a bit rusty. You three haven't caused any problems lately."

"We'll try to do better," Bubba promised.

"Thanks," said the deputy. "I knew I could count on you three."

Chapter 8
Sheep Kissing

The bobcats had seen enough for the day. They sneaked out of Rowdent Gulch. The bobcat cowboys didn't want the LaPurr sisters to see them. Billybob was especially worried. The bobcat sisters were a lot prettier than he had imagined.

He was afraid Bobbybill or Bubba might fall for them. He didn't need them going around with lovey-dovey smiling faces. No one would be afraid of them. He needed them to concentrate on their work. Now that they had sheep to ride, Billybob wanted to expand their business. It was going to take a lot more of their time.

He hoped they could start robbing steamboats, do a little duck rustlin', or even hire a few foxes to work for them. He had big plans. They didn't include any female bobcats.

He especially thought of Miss June LaPurr. She was the prettiest bobcat he had ever seen. Billybob thought of the way she looked walking down that aisle in the church. Her pointed ears and long whiskers were so lovely. Before he knew it, Billybob was puckering his lips.

"Baa," cried the voice.

"Did Billybob just kiss his sheep?" Bobbybill whispered to Bubba.

The two bobcats stared at Billybob. He had a goofy grin on his face. Suddenly, Billybob realized what he had done. He looked at his brothers.

"My lips were getting cold. The wooly fur warmed them up."

That was just the first of the strange things the bobcats did over the next few days. They all started taking baths every day. The bobcats stole new clothes. They even remodeled their cave.

"You know what this place needs," said Billybob as he looked around the cave. "Flowers, fresh cut flowers."

"I'll go pick some," said Bubba.

The wildflower patch was in full bloom. Bubba danced happily through the tall grass. He watched the butterflies. The bobcat was so happy. He enjoyed a bluebird singing at the edge of the woods.

"Hello, little birdie," said Bubba. "Isn't this a wonderful day?"

"It certainly is," answered a voice behind him.

"You know what, little birdie? You sound just like a girl bobcat."

The voice behind him giggled, "That's because I am a girl bobcat."

She tickled Bubba behind the ears with a daisy. Bubba jumped up. He was surprised to see April LaPurr. She was wearing a bright pink dress with a matching ribbon on her head.

"What are you doing here?" asked Bubba.

"I'm just picking some flowers for my sister," she said.

"You must like her a lot," said Bubba as he pointed to the basket that was on the ground behind them. "You picked her a lot of flowers."

"They're not for her, silly," giggled April. "She's going to use them in the wedding. Oh, I forgot. I'm not supposed to tell you about it. It's a surprise."

"That's okay," said Bubba. "But I hope you don't need too many flowers."

"Why is that?" asked April.

"Because a sheep just walked off with your basket," Bubba pointed.

"Oh no!" cried April.

She chased down the sheep. April tackled the surprised animal. The bobcat and sheep rolled around on the ground. Finally, she pinned the sheep down.

She made the sheep promise to leave her flowers alone. Then the wooly creature ran off to rejoin the rest of the flock. Bubba gathered up the flowers. He placed them in the basket and handed them to April.

Bubba was amazed, "You're a great sheep wrestler."

"Thank you," smiled April sheepishly.

She took the basket and started walking back to town. Bubba watched her. He had a big smile on his face. He thought April was the prettiest bobcat he had ever seen. Bubba just wanted to reach out and kiss a sheep.

Neither bobcat knew they were being watched. Walt Woodchuck was just coming back from the carrot patch. He was very concerned about what he saw. They didn't need another sheep wrestler in Rowdent Gulch.

Chapter 9
The Plan

That night, there was a secret meeting in the backroom of Walt Woodchuck's Bakery Shop. Only three critters were there. Things were not going well in Rodent Gulch.

Eweness Sheep was upset because daydreaming bobcats kept kissing her. Otto Muskrat was upset because the bobcats weren't stealing the things he couldn't sell. He had even taken down the NO STEALING signs. The muskrat was running out of places to store things.

"I just wasn't prepared for the bobcats turning honest on me," sighed Otto. "I have eight cases of gold pants I can't get rid of. Actually, they aren't pants anymore. I took them all apart."

"Why did you do that?" asked Walt.

"I was trying to make bridesmaid dresses out of them. Humph, it just wasn't good enough for that low-down, good for wedding plannin' bobcat, June LaPurr. She wanted something frilly. So, I cut holes in them. She still didn't like them. Picky, picky, picky.

That's not the worst of it. I had Starlet and Frazzle all signed up on the bridal registry. Everyone was going to buy the wedding gifts from me. I've been the official sponsor of the Last Saturday of the Month Playing for All the Wedding Gifts Checker Tournament for the last five years.

She got those rabbits signed up at the new Hare-Mart over by Mountain Creek. Now, the last Saturday of the Month Checker Tournament is called The Hare-Mart Invitational. Those female bobcats have got to go."

Walt spoke next, "I think those bobcat cowboys are sweet on those LaPurr sisters. We can't have that. Imagine Rowdent Gulch being overrun by bobcat cubs by this time next spring. We've got to put a stop to it now. I have a plan."

"All we need is some lumber, a lot of icing…"

Chapter 10
Two Hundred Children

There's something every rabbit couple should plan for. It's never too soon to start. A wise bunny couple always plans a nursery before they get married. The Fussybunny-O'Hare wedding was the next day. The LaPurr sisters had everything under control. Frazzle and Starlet were very pleased with April, May, and June.

Rabbits have lots of babies. They have them soon. They have them often. Starlet liked June's decorating tastes so well, they wanted her to plan the nursery. June was working on the drawings. April and May were helping, of course. The LaPurr sisters wanted to unveil the plans at the wedding reception. Baby bunnies always got the bobcats excited.

They couldn't help talking about the plans. The three bobcat sisters were very chatty. They didn't notice the shuffling of cowboy boots outside the window of their hotel room.

Billybob, Bobbybill, and Bubba couldn't resist any longer. They had come to court the bobcat sisters. They were totally smitten by April, May, and June. The sheep parking was behind the hotel, so they naturally had to walk right by the LaPurr sisters' window.

The sound of the lovely bobcat sisters' voices was like music to the ears of the bobcat cowboys. They just wanted to stop and listen. Billybob, Bobbybill, and Bubba listened to what the sisters had to say.

"I think the nursery needs to be bigger," said April.

"How many children are we planning for?" asked May.

"I think one hundred would be good for a start," answered June.

"You think that's enough?" asked May.

"Let's make it two hundred," said June.

Billybob, Bobbybill, and Bubba looked at each other. There was fear in their eyes. They thought five or six cubs was a lot. They couldn't even imagine two hundred.

"We'll probably have to knock out a wall," said June.

Billybob couldn't imagine how hard it would be to knock a wall out of their cave.

"By the way, April," asked June. "Did you arrange for Walt Woodchuck to deliver the cake tomorrow. We can't have a wedding without a cake."

"I saw Walt today," said April. "The cake is almost finished."

The bobcats hightailed it out of the alley. Once they got away from the window they were free to talk.

"That was a close one," said Billybob. "We almost courted those bobcats."

"Imagine two hundred cubs crowded into our cave. Where would we live?" asked Bubba.

"They're already planning to knock a wall out of our cave," said Bobbybill. "That sounds like a lot of work."

"Teaching two hundred cubs chicken thievin', ambushin', and bank robbin' is going to be a lot of work too," added Billybob. "That might take us a whole day!"

"Plus, we've got to share some of our brains with the cubs, like Momma said," added Bubba. "Are we going to have enough to think with?"

"We hardly have enough as it is," agreed Bobbybill. "And, what if they all turned out looking like me?"

"Don't even say such a thing," shuddered Billybob. "That's scary."

"I know," said Bobbybill. "Then I wouldn't be the best lookin' one anymore. I'd be just another purdy face."

"We've got to stop this wedding before it happens," said Billybob.

"It's too late," said Bubba. "Walt Woodchuck has already baked the cake. It's a real shame we were so smitten. We could have canceled the order. You can't have a wedding without a cake. That's what June said. She should know. She's a wedding planner."

Billybob smiled, "You're a genius, Bubba."

"Thanks," said Bubba. "I guess I can share some of my brains with my cubs."

"Don't get carried away," said Bobbybill.

"That's exactly what we're going to do," said Billybob. "We're going to carry that wedding cake away."

Chapter 11
The Bobcat Trap

Eweness Sheep carried the note to the hotel. She gave it to June LaPurr, and then rushed back to the bakery. June read the note to her sisters. Walt Woodchuck had a question about the cake. He wanted to see all of them right away.

The three bobcats went down to Woodchuck's Bakery. The lamps were turned off. It was dark inside. The bobcats looked into the window.

Someone carrying a candle was walking toward them. They recognized Walt when he opened the door. He told the bobcats to follow him. The woodchuck led them back into the kitchen.

"Just a little bit further," Walt instructed them. "A little further. Stop right there."

The bobcats didn't see a cake. The only thing they noticed was the strange rug under their feet. It was more like a net. Walt tugged on a rope. Four sacks of flour fell to the floor.

They were tied to a rope that ran through a pulley. The other end was attached to a net. It was right where the bobcats were standing. The net sprung up and the bobcats were lifted off the floor.

Otto slid what looked like a giant wedding cake under the bobcats. It was made of wood. Walt had covered it with icing. The inside was hollow.

Walt lowered the net into the opening in the top of the cake. Otto nailed the lid shut. The LaPurr sisters were trapped inside. Otto licked the icing off his paws.

"Our troubles are over," smiled Otto. "First thing in the morning, I'll come back and haul this cake right out of town. No one will suspect a thing."

"Do you have Davy's wagon out back?" asked Walt.

"I sure do. This is the perfect plan," said Otto. "Where do you want me to send the bill?"

"What bill?" asked Walt.

"The delivery bill, of course," said Otto.

"This is our plan. I'm not going to pay you," said Walt.

"Okay. It's not a perfect plan," sighed Otto as he followed Walt out the door.

Lurking in the alley behind Walt's Bakery were the three bobcats. They were surprised to see Walt and Otto leave so late. They were also surprised to find Davy Beaver's wagon by the loading dock of the bakery.

"This is going to be easier than I thought," said Billybob as he helped Bubba hitch their sheep to the wagon.

Bobbybill was picking the lock on the back door of the bakery. He was really struggling. Bobbybill was never very good at picking locks. Bubba lifted a mat by the door. He found a key and handed it to Bobbybill.

The lock clicked. The bobcats broke into the kitchen of Walt Woodchuck's Bakery. They immediately saw what they were looking for. The big white wedding cake was right by the back door.

The bobcats pushed it onto the back of the wagon. The licked the icing off their paws. Soon, they were heading toward their cave on Gooseberry Mountain. The bobcats drove the wagon into the garage door of their cave and parked it.

"What do we do next?" asked Bobbybill.

"We destroy the evidence," smiled Billybob as he passed out plates and forks, "One slice at a time."

Billybob tried to cut a slice with a knife. The blade wouldn't cut through the cake. Bubba got a large saw used for cutting trees. Bobbybill grabbed one of the handles. Bubba pulled the other one. Together they sliced off the top of the cake. Out popped three very relieved lady bobcats.

"Our heroes!" cried the LaPurr sisters.

April gave Bubba a big hug and a kiss. May gave Bobbybill a hug and a kiss. June gave Billybob a hug and a kiss.

"I guess we're married," sighed Bubba. "After all, we did hug and kiss."

"Married!" yelled June. "You haven't even met our parents yet."

"Or courted us," added May.

"Or wrestled sheep with us," added April. "Well, maybe just once. But we'll have to do a lot more sheep wrestling before I know if you're the one for me, Bubba Bobcat."

"And do you have rings?" asked June.

"I like diamonds," said May.

"We didn't know," said Bubba. "That wasn't on your order form."

"Order form?" asked April. "What order form?"

"Aren't you our mail order brides?" asked Billybob. "Haven't you been planning our wedding?"

The LaPurr sisters laughed. "We've been planning Miss Fussybunny and Mr. O'Hare's wedding."

"So, you don't want to have two hundred cubs that look like me?" asked Bobbybill.

The LaPurr sisters could see how disappointed the bobcats were. It was all quite flattering as they thought about it. Then there was the daring rescue from the bakery. On top of it all, the bobcat cowboys weren't even invited to the Fussybunny-O'Hare wedding. It had been a tough few weeks for Billybob, Bobbybill, and Bubba.

June gathered her sisters together. They whispered to each other. Then they turned to the bobcats.

"We're going to the Fussybunny-O'Hare wedding tomorrow. We don't have dates. Are there any strong, handsome bobcats here who want to take us?" asked June.

Chapter 12
The Wedding Day

The bobcats did go to the Fussybunny-O'Hare wedding the next day. Starlet could hardly say no. After all, they did save the wedding planners for her. She had to admit, without the bobcat cowboys, the wedding would have been a disaster.

The bobcats were on their best behavior. They didn't cause a single problem. Walt was beginning to think the LaPurr sisters might be able to tame the bobcats. He apologized for kidnapping them. April, May, and June were very forgiving. After all, they got to be rescued by the bobcat cowboys.

Even the wedding reception at the checker hall was almost perfect. The beaver family was happy that the bobcat cowboys brought the wooden wedding cake back to town. Davey cut up slices for his children. There was only one small problem. Otto Muskrat sat on Davy's last slice of cake. The icing washed right off. It was the splinters that caused the problem.

Even Otto's splinter problem worked out well. Starlet O'Hare won the checker tournament. She got to keep all the wedding presents. Otto came in second. When Otto sponsored the tournament, there was no second prize.

Now, The Hare-Mart Invitational gave the runner-up a gift certificate. It was to promote their new splinter removing clinic. Otto decided progress wasn't so bad after all. He may have lost a few sales. Not having to travel so far to find a professional splinter remover was going to save him a bundle of money.

A few days after the wedding, three mean looking female bobcats stepped off the noon stage. They were covered with stamps. The ferocious looking ladies were looking for a cave on Gooseberry Mountain. Walt Woodchuck talked them into a free piece of cake at his bakery. Later that day, Otto hauled a large wedding cake out of town. The tough looking mail order brides were never seen in Rowdent Gulch again.

Made in the USA
Monee, IL
19 June 2023

35668284R10109